Dreams Never Dreamed

A Mother's Promise That Transformed Her Son's
Breakthrough into a Beacon of Hope

Toby

Kalman Samuels

DREAMS *never* DREAMED

A Mother's Promise
That Transformed Her Son's Breakthrough
into a Beacon of Hope

The Toby Press

Dreams Never Dreamed
A Mother's Promise That Transformed Her Son's
Breakthrough into a Beacon of Hope

The Toby Press LLC
POB 8531, New Milford, CT 06776–8531, USA
& POB 2455, London W1A 5WY, England
www.tobypress.com

ISBN 978-1-59264-525-1, *paperback*

A CIP catalogue record for this title is
available from the British Library

Printed and bound in the United States

Dedicated
to my dear wife and life partner Malki

to our beloved children
Nechama
Yossi
Yochanan & Michalli
Avi & Debbie
Simcha & Yocheved
Shlomo & Orit
Sara

and to our delightful grandchildren
You are G-d's precious gifts to me
and a boundless source of love and care
for Yossi

Contents

Preface

Writing a book that necessarily exposes much that is private to myself and to my family was not in my plans. As my son Yossi became well known, good friends urged me to share his story and, in doing so, raise awareness of the issues it embraces. But it was my beloved father, Norman Samuels, who finally convinced me. A man of few words, he was dying of cancer when he took my hand in his and said urgently: "Promise me that you'll write that book!" Promise I did, and though it took many years, that promise is now fulfilled.

Much of what I have shared is based on my personal journals in which I recorded events, as well as my feelings and observations, in real time.

Some names have been changed to protect privacy and reputations.

Chapter 1

Early Days

The sixties, the decade that I so loved, that had so strongly impacted my generation, were over, and unbeknownst to me, "the times they were a-changin'." Drifting, seemingly with no choice, I found myself worlds away from my roots, in body and in mind, and dreams never dreamed were beginning to unfold.

It all began in Vancouver, Canada, which in 1951 was an extraordinary place to be born. The largest city in British Columbia and third largest metropolitan area in Canada, it was nonetheless able to retain its charm and unique character. Magically pinned between the mountains and the Pacific Ocean, it had an abundance of lush green parks and playgrounds seemingly on every corner, and a sense of serenity pervaded. The youngest of three children, I enjoyed all the privileges of middle-class life.

My father was a second-generation Canadian whose parents had come from the Ukraine at the turn of the century – brought west by great-great-uncle Mendel Shmelnitzky. Uncle Mendel was the owner of a general store east of Kiev, and it was on a business trip to England in the late 1890s that he saw a large sign in numerous languages at a London railway station that read: "FREE LAND IN CANADA! COME TO STAY!" Canada, he learned, was handing out land-parcels in its prairies. "These new farmers will need a general store just like the Ukrainian peasants I serve now," he thought. "It'll be the same – but without the pogroms."

Like many other Eastern European Jews, he wound up in Winnipeg on the eastern edge of the prairies, set up shop, and one by one summoned his family to Canada. Among them was his eighteen-year-old nephew Joseph, who was to become my grandfather. The Shmelnitzky clan prospered in Canada and in the 1930s anglicized the family name to Samuels. Grandfather Joe married Fanny and settled in Edmonton, where he established a successful network of women's clothing stores and was able to send my father to the University of Alberta to study law.

In 1943 Dad was drafted into the Canadian army, and along with his university buddies he served his country overseas in Europe as a platoon commander until the end of the war in 1945. He made sure to marry my mother Frances, a.k.a. Franky, just before he left, for safekeeping. When World War II ended and Dad was decommissioned, they moved west from Edmonton in favor of the balmier weather in Vancouver. My brother Jeff was born in 1946, my sister Marilyn in 1948, and finally me, Kalman, some three years later. According to a popular Jewish-names book of the time, the corresponding English names for Kalman were either Kenny or Kerry, and so I became known as Kerry Alfred Samuels. By the grand old age of six, I had seen the iconic Alfred E. Neuman character appear in so many *Mad* magazines that I insisted my middle name be changed. I must have driven my parents nuts because my Dad, who by and large didn't respond quickly, had my middle name legally changed to Allan.

We were a typical Jewish family of that time and place in that we were somewhat traditional but not religiously observant.

My grandparents spoke Yiddish and my parents adopted a form of Anglo-Yiddish, which they used when they didn't want us kids to understand. Our home was ostensibly kosher with separate dishes for milk and meat, and a special set of kosher dishes for Passover, but outside the house we ate in nonkosher restaurants. There were in fact no kosher ones. My first taste of a cheeseburger was at age sixteen at McDonald's following a Friday-night high school basketball game. It literally stuck in my throat and made me vomit, but with hard work I got past that.

While we didn't observe the Sabbath, we always had a Friday-night meal at which Dad said the traditional Kiddush on wine and the blessing on my grandmother's homemade hallas.

Occasionally we attended services at the large Orthodox synagogue, where among the worshippers there were perhaps half a dozen who were religiously observant – and that number included the rabbi and his assistants. After synagogue I came home and spent my day however I wanted. On the High Holidays we drove the three miles to attend, but Dad parked a block away out of respect, since Jewish law dictated that driving on the Sabbath and holidays was prohibited. I'd play outside or sit inside next to Dad listening to the services in Hebrew that I didn't understand. There were limits, of course, to my patience for synagogue attendance. When the Dodgers played their World Series thrillers, time was made for me to pick up parts of the games.

I attended the local Jewish day school, but by the end of second grade my teacher had had enough of me, telling Mom that "Kerry asks too many questions." I was delighted when Mom sagely moved me to the local public school. Despite my questions, my new teacher, Mr. Wellman, liked me and told Mom so. He once took me aside to ask why I wrote G-d with a dash instead of an *o* in the middle. I explained it was because of the third commandment, which forbids taking "the Lord your G-d's name in vain" – so we never write His full name, in case the piece of paper is thrown in the garbage. He was intrigued and wrote an end-of-year letter to my parents saying that he would miss me in class and foresaw a bright future for me.

I loved both school and sports and excelled at both. I was a good, albeit mischievous, kid and to this day fail to understand how both in third grade and again in sixth grade the principal called me into his office to tell me, "This is the straw that broke the camel's back!" On each occasion, he pulled out a flexible braided leather belt, eight inches long, three inches wide and half an inch thick, with a convenient leather handle, and ordered me to put out my hand. The first time I was fearless and defiantly did so. One swipe on my right palm was enough for me to realize I'd badly misjudged things. The pain was searing, coursing from my swelling hand through my outstretched arm all the way to my wounded heart. Appearances were instantly dropped and I broke into piercing wails. "The other hand!" he said. Like an idiot I produced the second hand, and the procedure was repeated, and then twice more on both hands. I was in enormous pain, and more significantly my pride was in shreds. And all I'd done was throw a girl's skipping-rope onto the roof.

The second time I was strapped, however, I fully deserved it. Caught reading *Little Archie* comics in sixth-grade library class, I was told to go to the principal's office. Knowing what was ahead, I calmly said to the teacher: "Mr. Burson, did anyone ever tell you that you have the brains of a kindergarten student?" It cost me an extra couple of wallops, but at least I went down fighting and earned roars of laughter from my classmates! What most worried me was what Mom would do when she saw my swollen hands. To her credit, she simply said, "You've had your punishment. I'm not going to add to it."

Since there was no Jewish instruction in public school, I attended after-school Hebrew and Jewish studies classes at the Schara Tzedeck Orthodox Synagogue three times a week until I was fifteen. My teacher was a young rabbi who had recently arrived from Brooklyn, New York, to serve as the assistant rabbi to Schara Tzedeck's venerable Rabbi Bernard Goldenberg. His name was Rabbi Marvin Hier.

While year-round attendance at Schara Tzedeck's Sabbath prayer services was scant, on the High Holidays it was a different story. For those three days a year, an additional service had to be held in the lower-floor auditorium to accommodate the tremendous overflow, and it was here, on Rosh Hashana, that the young newcomer assistant rabbi with his Brooklyn accent gave his first major sermon. I still remember the buzz that followed. "That young man is incredible! He speaks masterfully."

To prepare for my August bar mitzva, I made two major sacrifices. I was an avid baseball player, but Mom wouldn't take a chance on my getting hurt. Despite my endless pleading, she didn't allow me to play catcher for the Canadian team at the Western Boys Baseball Association (WBBA) playoffs in Bountiful, Utah, as I had done the previous year, nor did she allow me to be offensive and defensive halfback at the Walt Disney Tackle Football Classic in Los Angeles. Instead I labored for months on end learning to chant the reading from the Torah. But even with all my practice I couldn't quite get it right. My teacher solved this by writing coded arrows over each word, with numbers indicating whether I should take my voice up two notes and over one, or down two. It wasn't easy, but I finally managed.

As my bar mitzva approached, I regularly rode the bus to synagogue on Saturday mornings, where Rebbetzin Hier led the children's service. Just before my bar mitzva, Rabbi Goldenberg, with whom my family had developed a close relationship, left Vancouver and moved to New York to head a national Jewish educational organization. Years before, as a five-year-old, I had been troubled by a question that my mother couldn't answer. "If G-d created the whole world," I asked, "who created G-d?" Mom put me on the phone with Rabbi Goldenberg, who explained, "No one created G-d, Kerry. That is the difference between man and

G-d. We are created, but G-d has always been and will always be here." His straightforward answer eased my anxiety.

I was initially disappointed to learn that I was to be Rabbi Hier's first bar mitzva boy; he was and looked so young. But Rabbi Hier turned out to be an extraordinary teacher and friend. He was a visionary who would go on to found one of the world's foremost human rights agencies, the Simon Wiesenthal Center in Los Angeles, as well as win two Academy Awards. Knowing that I helped Rabbi Hier get his career started on the right foot has always brought a smile to my face.

In eighth grade, I moved to Vancouver's largest public high school, joining a student body of almost two thousand. I loved it! At five feet two inches, I was the third shortest of the 306 pupils in my grade, but that didn't stop me from running for president of the eighth-grade student council – and getting elected. The fact is, I probably knew more of those eighth graders than anybody else did: there were kids from the two elementary schools I'd attended, Jewish kids that I knew from the community, and a whole other group that I had grown up with in Little League. As president, I had the privilege of organizing ice-skating parties, concerts, and other events. One of the rock bands I brought to perform in the school gym for $300 went from those humble beginnings to international fame as The Guess Who.

At fifteen, I got my first real job, thanks to my Mom's smart advice. My friends and I had tired of mowing lawns for $2 and decided it was time to get proper summer jobs at no less than the more respectable hourly rate of $2.25. I interviewed on a Saturday morning at the exclusive Sheppard Shoes shoe store in downtown Vancouver, but left dejected when I heard they paid $1 an hour. I said to Mom, "I don't need this! The minimum wage is $1.10 an hour and they want to pay even less. It's slave labor!"

Her reaction was: "What exactly do you know about selling shoes?" I owned up to knowing nothing. "So why in the world would they pay you for something you don't know?" she said. "Take the job and they'll train you. Then they might give you a raise, and if not, you'll have some skill and experience to offer when you look elsewhere." I wasn't pleased. "How can I work for $1 an hour when some of my friends are getting $2.25?" I objected. I don't know who made my mom a prophet, but she sure knew the future. "The chances of your friends getting $2.25 an hour are very slim," she said flatly. "And if they don't accept that, then you may well be the only one with a summer job." How right she was. I worked very hard, learned to sell, tan, and polish fancy shoes, and earned $8 a day, which was $40 a week, and with tips, I came out with over $400 for the summer. At first, my friends couldn't stop telling me how dumb I was. But come September, when I had money in my pocket, no laughter was heard.

I continued working at Sheppard Shoes on weekends, and then the following summer I applied for work at a national department store chain called Woodward's. The shoe department manager turned out to be the father of Kelvin, a classmate with whom I laughed a lot. Kelvin was deaf, and nobody could curse out our teachers as eloquently and quietly as good ol' Kelvin! When his father learned we were friends, he gave me a job on the spot for – you guessed it – $2.25 an hour! Throughout high school, I worked Friday nights and Saturdays and always had my own cash on hand. My friends, always on the lookout for the big money, often remained unemployed.

From a young age, sports had always been my thing. Our Little League baseball league, the WBBA, was very popular up and down the West Coast. I was small but a fearless catcher, and at age eleven I was selected for the all-star team that was to compete in the WBBA regional playoffs in Bountiful, Utah, just outside Salt Lake City. We had never seen such a magnificent playing field nor had we seen such huge players, who could hit the ball 150 feet over the 200-foot home-run fence. This was well before the days when players' ages were verified. One pitcher was being scouted by the Los Angeles Dodgers, and while we were outmanned, I was pleased to actually get a hit.

In addition to baseball, I played tackle football as an offensive and defensive halfback and backup quarterback. My years of playing on the street with my older brother Jeff and his friends paid off. "Big Sam" and "Little Sam," as we were known, knew the game inside out, its highs and its lows. A memorable high came early one season when I took the snap and our quarterback took my left halfback position. We ran a wide sweep right and just before reaching the line of scrimmage, he paused and found me with a cross-field throw sneaking down the left sideline. I broke one tackle and raced the length of the field for a touchdown. Mom was on the sidelines cheering. As I was also the placekicker, I kicked the extra point and prepared for the kickoff. It was an amazing shot into the end-zone, but as my foot touched the ball I felt a searing pain in my upper thigh and I was down and out. My groin muscle was ripped and that was the end of my season and, in fact, of my football career.

I played soccer and golfed to a single-digit handicap, was on the tennis team throughout high school, and as a senior, captained both the tennis and basketball teams. Remaining short until almost sixteen, I finally sprouted a full six inches in the summer leading up to my junior year. Back in school that September, no one recognized me! In my senior year I was active in youth groups and was vice-president of the school student council. In addition to several academic scholarships awarded upon high school graduation, I received one of two provincial scholarships in recognition of my combined basketball, academic, and social excellence.

Chapter 2
The Road to Jerusalem

In September 1969 I began studying philosophy and mathematics at the University of British Columbia and what a blast that was! The hippie movement was at its height, and the university was a hotbed for Americans dodging the Vietnam draft. Anti-war activist Abbie Hoffman and his friends were frequent visitors, pot was everywhere, and there was no such thing as legitimate authority.

The anti-authority trend of the time is what made me take a unique course imported from Berkeley. Called Arts 1, it focused on the theme of "freedom and authority," and the course featured extensive reading, writing, and discussions on the subject. The reading material spanned the course of history, beginning from the Old and New Testaments and moving on to Plato, Chaucer, Hobbes, Rousseau, John Stuart Mill, Dostoyevsky, and others. It was stimulating stuff, accompanied by a strong message from our philosophy professor, Dr. Bob Rowan: "If you don't know the roots of your own culture, you have no yardstick with which to measure any other." At that time, traveling to India to experience the local culture and study with Indian gurus was in vogue, but without a real knowledge of one's own roots, Professor Rowan stressed, one would be stepping into a giant void without the tools needed to assess the experience. Given the number of zombies that the times created, I decided, along with a classmate from Pakistan, that he was absolutely right. If we wanted to understand who we were, we must use our undergraduate years to seriously study and gain a deep understanding of the roots of our culture, which for me was Western civilization. We set out to do just that.

My studies went well, but my midterm winter vacation in Hawaii didn't. I visited a magnificent beach up the coast from Honolulu and was amazed by its beauty: ten-foot waves rolled in one after the other, crashing loudly into the shore, where hundreds frolicked in the surf. On one side of the beach, razor-sharp volcanic rocks jutted out far into the sea. Wildly excited by the impressive scene, I entered and made my way out toward the breaking wall of water.

Never having seen such a thing before, I asked a swimmer how to get beyond these waves and was advised to just "dive at their base, and you will soon be on the other side." It was easier than I could have imagined, and I found myself relaxing and floating on the bobbing sea. Time passed and I decided it was time to swim in, but to my horror there was no beach in sight, and I suddenly realized that I was alone and had been swept out into the open ocean. I searched for some time to no avail, until I saw far in the distance an open area of beach. That was my only hope.

Fighting the panic welling up in me, I began to swim horizontally, hoping to place myself beyond the dangerous volcanic rock. Exhaustion was setting in. I sensed that it was either now or never and so I turned my face to the shore. As I came closer, the waves rolled higher, and I tried to make myself into a human surfboard and ride one. The cresting movement of an enormous wave lifted me and carried me a great distance until it suddenly dumped me with a painful thud on the sandy seabed. Stunned, I looked up, only to see another massive wave curling and then pummeling down on me. This was repeated until I finally reached the surf punch-drunk and saw people laughing and playing in it. I crawled up on the beach and collapsed, and stayed lying there for hours. As the sun began to set, I got onto a bus heading back to Waikiki, shaken by the thought that my short life came close to being over and that it was quite possible that no one would have even known of my whereabouts.

Since I had a full academic scholarship in place for my second year of university, as well as money I'd earned working on weekends, I had no need to work during the summer, so I decided to take a student charter flight leaving for London in mid-May 1970 and returning September 3. With a year of studies behind me, I was off to Europe with the goal of furthering my understanding of Western civilization and the roots of my culture. I registered for a six-week intensive French language course in the city of Lyon, where I would live with a French family. As a good western Canadian who had studied French as a second language for many years without speaking it, I wanted to perfect my spoken French. Fluency would be critical for any future public role I might have the opportunity to take in Canada, and – who knows – I might even have a good time along the way.

I showed my chock-full itinerary to my parents and Mom objected that Israel was not part of it. With the confidence gained from a year's worth of reading *The New Republic*, I assured them that Israel was an "apartheid state" and that I wanted nothing to do with. It took a mother's pleading for me to agree that my trip would include Israel, apartheid or not. My rearranged schedule gave me three weeks in Mother England and Scotland, two weeks in Israel, and six weeks studying in France, which left August to hitchhike through Europe and get back to London for my charter flight home.

The trip began as planned, and I kept a diary of it all. I arrived in London in mid-May and, with some guys I'd met on the plane, made my way to an inexpensive part of town to find somewhere to stay. The Arabic street signs and shop signs were unexpected, as I'd always thought of London as being English, but they gave me little pause. We slept at an inn where the Arabic-speaking staff spoke broken English, and the next day we all went our separate ways.

By rail and thumb, I traveled the country, taking in several music festivals en route and eventually getting as far north as Inverness, where I read a newspaper in daylight at 11:30 p.m. In Cambridge, I got to see a rowing regatta. What excitement! What culture! In Oxford, I remember sitting at a small, round wooden table in my room, watching an ant make its deliberate way across the surface. I noted in my diary: "How deeply troubling that this ant undoubtedly has a clear sense of both purpose and meaning to its existence, while I have neither."

Exiting the railway station at Bath, I encountered a dozen skinheads hanging about with their shaven heads and metal-spiked boots. They eyed me fixedly, and for a few moments I feared that, cool as I was in my brown-and-white-striped bell-bottoms, I was about to be their latest bloody victim. Somehow I managed to walk right past them, and though their stares continued, they made no move. Decades later, I vividly recall the fear and helplessness I felt in those seconds.

And then it was back to London and onto an El Al plane to Tel Aviv. I had the names and phone numbers of cousins I'd never met and only recently heard of, but I would be spending my first days in Israel in Tel Aviv staying with a classmate whose friend had a place there. Tel Aviv was hot, very hot. At a bus stop on Dizengoff Street, my friend and I politely asked directions from the many people waiting. The locals were happy for the opportunity to practice their English on us, and from the instructions we received from at least half a dozen people, in better and worse English, we understood that we should take the bus that was approaching. As we said thank you and turned to board the crowded vehicle, all those helpful folks pushed on ahead of us. The bus's doors closed with a decisive thud, and we were still on the sidewalk, our mouths open in disbelief. Welcome to Israel!

On Saturday morning, we got a ride up to Jerusalem. As we approached the city's foothills, I had a strange feeling that they were different from anything I'd ever seen, an unusual feeling for someone who had grown up surrounded by mountains and traveled the Rockies.

On our way to the Western Wall and Temple Mount, we stopped for a drink in the Old City's Muslim Quarter. Thinking that I was playing it safe, I asked for milk. It looked kind of rich but nothing could have prepared me for my first taste of warm, unpasteurized goat's milk. I somehow managed to hold it down and finished the glass. Suffice it to say, I have never touched unpasteurized goat's milk since.

We walked through the narrow bustling alleyways of the Old City market until suddenly, straight ahead of us, was the breathtaking view of the Western Wall with the gold-domed mosque beyond it. Despite my Sunday-school education in the Orthodox synagogue, I'd never heard of either the Temple or its Western Wall. At the walkway leading up to the Temple Mount, I stopped in my tracks. A large sign informed us that this was a holy site which, "according to Jewish law, it is forbidden to enter." A strange feeling welled up inside me. "I'm not going further," I told my companions. "I'll wait for you here." Their response was understandable. "What are you talking about? Are you crazy? That sign is meant for Orthodox Jews, not for you. You have no idea how beautiful it is up there!" And, with that, they took me by the arm and led me unwillingly up the walkway.

The Temple Mount was indeed very beautiful, but I didn't enjoy it. The entire time, I had one incomprehensible thought gnawing at me: "You're going to regret this to the end of your days." At the Western Wall, which we visited next, I posed for a photo, as if weeping.

The next day, I began contacting my relatives. I met cousins who lived in the Tel Aviv suburb of Givatayim, and to my surprise they were super warm and friendly. Dussi and Shmuel Frankel took me to Arad in the northern Negev and then on to the Dead Sea and Masada, all of which was a total revelation for me. They arranged for me to travel north the following week to visit their children Hagai and Rivka, who lived on Kibbutz Maayan Baruch. In the meantime, I met other cousins: Yitzhak and Yafa Shimshon and Aaron and Mira Botzer. They too were warm and welcoming. Aaron took me to a well-known eatery in Jaffa for my first falafel and hummus. He worked for the Israel Electric Corporation but spent most of his time pursuing his real passion, windsurfing, and I never figured out when he found time to work. He later became head of Israel's windsurfing organization, an international windsurfing judge, and a member of the International Olympic Committee. He made headlines at the 1988 Olympics in Seoul for disqualifying two Israeli windsurfers for sailing on Yom Kippur. Aaron isn't observant and I later asked him why he did it. His answer was, "Yom Kippur? Israeli windsurfers had the audacity to break our rules and practice on Yom Kippur? They were no longer worthy of representing their country."

I bused down to Eilat at Israel's southern tip, snorkeled in its reefs, and slept for a few nights on its magnificent beaches. Growing up, I'd thought that my native Vancouver lay at the center of the world. Standing on the beach just south of Eilat in what had been Egypt until the Six-Day War three years earlier, with the coasts of Jordan and Saudi Arabia looming across the Gulf of Aqaba, and Israel to the north on my left, Vancouver suddenly seemed a wonderful place – but so very far from civilization's hub.

On my way back to Jerusalem, I ran into friends from home and went with them to the Western Wall. This time, though, I didn't go up onto the Temple Mount. Leaving the Old City, we boarded a number 9 bus to the Hebrew University. It was packed with numerous people standing and it was brutally hot. As I made my way toward the back, I spotted an empty seat next to a fellow dressed in black clothing with an enormous black felt hat and a long beard. I was too hot to worry about him and sat down. After a minute he began to talk to me in broken English. What was I doing in Israel? "Touring." Where was I going? "To study in France." Would I like to come to his home, study Torah with him, and stay for the Sabbath? This was not what I had in mind, but I suddenly thought that, after all, had this been India and a native invited me to join him in his home environment, I probably would have leaped at the opportunity! What an experience to relay back in Vancouver. I asked him whether he had a family and he said of course. "You know what, I'm heading north to visit a kibbutz this week," I told him, "but I'll be back on Friday and will possibly spend the Sabbath with you and your family and then head to France on Monday." He gave me his details and I went back to my friends, and on to the Israel Museum and the Shrine of the Book with its Dead Sea Scrolls.

The following day, Monday, I boarded a bus for Kibbutz Ma'ayan Baruch in northeast Israel, positioned where the country's border intersects with those of Syria and Lebanon. There I met my relative Hagai, who showed me the kibbutz watchtower, where lookouts stood alert for terrorist infiltrators. It was another rude awakening for me to learn that Israelis routinely lived under armed guard.

Working in Ma'ayan Baruch's fields that week, my childhood experience of picking strawberries was put to good use. There were many other young English-speaking volunteers from all over, so I had good company. After hours picking fruit under the sun, the young Israeli tractor driver suggested a dip in the nearby Jordan River, which was gushing and refreshingly cool. It was not an overly impressive river, but even in my ignorance it was somehow very meaningful.

I had unwittingly chosen a troubled time to visit the kibbutz. There was a massive Syrian tank buildup underway, the largest since the Six-Day War three years earlier, and Israeli fighter planes were busily engaging them, strafing and bombing the nearby Hermon hills. My little bed at the kibbutz was rocked repeatedly by the explosions and at times I wasn't sure I was going to make it out of there. The kibbutz was under total blackout and I walked through the pitch dark to the dining hall each evening, bats soaring between the trees and zipping past my head. I was more than a little concerned.

Back in Tel Aviv on Friday, my Israeli host let me have it with both barrels when I told him I was spending Shabbat with a Hasid and his family. "Are you totally crazy? You're spending your last weekend in Israel in a hasidic ghetto?" He made sense. It was mid-June and stiflingly hot. The inviting blue Mediterranean and its beaches were only three blocks from his apartment. But…I boarded the first of several buses en route, clad in white bellbottom pants and a bright green golf shirt with my backpack.

My Tel Aviv host certainly knew what he was talking about. The streets of the hasidic community were bustling with people rushing with last-minute shopping. And what strange people these were. The men wore long black coats and big felt hats in the sweltering heat. The women wore long sleeves and skirts that reached almost to their ankles.

The address I was given led me to a humble apartment. At the top of rickety wooden stairs, the door opened, and there was my host sitting with a hippyish long-haired young fellow, also invited for Shabbat. One glance told me the guy was half-stoned – certainly not anyone with whom I wanted to share a room. He was expressing reservations about the Shabbat, so I seized the opportunity and told him, "You know, soon you won't be able to get a bus or cab out of this place till Saturday night, so you should decide now if you want to leave while you still can." It worked, and he bolted!

I was now asked whether I wanted to come to the *mikve* before Shabbat. "What in the world is a *mikve*?" I inquired, and learned it's a communal bath in which to purify in preparation for the holy Sabbath. I told him I'd already showered, thank you, but the *mikve*, it seemed, was spiritual in nature and had nothing to do with physical cleanliness. Thinking that this would be one more experience, I agreed to go. I found myself undressing in a crowded room along with more Hasidim and then dipping into the warm water of a mini-pool. I was not a happy camper.

Shabbat began and we went to pray in a hasidic synagogue. I think the people there felt about me pretty much how I felt about them. They were so strange to me, dressed in long black silky coats with big furry Cossack hats called *shtreimel*s on their heads. But I guess I looked weirder still to them in my brightly colored cool clothes. It was odd to be among Jews, yet be so totally out of place, so far from what I saw as normal.

Saturday evening was long-awaited and I knew I was getting out of there on the first bus. I gathered my meager belongings, said thank you, and headed for the exit. "Wait just a minute. Before you go, I want you to meet a Rabbi who speaks good English." Against my better judgment I walked several blocks to a much nicer apartment and was introduced to a striking individual, a man in his late thirties with a flowing, well-kempt brown beard and a mustache that drooped over his upper lip. When he spoke I heard with astonishment that he was Australian, and we began to talk. I was leaving in two days for a six-week French course in Lyon, I told him, and would be living with a French family. He looked at me thoughtfully and quietly asked, "Are you aware that it might be uncomfortable for you to live in the home of a devout French

Catholic family, who probably don't yet know their guest is Jewish?" Sensing my shock at his comment, he shared that he was raised Catholic and later became a journalist, searched for meaning and found it in Jewish thought. He converted and ultimately became a Rabbi and a Chabad Lubavitcher Hasid. He continued, "No doubt you will improve your French, but I sincerely believe that you will have a far more enriching experience in the intensive Jewish studies program that I head. In six weeks you will learn about your Jewish roots. You'll be studying with bright young men visiting from Ivy League colleges and you'll have a truly stimulating summer. Have you ever studied Talmud?" "What's that?" I asked. He continued, "Have you ever studied Mishna?" "What's that?" I repeated. He answered with another question: "Would you consider studying in a yeshiva?" and yet again I asked, "What's that?" He clarified, "It is a school that teaches Torah and it will give you a taste of your heritage."

In spite of my severe reservations, the Rabbi unwittingly struck a deep chord within me. This, I immediately thought, is precisely what Professor Rowan had been talking about. Here I was, trying to get a handle on Western civilization, when I was not adequately familiar with my own, upon which much of Western civilization is rooted. My mind was racing and my gut was being ripped in pieces. I told the Rabbi with an uncomfortable smile, "I sincerely don't believe what I am about to say, but OK, I'll give it a shot." I did not fully realize that this was not an academic study of someone else's heritage but a journey into my own.

The next morning, I canceled my France arrangements, said *au revoir* to my friends, heaved on my backpack and sleeping bag, and headed for Kfar Chabad, a small Chabad-Lubavitch village south of Tel Aviv. The trip was miserably hot, and as I walked the two miles down the dusty, narrow road from the highway to the village, with giant spiky cacti standing sentinel on either side, I had second, third, and even fourth thoughts. But nothing could have prepared me for the yeshiva, where I was warmly welcomed by dozens of men my age and older. All had beards of different shapes and sizes, from scraggly whiskers to long and flowing. I too had a small beard, but the reason I had grown mine was quite different: I had stopped shaving the day I left Canada as a statement of independence, while they had never shaved and theirs were statements of conformity.

A young man warmly greeted me with the traditional Jewish greeting, *"Shalom Aleichem,"* which, after having heard it countless times during the previous Sabbath, I knew meant "Peace be upon you" or *Hi, how are you?* I even knew the correct response, *"Aleichem HaShalom,"* meaning "Upon you may there be peace" or *The same to you.* He asked me in heavily accented English where I was from. When he heard my answer, he responded: "I am too from Canada, from Mon-tree-all!" Given his thick accent, I asked him where he'd been born before moving to Montreal. "I born in Mon-tree-all," he responded indignantly. This didn't make sense, so I tried again, speaking very slowly: "I understand that you live in Montreal, but where were you born? No one born in Canada speaks English like you do." More than a little put out, he repeated: "I born in Montreal and lived my life in Montreal and now study here." This young man, raised in an insular Yiddish-speaking hasidic community, turned out to be a real gem, and though we didn't always understand each other perfectly, we spoke many times in the weeks ahead.

A decade later, in different circumstances and far from Israel, I was introduced to an impeccably dressed young rabbi who spoke English eloquently and with something familiar about him. I asked him, "Did you study in Kfar Chabad?" "Yes, I did," he answered. "Were you there in the summer of 1970?" I asked. "Yes," he said. "Did you meet a newcomer there named Kalman?" "Yes, of course." "Well that's me," and with that we were hugging each other. "How," I asked, "did you master English?" and he answered simply: "I had to, so I could get a job teaching Torah." His metamorphosis was astonishing.

My days in the Chabad yeshiva were, as promised, fascinating and stimulating, and despite the gaping cultural differences I felt oddly comfortable there. Although our family in Vancouver was decidedly secular, we had, I came to realize, retained a substantial amount of tradition in our lifestyle. So when I immersed myself in yeshiva studies, I wasn't a total stranger in that uncharted territory, even though the study hall with its hundreds of spirited young men chanting and shouting at one another over large talmudic texts was light-years away from the silence of the pristine university library I was used to. I studied Hebrew, struggled to recite Hebrew prayers, and encountered Mishna, Talmud, and hasidic thought. I learned that Jews recite blessings not only on bread on Friday nights but throughout the day, before and after eating a meal, after using the restroom, and on many other occasions.

On my first Friday afternoon there, I joined the others at the *mikve* before the Sabbath. I felt uneasy when I noticed some young men staring at me. Once outside, I asked a more knowledgeable friend why they were staring, to which he replied, "Nothing to worry about. These guys have simply never seen a six-pack before." Sadly, it didn't take too much physical inactivity before those stomach muscles were gone – and with them the stares.

There were a number of bright young men from Harvard, Yale, MIT, and other fine schools at Kfar Chabad that summer, and we engaged in animated philosophical discussions well into the nights. It was invigorating and there was an unidentifiable something about it that called me to delve deeper. But with my six weeks rapidly coming to a close, time was running out.

To the shock and consternation of family and friends, I decided I'd take a year off university to pursue Jewish studies in Israel. My parents immediately assumed I was a victim of brainwashing and had become incapable of rational decision-making in my closed, all-male environment. They urged me to come back to Canada for my second year of university, confident that among clear-thinking, balanced, open-minded people I would regain perspective and be restored to life's proper path. I argued that the university has its own powerful agenda and is no less of a biased environment.

One day, two guys and two flimsily dressed girls arrived unannounced at the yeshiva, creating quite a stir. They were friends from Vancouver summering in Israel, and had come to convince me I'd been ensnared in a Moonie-type cult. We talked until I agreed to go with them to Tel Aviv overnight – where they put forward every possible argument to show me I'd lost my mind, triggering many doubts and questions. The next day, I took a bus to Jerusalem and sat in the Hebrew University library to think through my life and the direction it should take.

I spent five days writing a lengthy entry in my diary, tracing my thinking regarding how I had arrived at where I was now and where I should be heading. I noted that I felt I was carrying an enormous weight, a weight greater than I could bear, which I identified with the biblical story of Jews redeemed from Egypt who then wandered in the desert for forty years before reaching the Promised Land. But my situation seemed even worse, as I felt figuratively doomed to wander all those years only to die in the wilderness without ever seeing the Promised Land. Despite the weight and darkness, however, I saw a pinpoint of light at the end of this long, gloomy tunnel – and although I felt that I would not survive, I sensed that I must follow its current course for the sake of those who would come after me.

Leaving the library, I went to see a display of biblical dioramas at the Heichal Shlomo Museum, which was then the seat of the chief rabbinate in Jerusalem. Looking at them, I realized I'd learned a great deal in my six weeks at Kfar Chabad. Instead of viewing the dioramas simply as art and with the eyes of a stranger, I recognized each scene and identified with the characters. As I carefully examined a beautifully ornamented, silver, Sephardic-style Torah cover, I felt a strange rush inside and suddenly knew that while my university education was important, this was the experience that was meaningful to and necessary for me now. My decision was made: I'd move to Jerusalem and enroll in a Jewish studies program for university students. My only problem was that I had no idea how or where to do so.

Chapter 3

My New World

The next day was Tisha B'Av, the ninth day of the Jewish month of Av, a day on which several catastrophes in Jewish history took place, most notably the destruction of both the First and Second Temples. It is a day of fasting and intense mourning. Midday, I arrived at the Western Wall – the last remnant of the Second Temple – donned my *tefillin*, and began to pray amid sobs and lamentations all around me. It was a powerful experience to pray at the Wall on this historic day of Jewish destruction and tragedy, together with thousands of others who mourned Jerusalem, at a time of miraculous rebirth for the Jewish people in their homeland – especially when I myself was at a crossroads, staggering under the weight of my burden of spiritual introspection.

Standing at the Wall in the intense heat of an August afternoon, I prayed and prayed, asking G-d for help and guidance, reciting psalms in English. It must have been quite a sight, because several weeks later my Tel Aviv cousins told me they hadn't known I was still in the country until they saw me on that evening's TV news, absorbed in prayer with my *tefillin* melting! I knew nothing about the TV cameras, but I did know that I wouldn't be returning to UBC in September.

Back in Kfar Chabad, two newfound friends told me they were on their way to Jerusalem to study at Hartman College under its dynamic twenty-nine-year-old rabbi, a Yeshiva University graduate named Chaim Brovender. They invited me to join them. A Jewish studies program for university students had fallen into my lap. Rabbi Brovender was an impressive figure and graciously accepted me into the program. My parents were relieved that I was leaving the yeshiva and could accept that I was to be engaged in Jewish studies at a "college." I was now free to focus exclusively on Torah study.

I said my goodbyes at Kfar Chabad, leaving friends and teachers who were disappointed to see me go. At Hartman College, once again I met an amazing group of young men. They were all university educated, and many had advanced degrees. My roommate was David Fink, a kind and quiet genius who in many ways took me under his wing.

On a Friday evening some weeks later, David took me to Jerusalem's ultra-Orthodox Geula neighborhood to join the Gerrer Hasidim at their Friday-night Sabbath *tisch,* meaning "table," at which the Hasidim would gather with their Rebbe in study and uplifting song. We reached the enormous hall early, stood to one side, and studied Maimonides' writings while we waited. The chamber soon filled until it was standing room only – close to a thousand Gerrer Hasidim, dressed in their tall fur hats, long black coats, and dangling *peyot* (side curls). There was a sudden hush. A diminutive figure made his way slowly through the tightly packed crowd, which parted before him like the Red Sea before Moses. This was the famed Gerrer Rebbe. At David's suggestion, I stood on my chair in order to see him, and what a breathtaking sight it was! The Rebbe's golden beard and long *peyot* gave him a countenance I can only describe as saintly. As he passed by a mere five yards from me, my heart soared heavenward and I was consumed by the experience, until the human chain suddenly lurched back and the elbow of a burly Hasid inadvertently smashed into my lower parts. I reeled in hellish agony. Heaven, it seems, was not to be so easily attained.

My days and nights were occupied with my single-minded efforts to master the age-old Hebrew and Aramaic texts of the Babylonian Talmud, with their unique logic and mystical holiness. Hour after hour, I plunged deeper and deeper, yet rather than ending the day with a headache as had been the case when I was studying calculus, my entire being was invigorated. Never in my secular studies had I experienced the raw intellectual challenges of Talmud. As time went on I realized this was what I enjoyed, this was what fulfilled me and what I wanted to do, and I felt comfortable with my path. University would wait.

I met extraordinary people while I was there. One was Rabbi Noach Weinberg, of blessed memory, who a few years later would establish Aish HaTorah, the Jewish outreach organization that is a world leader in creative Jewish educational programs and leadership training. I vividly recall studying one Thursday night in his home. Reb Noach suddenly pointed to the window, emphatically declaring: "Do you see that darkness outside? It's overpowering, but we're studying in a lighted room – which teaches us that even a little light can dispel much darkness." In the ensuing fifty years, Reb Noach lived his life according to that belief and brought his light to so many.

After eighteen months of studying in an English-speaking environment, I began looking for a new challenge, figuring that if I had gone to India with friends I would not be hanging out with English speakers but would have sought out an authentic local spiritual experience at an Indian-speaking ashram. So I decided it was time to seek out the Jewish equivalent. I bought a college textbook of Yiddish, studied it intensely for a month, and approached Rabbi

Yitzchok Shlomo Ungar, the head of a Yiddish-speaking yeshiva in Bnei Brak named Chug Hasam Sofer, after a leading Orthodox rabbi who lived in Europe in the early nineteenth century. Rabbi Ungar was a highly esteemed, no-nonsense Hungarian hasidic rabbi. He tested me thoroughly on my knowledge and language, and although he had never had a student from my background before, he accepted me warmly. Prior to World War II, Rabbi Ungar had been a brilliant young man who knew the entire body of rabbinic literature verbatim. Thrown from a four-story building by the Nazis, he survived the fall but lost his memory. After the war he spent many years restoring his broad Torah scholarship.

Right before Passover, when there was a four-week break in the yeshiva schedule, Rabbi Ungar permitted me to move into the yeshiva dorm with a few other young students. One was a hasidic New Yorker who spoke fluent Yiddish but very broken English. We quickly became friends and studied Talmud together in Yiddish, enabling me to improve my Yiddish language skills.

There was also a sweet, scrawny, sixteen-year-old Hasid with *peyot* wrapped around his ears, who wore a long black coat, knickers, and black knee-high stockings, and who spoke Yiddish and Hebrew but didn't understand a word of English. He spent a lot of time each day reading entire books of miraculous stories about Elijah the Prophet. When I asked him why he did this, he answered simply: "I don't know. I can't explain it. I just love these stories." Some twelve years later, I heard about a Hasid who was an internationally known advisor on medical issues who often lectured in English. The name rang a faint bell, but I was in total shock when I verified that it was none other than my young class-mate Elimelech Firer. Over the years, Rabbi Firer has received a multitude of prestigious awards and honorary doctorates for his volunteer work providing medical advice to everyone from simple folk to prime ministers and presidents. He never altered

his hasidic dress or his humble demeanor. For most, his mete-
oric rise is inexplicable, but to me it is clear: Elijah the Prophet
is at his side.

My schedule at the new yeshiva was rigorous. I rose at
4:30 a.m. and immersed myself in the *mikve* downstairs. I drank
a coffee, studied Jewish law from 5:00 to 7:15 a.m., prayed morning prayers with the others, studied for twenty minutes between
prayers and breakfast, then studied again from 9:00 a.m. to 1:00
p.m., breaking only for lunch and a thirty-minute doze, followed
by more intensive study until 11:00 p.m. My intellectual and spiritual hunger was insatiable, and all week long I didn't step outside
the yeshiva building.

Each day from 11:00 a.m. to 1:00 p.m., Rabbi Simcha Kessler,
of blessed memory, delivered a brilliant two-hour Talmud lecture
in Yiddish. During the first week I jotted down every word I didn't
understand and looked it up after class, but once I got the hang
of it I was sailing. Rabbi Kessler was a *tzaddik*, a righteous man,
who lived in a tiny apartment nearby with his ten young children.
One summer evening, he invited me to his home to review a long
passage from the *Tosafot*, a medieval commentary on the Talmud.
We studied on a little porch off of his nine-by-twelve-foot "living room," which I was advised to cross carefully, treading gently
between no fewer than six sleeping children neatly arranged on
mattresses on the floor. Rabbi Kessler had minimal physical means
but was a giant of the spirit.

By the time I turned twenty-one, I was light-years away
from my upbringing, a hasidic man complete with *peyot* and the
distinctive clothing. I was also an eligible bachelor.

Chapter 4

Matchmaker

In the world that was now mine, the way to meet a virtuous young woman was through a *shidduch*, an introduction by a matchmaker, an efficient and time-honored practice that nonetheless horrified nonobservant parents like mine.

My *shidduch* came about unexpectedly. On Friday mornings, the only free time in my rigorous learning schedule at the yeshiva, I'd go out to run errands and pick up odds and ends for the Sabbath. My route took me past a small store which made and sold the fur-rimmed hats known as *shtreimels* that I'd first seen during my initial Sabbath. Custom-made for each purchaser, their cost ranged from hundreds to thousands of dollars. The *shtreimels* in this shop were made by an elderly and diminutive Hungarian Hasid named Reb Chaim Hersch Schwartz, whom I'd first met outside his shop. There was immediate chemistry between us, and we fell into the habit of schmoozing at length each Friday.

One week, I sensed he'd been waiting for me. "I have a friend who is the principal of a girls' school in Jerusalem," he said. "He tells me there's a unique young lady studying there. She needs to meet someone who is very Orthodox, hasidic, but not run of the mill. I hear she's exceptional. Would you like to meet her?" Naturally my answer was in the affirmative.

As was the custom, Malki and I were introduced in the Jerusalem living room of one of her married friends, Ita. I realized that I had in fact spent just over two years preparing for this meeting, transforming myself from a secular, eighteen-year-old university student and sports jock from Vancouver who ate cheeseburgers, into a devout young man dedicated to Torah study. Two years ago, Malki had been a sixteen-year-old, sheltered, ultra-Orthodox Jerusalem schoolgirl, demurely clad in a long skirt and long sleeves. Clearly, for us to come together, one of us would've had to change dramatically – and that one had been me.

Malki blew me away from the first moment. She was stunning but modest, European by birth, New York and Jerusalem educated, and at home in six languages. I felt as if I'd known her forever. Miraculously, my interest in her was returned and we were married in March 1973, eight months after we had first met.

Our wedding was performed by Grand Rabbi Avrohom Yitzchok Kahn, of blessed memory, the illustrious Toldos Aaron Rebbe from Mea She'arim who headed a very pious and closed hasidic sect. On my head was the *shtreimel* specially made for me by our matchmaker, Reb Chaim Hersch Schwartz.

Despite the religious chasm that now yawned between my family and me, my parents, grandmother, and sister Marilyn came to Israel for our wedding. They took it well and ultimately were filled with immense pride. For most others among my Vancouver friends and relatives, Kerry Samuels had fallen off the face of the earth.

Malki and I had grown up at opposite poles of mid-twentieth-century Jewish life. My childhood was spent in tolerant secular Western Canada; hers in Eastern Europe, too recently shattered by war, with millions having died under the Nazis, suffocated in gas vans or transported to death camps. Lurching from fascism to communism, it had been torn apart and re-stitched, much of it in blood and betrayal.

Among those murdered by the Nazis were Malki's widowed grandmother and nine of her mother's brothers and sisters. Between 1943 and 1945, while my father fought the Nazis as an Allied soldier and my newlywed mother waited for him in the safety of provincial Edmonton, Malki's family knew fear, hunger, deprivation, and death. Rounded up and transported, they were disgorged at Auschwitz on the second day of the Shavuot holiday, Monday, May 29, 1944. Manhandled by SS guards, prodded by guns, and petrified by growling, snarling dogs, the family huddled together as they shuffled toward Josef Mengele and his infamous railway platform inspection.

Malki's aunt, Sarah Tobah Alti Bracha, was clutching her two-and-a-half-week-old baby. The infant was wrenched away from her by a Jewish *kapo* and thrust into the arms of her grandmother. Minutes later, at the flick of Josef Mengele's wrist, baby, grandmother, and several of Malki's other uncles and aunts were sent to die in the crematorium, while nineteen-year-old Alti and her fourteen-year-old sister Leah were sent to debilitating slave labor which few survived. Daily, for the next eight months, Alti and Leah cared for each other. Daily, even as temperatures plummeted far below freezing, the two sisters bathed in the horse trough, trying to keep themselves disease free. And daily, the sisters were inspected naked together with all the female prisoners to determine whether they should work or die. Despite a leg damaged by childhood illness, Alti was inexplicably deemed fit for work each day – protected, she believes, by a blessing she had received from the holy Belzer Rebbe who, at the height of her illness, had promised that she would live to a ripe old age and had bestowed upon her two additional names, Alti and Bracha, meaning an "elderly blessing."

Leah lay languishing in the bunk with countless others, suffering from typhoid and starved almost to death. Suffering from near-starvation herself, Alti made her way slowly toward the other end of the barrack, supporting herself on the shaky walls. In the courtyard outside, Sori, a fifteen-year-old inmate who worked in the kitchen, spotted her and asked where she was going. Alti shared that she was headed to the garbage in search of a potato peel. "You know they will shoot you on the spot," said Sori. "Yes, I know," Alti replied, "but I have no choice, because my sister is about to die."

With deliberate movements young Sori slowly opened her apron and, at the risk of being shot herself, whispered, "Would you like a sweet white beet for your sister?" Alti could not believe her eyes or her ears. "Yes, thank you," she stammered, and taking the beet carefully with her ebbing strength, she turned back to the barrack. Again she heard Sori's voice: "Would you like another beet? Your sister needs it." In disbelief, she took that too, made her way back, and morsel by morsel fed them to her younger sister. Leah was revived.

Scores of Malki's family members were murdered in Auschwitz, but Alti and Leah survived and later built families of their own. Their survival was a direct result of one young girl's truly audacious sacrifice, made in order to help another human being, an unexpected uplifting moment in the darkest days of Auschwitz. Sori Kohn too survived.

Each person's life marches to the beat of its own drum, and the "beets" that saved Alti's and Leah's lives had a critical and unforeseeable impact over generations on many lives, including that of Leah's daughter Malki and my own.

"Many people came out of Auschwitz changed, with their faith either destroyed or indestructible," says Malki's aunt "Mima" Alti. "My sister and I came out yet stronger believers." That powerful belief in G-d became an essential part of Malki's DNA.

* * *

Newly married, we set up our home in Jerusalem. I was accepted into an intensive, Yiddish-language rabbinic ordination program, and my days and nights remained steeped in Jewish learning. Malki and I often discussed my studies, and by the time I was ordained as a rabbi in 1977 and qualified as a Torah scribe the following year, she was no small maven in Jewish law and thought herself.

We had been married for about eighteen months when Malki's dear friend Ita suggested we go to a very special Mea She'arim rabbi known as the Tchaba Rav for a blessing. Happy as we were, there was as yet no sign of a baby, and in our society, if there was no pregnancy in the first year and a half, there was cause for concern. We made an appointment, and when the time came we entered the esteemed rabbi's small austere apartment at 3 Mea She'arim Street and waited to meet him. An elderly lady eventually ushered us into a book-filled room and presented us to an even older man. I was completely unprepared for what followed.

The Tchaba Rav had been a rabbi in the Hungarian town of Tchaba (Békéscsaba) and was a Holocaust survivor. Now almost ninety years old, he stood straight and tall at six foot four inches, with a long, flowing white beard and a countenance as holy as I imagined that of Elijah the Prophet to be. A man without airs, he was dressed in a long black coat and a very large black-brimmed felt hat. Everything about him was open and unambiguous. In quiet simple Yiddish without pretense, he told me things about myself that were nothing short of spooky. He knew me better than I knew myself. He gave us each a red thread to wear round our wrists, explaining this was no ordinary thread. It had been wound around the tomb of our biblical matriarch Rachel near Bethlehem and a special sequence of psalms had been recited by a *minyan* (a Jewish prayer quorum of ten) of scholars while it was being wound.

The rabbi then asked for a charitable gift, clarifying that it was not for himself but to help provide Sabbath meals for the poor, and in that merit hopefully our prayers would be answered. Finally, he took a *kame'ah,* an amulet made from parchment on which the names of G-d are written according to Kabbala, held it aloft with his outstretched right arm, and began chanting a *lahash,* a kabbalistic incantation in Hebrew: "Elijah the Prophet met the angel." He repeated this and other phrases over and over, with intense concentration and fervor, building up to: "The angel blessed Elijah in Your great name!" At that point he lowered his head and shoulders toward the table in front of him and began pronouncing kabbalistic names of G-d that I could not understand. To me, the words seemed to literally roll out from under his long beard and make the whole room tremble. I consider myself a rational being, my feet planted firmly on the ground, but I witnessed this several times over the years and it was always the same unfathomable and unforgettable experience. The Tchaba Rav told us that we would be blessed with four children who would arrive in rapid succession, but he underestimated the power of his own blessing. Nine months later, on July 24, 1975, Malki gave birth to our daughter Nechama Leah and then to five boys, all in the span of six years. Our seventh child, our daughter Sara, arrived seventeen years later. The first four were born in the Tchaba Rav's lifetime.

Nechama Leah means "comfort for Leah." Malki's mother, Leah, of blessed memory, died at age forty-five, four months before our baby's birth. After having survived Auschwitz, its subcamp Hindenburg, and Bergen-Belsen, she was walking in a pedestrian crossing on a green light when a car plowed her down. She did not live to see her first grandchild.

Nechama Leah's birth made us proud and joyous parents. Fifteen months later, on October 30, 1976, Shalom Yosef, nicknamed Yossi, was born. It was a Sabbath morning and I was floating on air as I ran from the hospital to share the news. Malki and I were still in our early twenties. We had a daughter and a son. We were totally elated and felt our lives were blessed. By the time our third child Yochanan was born thirteen months later, our lives had forever changed.

Chapter 5

In Silence and Darkness

A downtown Jerusalem clinic was where it began. None of the clinic staff will talk about what happened there that day. It was October 16, 1977. Yossi, then two weeks short of his first birthday, remembers nothing of course. But every detail of that afternoon, now over forty years ago, is seared into the memory of my wife, Malki.

"I never liked the well-baby clinic," she says. "Maybe it was intuition. It wasn't that I knew anything could go wrong. After all, this was 1977. Information wasn't out there, the way it is now. There were no PCs, no internet, no mobile phones, no social media. And anyway, it wasn't for parents to second-guess doctors and nurses. It was a hot day and I was at the end of my third pregnancy. I thought about postponing the visit but decided I must go. I'd be having the new baby any day and then Yossi's second immunization would be delayed for weeks. I slowly walked the few blocks to the local well-baby clinic and climbed the stairs carrying my beautiful little boy. The pediatrician, Dr. Neiman, ran the usual checks – psychomotor, sight, hearing, weight, height. She entered Yossi's developmental milestones on her medical chart and told me he was doing well. Then the nurse sat my alert and smiley baby in my lap and gave him the shot."

On that hot October afternoon, Israel's health authorities had already known for almost five months that the vaccine batch they were using for the routine triple immunization against diphtheria, pertussis, and tetanus (DPT) was dangerously flawed.

"I took Yossi home and followed the instructions they'd given me at the clinic," Malki recounts. "I bathed him, gave him baby paracetamol, and let him sleep. The moment he woke, I knew my baby was gone. He looked up at me with shiny eyes as if to say: 'What have you done to me?'"

On that terrifying afternoon, when Malki picked up our beautiful little boy from his nap and saw he was "gone," she had no way of reaching me. She called the clinic and was told not to worry. There was no phone in the yeshiva where I was engrossed in my studies, and I knew nothing until I got home at about 7:15 p.m. As I walked in the door, my panic-stricken wife propelled me into the children's room. Yossi was in his crib, lying on his back. "Look at him! Look!" she cried. "Look at his eyes! It's not my Yossi! It isn't him! He's not responding! Something's terribly wrong!"

I picked Yossi up and he smiled painfully. I looked at his eyes and saw that there was indeed something amiss. His eyes were glassy with a shimmer that had not been there that morning when I left him. Malki wanted to call the pediatrician immediately. "No," I told her. "It's probably just a cold. We'll let the baby sleep and call the pediatrician in the morning, if we need her."

The next morning Yossi was worse. He was running a fever, his nostrils were blocked, and he was clearly in distress. We called our pediatrician, Dr. Kanner, who was well qualified and affiliated with Jerusalem's Shaare Zedek Hospital. Arriving at the house a few hours later, she examined Yossi thoroughly, diagnosed a viral infection, and prescribed paracetamol and fluids. Several days later, with no improvement in Yossi, she decided it was time for antibiotics. Diligently we dosed him, but as time passed not only was he getting worse, he also began making sudden jerky movements.

We didn't know what to do for our baby and felt utterly helpless. Malki could take no more. I called the doctor demanding that she come that very day to see the child again. She came in the evening at 9:00 p.m., after her day at the hospital. This time, she was visibly concerned. She asked to use our phone and spoke to Dr. H., a leading neurologist at a Jerusalem hospital. We were told to be at her clinic first thing next morning for a full examination. Clearly, this was something more than a virus, but who were we, as young parents, to be told what it was? Obediently, we brought Yossi to Dr. H. as directed, at nine the next morning.

With a medical assistant present, Dr. H. spent five minutes examining Yossi. She then sat down and slowly spoke words we will never forget. "Did this child recently receive a DPT vaccination?" Her words hit us like a tidal wave. Malki and I looked at each other and said almost in unison, "Yes, he did, and that's when all this began."

Dr. H. said nothing but got up and left the office with her assistant. When she finally returned after what seemed an eternity, she handed us a sealed envelope and told us to wait down the hall for the eye specialist. In hindsight, it amazes me that we meekly heeded her without asking any questions, but she was a top neurologist and we were young parents. We made our way down the hall to wait for the doctor. He examined Yossi thoroughly, and when we asked him what he saw in Yossi's eyes, he didn't respond but rather wrote notes on Dr. H.'s piece of paper, resealed it in the envelope, and told us to return it to her.

After another long wait, Dr. H. called us in again. She read the ophthalmology notes and told us to come back two days later, on Sunday morning, for an EEG. We asked what was going on.

She said it was too early to tell. First we had to check the electrical activity in Yossi's brain.

Malki and I left the hospital distraught. We'd been told nothing about what was wrong with Yossi, and we felt bypassed and powerless. In retrospect, our treatment seems unreal, but this was Israel in 1977. We got through the two days, playing with our daughter and comforting our son, until we were due back at the hospital. Early Sunday morning we brought Yossi in for his EEG.

Dr. H. said she saw nothing amiss on the scan and that his brain activity was normal. "Yossi's fine," she said. "Come back in six weeks for a further check."

But Yossi was not fine. The movement in his eyes became far more acute, with his eyeballs seeming to roll in his head. He was making frequent, sharp, and sudden jerks, throwing his head forward and backward, knocking it against whatever was in range. None of the doctors had told us Yossi was suffering from convulsions, and certainly no one notified us that the pertussis vaccination could in rare instances cause them and to be alert for that.

We called Dr. Kanner to update her. Hesitantly, she told us that she knew of another baby recently injured by the DPT vaccine. That incident had occurred in June, four months before Yossi had received the vaccine, and that baby had died.

We called in a big-name physician for a home visit. After he examined Yossi, we told him about the triple vaccine and asked him what he thought. His words still ring in my ears: "Sometimes, at the age of one year, children become retarded. May I now use your phone to contact my next patient?" And that was it. He rushed to another house call, only stopping long enough to be paid.

Our feelings of fear and frustration were boundless.

On December 3, some seven weeks after Yossi's vaccination, Malki gave birth to Yochanan, who weighed in at over ten pounds. With all the joy our new baby brought us, life was very difficult.

Our eldest child, Nechama, was two and a half years old. Yossi continued convulsing and his health continued to deteriorate. I recall taking him to visit two elderly Canadian aunts at a Jerusalem hotel. One of them was holding him when he gave a sudden and immense jerk, arching backward and banging his head on the lobby's glass table. I still had no idea that these jerks were called convulsions.

I took Yossi back to Dr. H. in late December 1977 for his six-week follow-up. She examined him briefly, then gave him a large ball to hold and spent a few more minutes with him. Then she said: "He seems fine. There's nothing more I can do at this time. He'll be OK." I asked when we should next bring him to see her. "No need to come again," she said. "He'll be OK."

Either I was a total fool or so anxious to believe my child was well that I suspended common sense. I came home upbeat with the wonderful news that Dr. H. said Yossi was fine. Malki saw things more clearly. Holding our little boy tightly, she cried: "Kalman, this child is fine? This child is healthy? What kind of doctor is she? She's not blind and she's not stupid – so tell me, what is she talking about? Why isn't she telling us what's wrong with him?"

Dr. H. had given me a sense that the situation would resolve itself. Clearly, that was what I needed to believe at the time.

Today I am wiser.

Today, I know that her behavior was collusion, and that she, with many of her colleagues, turned her back on both her medical ethics and her sense of human decency. And today I also know that Yossi was one of many children damaged by the faulty DPT vaccine during the six months it was administered, killing some and putting others into a lifelong vegetative state.

On December 5, 1977, seven weeks after Yossi had been irreversibly injured, the government ordered the country's well-baby clinics to halt all DTP vaccinations. They initially admitted that six children had been harmed, later expanding that figure to eleven and then twelve, among whom they did not number our son.

Two weeks later, on December 19, an almost unimaginably long interval in today's world of instant news, the story hit the Israeli press. The headline in the daily *Maariv* paper read:

Triple Vaccine Halted!
Six Severe Reactions in Six Months

The supervisor of Israel's well-baby clinics has announced that, two weeks ago, all clinics countrywide were ordered to cease administration of the DPT vaccine. Well-baby clinic directors were instructed to return all unused DPT vaccines and not to administer any part of the triple vaccine until further notice. The DPT has been stopped because of six severely negative reactions, two of them resulting in death. The matter is being thoroughly investigated.

According to Health Ministry Director-General, Dr. Tibor Schwartz, the problem is in the pertussis component. "We have decided to bring in a new vaccine batch so that children won't go unvaccinated," he said. "We are bringing it in from Europe. We won't stop the vaccination program. Our statistics show the same results as European studies, with a problematic reaction in one out of 50,000 cases, with some countries having a lower percentage of incidents, namely one problematic reaction out of 100,000 cases. This is an acceptable and known risk. Six severe reactions in six months are unusual and unacceptable. We don't know what occurred and if there is, in fact, a link between the DPT and the negative outcomes. We have our suspicions, but no clear answers, as yet.

Two months after that, on February 6, 1978, Israel's largest-circulation daily, *Yediot Aharonot*, announced:

Vaccine to Be Restored: "It's Safe"

The triple vaccine has been declared safe and will be resumed within the next two weeks. In 11 cases of severe complications following DPT vaccination, investigation has revealed that the pertussis component was the culprit. Three of the 11 affected infants died. No direct causal relationship has been found between the vaccine and the complications. Despite this, the Health Ministry decided on its withdrawal because of the Ministry's concern for public well-being.

A comparison between the number of injuries in Israel from this batch and those outside [from other batches] showed that serious complications in Israel were five times more frequent than in the UK. A British batch is now being used in Israel. A large amount of this vaccine arrived here during the past two weeks and is now being checked.

I didn't see these newspaper accounts at that time. We were totally occupied with Yossi. He was not "OK," as Dr. H. had assured us he would be, and his problems, rather than passing, continued to become more and more severe. Our lives revolved around our injured child, with never a quiet or tranquil moment, as we tried to protect him from himself and from others. Worse than all of this was seeing him desolate, locked in his own world, a small, lonely being with whom we couldn't communicate.

Malki cried a lot. She saw her child was in pain and didn't know how to help him. That, for her, was the most difficult thing in the world: to know your child needs help, is crying out for help, and you cannot provide it.

We visited many doctors. Those lower down the food chain had no idea what was wrong. Those above them knew only too well, but no one would talk about it. It was clear that an order had been issued by someone powerful and highly placed to conceal these vaccine-related injuries, thus sealing all medical doors tight.

Meanwhile, Yossi's situation continued to deteriorate. His eyes still rolled, and he was unable to focus. His nose, swollen and blocked from his falls and knocks received during convulsions, defied all efforts to clear it and he could breathe only through his mouth. He was beginning to walk, but his gait was awkward and he fell often. Unable to see, Yossi's world was restricted to what he could touch.

Using the very limited sensory information available to him, Yossi was desperately trying to make sense of his universe. And we, with no experience but with all the love in the world, tried to help our child with his extraordinary challenges.

Yossi was a good teacher. Startled if approached or touched too suddenly, he taught us that in his world, things appear out of nowhere and disappear into nowhere. He showed us that he needed gentle cues before being approached so that he could gather information and prepare himself to make his world intelligible and safe. He needed routine and, no less important, stimulation.

Desperate to find a way to help our child, we continued trudging from doctor to doctor – never receiving an explanation, a diagnosis, or any concrete help. When my father's brother Herschel urged us, late that year, to come to New York and meet expert doctors who would speak with us, we were out of other options. Uncle Herschel, thirteen years younger than my father and a brilliant man with a photographic memory, was at the time the co-director of orthopedics at the Maimonides Medical Center in Brooklyn.

And so we made a painful decision: we would take Uncle Herschel up on his suggestion in the hope that we would find out what exactly was wrong with Yossi and in turn learn how we could best help him. Nechama was three, Yossi was two, Yochanan was just over a year, and unbeknownst to us when we left Israel, Malki was pregnant and Avi was on the way.

Chapter 6
New York

Iwas January and freezing when Malki and I arrived in New York with our three children and made our way to Mima Alti's home in Williamsburg, Brooklyn. She had graciously offered to put us up until we found our own accommodations.

Her apartment was compact, and Malki began looking for an apartment for our family of five the day after we arrived. I was still jet-lagged and would have been happier to wait a little, but that didn't stop Malki from combing the ads in the local paper. A few days later, en route to see a number of these possibilities, we found ourselves in Brooklyn, walking down Boro Park's Forty-First Street with Yochanan in his carriage. The temperature was in the teens, with the windchill making it feel even colder. Malki felt terribly nauseous and we stopped frequently. As the nausea continued in the following days, she realized that she was pregnant.

We settled on a small basement apartment, and within a few days we had rented it and were living in Boro Park. This began the next stage of our odyssey to find help for Yossi.

Uncle Herschel referred us to an associate of his, Dr. Arthur Wolnitz, a most impressive man who was known as one of the fathers of neuro-ophthalmology in New York. He was warm and patient during the examination and then, pushing his equipment away from his face, he paused, looked at us with great sympathy, and said quietly, "Your son has a vertical nystagmus and atrophy of the optic nerve. The eye movement is not circular, as it appears, but vertical. I am so sorry to have to share this with you, but your son's optic nerve appears bleached – he will never see again. The connection between the physical eye and the brain is damaged and nothing can be done to either the retina or the physical eye to repair it."

There was an emotionally charged silence. Our flame of hope was extinguished. Numb with devastation, we staggered out of his office in a daze, hit with the finality of a new reality.

Life, however, is a powerful force, and we still held onto hope. Not long afterward, Malki read in the paper about a prominent ophthalmologist who had returned from Europe with a new breakthrough in vision. She contacted his office and made an appointment, hoping that maybe someone like him, a man at the cutting edge of his field, would be able to help our Yossi. So, in those pre-Waze days, I studied my roadmap, helped my wife and son into our jalopy, and headed into the wild blue yonder to find his clinic on Long Island. Driving was still somewhat unfamiliar to me after not having driven since leaving my native Canada a decade earlier, but I managed to find my way along the New York highways, the likes of which I had never experienced. We arrived without major difficulties and met the famous doctor. He and his assistant examined Yossi carefully and confirmed the earlier diagnosis.

Malki asked, "Doctor, Yossi still has a little vision despite his rolling eyes. Do you think that glasses might help?" He motioned with the back of his hand and croaked: "It's hard for me to talk," and with that, we were ushered out of his office. After a few stunned seconds, Malki burst into tears right there in the crowded waiting room. No one moved or asked us what was wrong. In her eloquent Yiddish Malki said, "My three hundred dollars [an exorbitant sum] he took with no problem, but to answer a mother's plea he couldn't respond. We're getting Yossi glasses."

And so we did. Several days later, we were in the office of a kind optometrist. "Let's sit the boy on the chair and I'll show him this chart," he began. Malki explained that Yossi couldn't see the chart because he was almost blind. Baffled, the fellow asked, "Then how can I know what lenses to give him?" "It doesn't really matter," Malki responded. "Just give him something to make the most of whatever minimal vision he may still have." Yossi soon had his first pair of glasses.

In addition to his visual problems, Yossi was acutely hyper-active, and there was never a moment that he wasn't up to some kind of mischief. Literally a little demolition machine, he couldn't be left alone. Unable to see, he experienced everything by touch, and anything he touched wound up dismantled and broken. Curious about how things worked, over the years he took apart every-thing from air conditioners to vacuum cleaners. The one thing he never removed or broke intentionally were his glasses. He put them on first thing in the morning and took them off last thing at night. Did they help him see? Clearly, they gave him something.

We were referred to a leading Brooklyn pediatrician whose diagnoses were said to be thorough and accurate. The waiting room was packed, and we spent the time there trying to keep Yossi under control – a task both exhausting and impossible – and apologizing to all those around us. After what seemed like eons, our turn came. The doctor asked many questions and examined Yossi. "The child needs medication," he concluded, naming a drug that "will make him less hyper and better able to function."

Malki had some questions about how the medication worked, whether it was habit-forming, and whether it had long-term effects, to which the doctor responded with the assurance that there were none to be concerned about. I thought it was a great idea, but Malki thought differently. "Kalman, I'm not playing with Yossi's mind and drugging him up to make our lives easier," she said after we left. "It might make things easier for us now, but we have to think of the long-term effects. It'll make him docile, giving his young mind less of a chance to develop as fully as possible." I understood her concerns but objected, reminding her that the doctor said there were no long-term effects. Her concerns were not allayed. I would have given a lot for a little less hyperactivity around the house. Mind *shmind*, I thought. She's worried about the state of his mind in the future, but I don't know how we'll survive the present!

It became abundantly clear that we had to stay on in New York for longer than we had originally planned because there was a wealth of doctors who were prepared to talk to us honestly about Yossi's condition. While they were definitely uncomfortable with the words "vaccine related," they were at least willing to give candid diagnoses. Therefore, I had to find a way to support our family of five, soon to be six.

My qualifications, at the time, consisted of one year of university, almost a decade of Torah study, rabbinical ordination, and certification as a Torah scribe. It was thus in the Orthodox Jewish world that I began looking for a job.

My first call was to Rabbi Bernard Goldenberg, the rabbi with whom I'd grown up in Vancouver and who'd left his pulpit just before my bar mitzva. He was now a leading figure in the Orthodox national day-school system and had an office in Manhattan. He was delighted to hear from little Kerry Samuels. We met and caught up on family and old-time Vancouverites. I filled him in on our situation and my need for employment, and he immediately presented what he thought was the ideal opportunity for me. One of America's most prominent pulpit rabbis, located in the south, was currently looking for an assistant rabbi, and Rabbi Goldenberg thought I'd be perfect. The salary was higher than I could have imagined, with amazing conditions, and I was shocked that I could be worth that kind of money to anyone. Despite my excitement, however, I knew that this was a nonstarter.

"I can't thank you enough, Rabbi Goldenberg, for thinking of me for this position," I said, "but it's not something I can undertake. We came to the US not for my future, but in the hope of improving my son Yossi's, and it's New York City that offers him the most and best opportunities, medically and educationally. In any case, he needs a stable environment, and if I take that position I will eventually become a traveling salesman, since if after a couple of years I am not successful, I will be looking for another rabbinical position in another city, and if I am successful, I will be seeking a bigger position elsewhere. Either way we will be moving house. It seems clear to me that we now need to stay put here in New York."

Soon thereafter, I was hired by a Jewish communal organization that was trying to prevent fraud in the buying and selling of Jewish religious artifacts through public awareness and consumer education. Although it was a good start, it wasn't what I was looking for. It was at this point that our friend Rabbi Aaron Fischer made a suggestion. Rabbi Aaron was a successful New York businessman and a uniquely kind individual who possessed both enormous worldly wisdom and extensive Torah knowledge. Twenty years my senior, he had also known Malki's family in Europe and as a youngster had lived through the hell of the Holocaust, surviving to raise a large family and devote himself to helping his community. We bonded immediately upon meeting and often talked late into the night in his study, but that never stopped him from rising at dawn for morning prayers, ready to face the new day.

"Try computers," he suggested. A Jewish communal organization would soon be opening an intensive four-month computer course in affiliation with New York University, which he thought would be perfect for me. "I feel very strongly about this opportunity and believe that you will be successful," he said.

I called the organization the next day and showed up as instructed at their Beekman Street office in Lower Manhattan. After filling out an abundance of forms, I was called in for my interview. It did indeed sound like an intensive but excellent and rewarding course. It ran from 9:00 a.m. to 5:00 p.m. five days a week, and I learned that the top students would be placed in good jobs upon graduating.

To my surprise, I was very far from the only applicant. There were over seven hundred candidates vying for forty-two places. Acceptance was based on an aptitude test to be held in two weeks' time. The course would cost $1,700, but there were eleven merit-based, full scholarships available, which also included a weekly stipend. I liked the sound of the course, but would I get in? I knew that in order to make this viable I had to be one of the eleven.

I went home with examples of the aptitude test questions and the name of a book I could purchase to help me prepare for it. The test, I learned, would run ninety minutes, divided into three half-hour segments: multiple-choice math questions, English-language logic, and a section called logical reasoning, in which we had to identify patterns in sequences of diagrams. I bought the book and spent afternoons and evenings in the local library trying to get the hang of it. This kind of test was foreign to me, since in Canada we never had to write exams in that format for university acceptance.

The entrance exam was in a Brooklyn high school gym with hundreds of anxious, young and not-so-young Jewish adults. For me, it went very smoothly. There were two questions about which I was uncertain, but the rest were crystal clear.

The days passed without news. Finally, I called to ask about my score. "Your score is borderline," I was told. I asked what grade was required to get in. "About 42 out of 50 in each of the three sections," he told me. "So what's the problem?" I asked. "I scored far higher than that." Sounding more than a little surprised by my moxie, he asked, "What precisely do you think you scored?" He was even more surprised when I replied that I'd correctly answered a minimum of 49 in both math and English logic and no less than 48 in the logical reasoning section.

There was a pause. I was asked to wait on the line while my test was retrieved. "How did you manage time-wise on the logical reasoning test?" he inquired upon returning to the phone. "It took me twenty minutes to answer the questions, and ten more to check it through twice," I replied. "Well," he said, "I must tell you, that you got 50 in math and 49 in English logic, but you scored only 39 with the logical reasoning diagrams." "That's not possible!" I objected. He was very decent and patiently explained: "You didn't answer the ten questions on the last page. I'm assuming you didn't see them." He generously offered to make an exception, and asked me to come to their office the next day where I would do another logical reasoning test, and my grade would be based on that one. I took the test the following day, got 49 out of 50, and was accepted with a full scholarship.

A friendly guidance counselor explained the course parameters and assured us that once we were qualified, she'd help us find jobs. It took a good five years to succeed in the field, she said. When I told her I planned to be back in Israel in five years, she laughed and said, "Dream on! Once you're in a good job and have a growing family, it's simply not realistic." I smiled and said, "I guess I've never been much of a realist."

The four months of the course were difficult, but youth is wonderful, and Malki and I had both energy and boundless love for our children. I would leave at 8:00 a.m. each day after attending morning prayers at the nearby synagogue and after insisting on helping Malki diaper three toddlers and cope with Yossi. I arrived home at 6:00 p.m., spent quality time with Malki and the kids, and then sat down to study the voluminous course materials until well after midnight.

Malki, pregnant with Avi, was fully occupied with Nechama, Yossi, and Yochanan, all of whom – and especially Yossi – needed her constantly. It was Shlomo Carlebach's Jewish soul music that gave her strength and comfort during this taxing time. Highly musical herself, she'd play his songs nonstop on our small tape recorder, fervently singing along. It grated on me, but it certainly empowered Malki. So it's no surprise that after having heard Reb Shlomo's music for most of his life in utero, Avi has unusual musical talent and sings and *davens* with Reb Shlomo's tunes in a uniquely sensitive way.

Our first New York summer arrived along with its characteristic humidity and heat. My computer course was coming to an end, as was Malki's pregnancy. Well into her ninth month, she called to make an appointment with her well-known ob-gyn and was advised that since she was away on summer vacation Malki would be seen by another doctor in the office who was filling in for her. He examined her, and after measuring her blood pressure, said matter-of-factly, "Your blood pressure is very high. How many children do you have?" "Three," Malki replied. "So after this birth, there will be four orphans," he calmly continued.

Twenty-four-year-old Malki held herself together and rushed as best she could to the first pay phone she found. Once on the phone with me, she sobbed, "That doctor will NEVER deliver my baby! I'd rather give birth like a cat on the street. How could anyone be so cold-hearted, so insensitive?"

She arrived home and we called Mima Alti's daughter Blimi for another ob-gyn recommendation. We met the new doctor the next day, a very pleasant fellow, and hired him to deliver the baby.

Labor began two days later and we hurried to Maimonides Hospital. Standing at admissions was the first ob-gyn, who greeted us, clearly thinking his patient had arrived. Malki looked straight through him and asked the nurse to call the second doctor. Several hours later, seven months after our arrival in New York, Avi was born, weighing in at nine pounds five ounces, a source of great joy at a very difficult time.

Chapter 7

By His Own Yardstick

W e had come to New York to help Yossi, prepared to go any distance to do so. But there was something critically important that I hadn't thought of, something that was very close to home. It took a visit from my sister Marilyn to open my eyes to it.

A professor of child developmental psychology and head of the Calgary Learning Center, Marilyn was in town for an academic conference, and we picked her brain about where to send two-and-a-half-year-old Yossi to school. She favored the Lighthouse for the Blind school in midtown Manhattan, which was part of Lighthouse International, the respected one-hundred-year-old pioneer organization in the field of vision rehabilitation. This was a difficult decision for me. I wanted my son in a religious Jewish school environment. Marilyn spelled out a hard truth in words that made a deep and lasting impression.

"Listen, kid brother," she said. "The problem here isn't Yossi. It's you. You've got to realize your son will never be the Torah scholar or the athlete you dream of – and that's not *his* problem;

51

it's *yours*. He's blind with additional challenges, and he needs the best school that will give him the tools to function in life. He won't get these at a religious school. He'll get them at the Lighthouse. He will get his religious education at home, but for G-d's sake, don't burden him with your dreams! You're going to be a frustrated father and have a frustrated son if you don't accept that he has his own life to live, his own journey, and his own goals to accomplish. And those goals can only be measured with his own personal yardstick. He'll achieve everything he can, but at the end of the day, if all you can do as a parent is keep him warm, comfortable, and as happy as possible, so be it. Kalman, wake up!"

Marilyn's words hit me like a ton of bricks and I wept like a baby. I knew she was right, but it still took me years to get from acknowledging this in my head to truly accepting it in my heart. It's not easy to give up on your own dreams so that someone else can live theirs – but oh so critical.

Marilyn arranged our first visit to the Lighthouse. It was very difficult to walk in and see people of all ages who were blind navigating the hallways with their canes. Surely this place was not for us, I thought. Of course, it was a fine place to visit, and of course we personally cared about the blind and would happily contribute to their care, but to realize that our beautiful little boy was part of this world seemed too painful to bear.

Mrs. Putterman was a Lighthouse social worker, a kind middle-aged woman, who saw our shock and received us with warmth and empathy. We also immediately took to the school's director of education, Dr. Mary Ann Lang, who was young, friendly, and beamed like a light bulb. She clearly loved every child who came into her care, and she gave us instant hope. After a long morning of seeing Yossi in different situations, Mrs. Putterman invited us into her office and said, "I am pleased to share that Joseph is accepted to the Lighthouse. The annual cost is $10,000." I almost fell off my chair upon hearing what was at the time an exorbitant amount, but she kindly clarified: "Mr. Samuels, it does indeed cost $10,000, but our policy is that while your child is with us, no one pays fees. We will never differentiate between those who pay and those who don't. In the future, after Joseph leaves, you'll have a moral obligation to help us in any way you can." "Sure, sure, of course," I said, relieved that not only could Yossi attend, but that he'd be no different than any other child. It was a lesson that Malki and I would remember.

And so the Lighthouse minibus began arriving every morning at 8:00 a.m., and Malki or I waited with Yossi on the street in front of our Brooklyn home to help him aboard for the hour-long drive to midtown Manhattan. He loved getting out each morning, and everyone at the Lighthouse loved him. Though he walked awkwardly, he was a fighter and walk he did. He was always neat and clean, so impeccably dressed that the Lighthouse staff assumed he was an only child. Working with children with disabilities at close range is hard, and Malki felt that anything she could do to make it as pleasant as possible for the staff to be close to him was a contribution to Yossi's education.

After several weeks at the Lighthouse, Yossi began making odd spastic movements with his arms and hands. Malki and I were deeply troubled, but leave it to a mother to figure out what the issue was. Malki discovered that on the school minibus Yossi sat next to a child who did exactly the same thing during the sixty-minute journeys there and back. Yossi was moved to a different seat and, sure enough, it ceased. What amazed us was Yossi's ability to mimic movements that he could feel but not see.

His energy remained seemingly limitless. Arriving home from the Lighthouse around 1:00 p.m., he was ready for action – action that had to be constantly watched. With three other toddlers, Malki rarely got a break and despite all her love, she was exhausted. We looked for help, but it proved difficult to find. One woman quit after two days, saying she could handle ten children at a time, but our little Yossi was too much for her.

Yossi was constantly curious and wanted to be involved in everything around him. It was clear to us that there was a keen mind locked inside him that we couldn't reach. One of his obsessions was our Electrolux vacuum cleaner. He loved it so much that Malki made it his and bought another one for her use. Yossi would switch it on to feel the air current and try to figure out how it worked. He did the same with everything he could lay his hands on, and while I sometimes viewed this as problematic, it made Malki happy. She knew that as long as he was actively trying to understand his surroundings, there was hope, and she went to great lengths to ensure that he wouldn't wind up sitting in a corner and giving up on the world.

On Sabbath afternoons, Yossi would somehow drag the mattresses off the beds in his bedroom and take them to the stairs, gathering his younger brothers to slide down on them together to the living room. He would then climb up with them in order to slide down again and again, all to the sound of his and their joyful laughter. He was so full of life and found ways to connect with everyone.

From a very young age, no keys were safe near Yossi. He was the ultimate pickpocket, and if keys were missing we knew the first place to look. He knew they were important and that if he hid them, we'd all have to look for them. He had his own key ring with a dozen keys of all makes and sizes, a few of which actually opened locks we used. These keys, however, were never enough, and Yossi would slide his delicate little hands into others' pockets to augment his collection. As careful as I was to keep an eye on him, when he leaned on my leg or sat on my lap, he'd wait for his moment and stealthily extract his treasure. When caught, a sheepish smile would spread from ear to ear, expressing as clearly as words: "Whoops! You caught me!"

His fascination with keys wasn't without its uses. One rainy winter evening, returning home with tired and cold children, most of whom urgently needed the bathroom, the outside hallway was pitch-black and we stood in utter darkness. I was fumbling through my half dozen keys for the two that opened our front door locks, until an exasperated Malki said: "For goodness' sake, give your keys to Yossi!" In the dark, he quickly ran his fingers delicately along the faces of the keys and within no time he had found the right ones and the door was open.

One very unpleasant surprise at this time was our neighbors. It hadn't occurred to us that people would feel uncomfortable living next door to a child with disabilities, but for two years one neighbor whom we ran into almost daily never spoke to us. To him, Yossi was contagious and he didn't want his children anywhere near him or near us. This was painful.

Our neighbors on the other side were friendlier but, as events bore out, there were serious problems of education there too. Yossi loved to play alongside his brothers and sister, and one afternoon he was in the backyard with them, holding on to the metal-mesh fence that separated our yard from that of these neighbors. Suddenly Malki heard him scream and feared the worst. She rushed outside and saw the neighbors' children laughing and running into their home, clutching sandy spades. Yossi's eyes, nose, and mouth were plastered with the thick, wet sand that they had thrown through the fence into his face. Their mother came onto her back porch to apologize.

"Don't you dare apologize to me!" Malki threw at her, anger erasing all inhibitions. "It isn't your children who are guilty! You're the guilty one! They're capable of cruelty like this only because they're aware of the disdain you bear toward my child." It was a horrible scene, and one that spoke volumes about the values parents instill in their children.

Meanwhile, I was looking for a job. I'd completed the computer course with high grades and had interviews lined up. I accepted an offer from a small consulting firm that specialized in programming what was then a very successful mini-computer produced by Wang Laboratories, widely used in small- and medium-sized businesses worldwide. My modest starting salary would be reviewed, I was told, after my first three months, and if warranted, would be significantly increased.

The work was stimulating. Within weeks I was part of a consulting team at the firm that was developing software onsite for a large Long Island eyeglasses retailer. The jump from academic theory to reality was cosmic. While I'd done well in my studies, the real world was more challenging. Once, I inadvertently hit the wrong key and watched in horror as the computer deleted, one by one, all eighty-five Cobol programs that the team had spent months developing. My heart dropped, but my colleagues were kindness itself. The source codes were not lost, they explained, and could be retrieved and recompiled. It would simply take most of a day to do so and get back up to speed.

My next assignment was with a different team, working on a project at Citibank. More experienced by now, I knew what was expected, had developed a wider range of skills, and was able to easily pick up what I didn't know, quietly and quickly. The bank was very happy with my work.

This was where I was when my three-month trial ended, but the promised review didn't happen. I called my boss at the consulting firm to ask about it. "Come in tomorrow at 5:00 p.m.," he told me.

Malki now had her driver's license and often drove in from Brooklyn with the kids to pick me up in our little red Ford. That day, she picked me up at Citibank and drove me to the firm for the meeting with my boss. Half an hour later, I was back at the car, and she could see from my face that things hadn't gone well. "He said I was a very diligent worker and greatly appreciated," I told her, "but, according to Citibank, I'm not yet churning out the latkes fast enough, so I'll have to wait another three months for another review. When I tried to tell him that I know Citibank is delighted with me, he wouldn't listen."

Malki was livid. She flung open the car trunk, where I had a dozen large Wang manuals. "Take these up to the office, put them on that man's desk, and tell him to lock away a shirt in his safe! If this is how he manipulates such dedicated, hardworking employees, he'll have neither a company nor a job in a year's time – and he'll need that shirt." I told Malki I couldn't do that. I had a family to feed. Our fifth child, Simcha, was on the way. I'd begin looking for another job at once, but I couldn't walk out of this one until I had something else.

I may as well have been talking to the wall. "Where there's injustice," said Malki, "money isn't an issue. I don't want you working for this man another day!"

And so, very much against my better judgment, I gathered the manuals and reluctantly made my way back to the office. I knocked on my very-soon-to-be-ex-boss's door. "What's all this about?" he greeted me. "These manuals," I replied, unloading them all over his desk, "I won't be needing them, because I'm quitting, effective immediately. I won't work for someone who brazenly lies to me about what clients say about the quality of my work in order to avoid giving me a raise that was both promised and deserved. And, by the way, I strongly suggest that you put a shirt away in a safe place. If this is how you treat dedicated employees, you'll have neither a company nor a job in a year and that shirt will come in handy."

There, I had gotten the words out. He was shell-shocked. Nothing came out of his mouth as I turned and walked quickly away. I, too, was in shock. What was I going to do now?

The next morning, I called my employer at Citibank to apologize for being unable to continue. When pressed, I shared that I'd been told the bank was unhappy with my performance. This information was met with several juicy expletives. Citibank, he told me, had been paying the consulting firm the obscene sum of $450 a day for my services and had balked when they'd asked for even more. Now it was my turn to be shocked; they were charging so much for the services of a novice and still refused to increase my meager starting salary?!

"Here's what I suggest," said my Citibank employer. "From tomorrow, work for us directly until the project is completed. We'll pay you $150 a day." Well, $150 may have been a small fraction of $450, but it was more than what I'd been paid until now. "What about my pledge not to take the firm's clients?" I queried. Amid more expletives, he assured me I had nothing to be concerned about. He'd let the consulting firm know that Citibank would release other members of their consulting team and countersue if they came after me.

During the five weeks it took to complete the project, I tasted the lucrative fruits of computer consulting. The bank was delighted with what I did and only sorry they had nothing further to offer. Every now and then, I saw my former employer from the consulting firm lurking in the shadows, but we never spoke.

Malki's clear-sightedness had let me hold my head high and had taught me yet another valuable lesson: in computers, consulting pays far more than a secure corporate job, and experience doesn't have to be a factor if you prove yourself as having the skills. With the pressing need to support my family, consulting was clearly for me.

Chapter 8

The Pact

I'm a firm believer in the power of blessings. Nine months after the blessing given us by the Tchaba Rav in Jerusalem, Nechama had arrived, rapidly followed by younger brothers. New York gave us access not only to some of the world's best physicians for Yossi, but also to some of the Jewish world's most spiritual rebbes.

One was Rabbi Chaim Zanvl Abramowitz, the Ribnitzer Rebbe. A righteous man believed by his followers to be a miracle worker, he had been revered even by the Russian gentiles among whom he'd lived until 1970, with members of the KGB bringing their wives and children to him for blessings. We'd met him in the seventies when he lived in Israel. Now he was based in Seagate, a gated community at the western end of Coney Island in Brooklyn, and we took Yossi to him for his first haircut.

Cutting a boy's hair for the first time at age three and leaving *peyot*, or sidelocks, is an age-old custom among ultra-Orthodox Jews, and for us it was a meaningful rite of passage. We arrived at the home of the Ribnitzer Rebbe in the early evening. Predictably, his waiting room was packed with people of all types and ages, waiting to see the Rebbe even for a couple of minutes and get his blessing. Yossi was inexhaustibly running around the room and up and down the basement stairs despite my best efforts to control him. It was very hot, I was sweating and, oh Malki, what I wouldn't have given for a little calming medication for Yossi just then! It was over an hour until we were called in. Picking Yossi up, we entered another large room. The Rebbe was seated with two men standing beside him. One was a well-known hasidic singer, Mordechai Ben David, and the other a well-known cantor, Ari Klein – two worldly young men who had become deeply attached to the Rebbe and spent hours helping him. They briefed him about Yossi and why we were there.

The Rebbe directed his helpers and me to sit Yossi down on a chair directly in front of him. Oh sure, I thought. Perfect! We're going to try to sit Yossi on a chair in front of the Rebbe. We're beginning with Mission Impossible! I was about to explain that this wasn't going to work, but they urged me, "Just do what the Rebbe says." So I gently placed Yossi on the chair. The Rebbe gave Yossi his hand and Yossi played with it. Then he reached out and touched the Rebbe's beard, something he was familiar with from me. I worried that the Rebbe wouldn't take to this kindly, but he patted Yossi's cheek and placed the child's hands in his. I told the Rebbe that Yossi's lineage leads directly back to King David. This may not get him into an Ivy League school, but it's important information for rebbes. The Rebbe leaned forward, placed his face close to Yossi's, and began to recite slowly, over and over, more and more loudly, the age-old Jewish expression, "*David melech Yisrael, hai vekayam*" (David, the king of Israel, lives and endures).

Amused, the Rebbe asked for the scissors. For over forty minutes, Yossi sat cooperatively still while the Rebbe cut off his long locks, piece by piece, chanting the sentence as he did so. At one point, a grumpy elderly man entered the room and said loudly in Russian-accented Yiddish: "Rebbe, we must recite the afternoon prayer. It's late and people are waiting." When the Rebbe ignored him, he repeated it louder. Scissors in hand, the Rebbe looked up slowly and motioned him away, saying, "*Loz mich ton vos ich vill*" (Leave me to do what I want). The Rebbe continued with Yossi, and Yossi continued sitting still. Mordechai Ben David literally lay on the floor to see better, saying to us, "This is incredible! I've never seen the Rebbe do anything like this before."

When the job was done – it was a messy haircut! – the Rebbe put the new yarmulke we'd bought on Yossi's head and gave him his heartfelt blessing for good health and a happy life. We thanked the Rebbe and walked out in a daze, full of hope that Yossi's condition would somehow improve. The forty minutes of calm evaporated in an instant as Yossi reverted to his frenetic self on the drive home.

Sometime later, we received another blow when Malki got a phone call from Barbara, Yossi's beloved Lighthouse teacher. "Malki," she said, "before working with blind children, I worked for many years with the deaf. I think that Yossi's tendency to go his own way isn't because he's ornery but because he has a significant hearing deficiency. He must be tested."

"I can't listen to this, Barbara!" Malki responded and uncharacteristically, she hung up the phone. How could an already overwhelmed young mother hear that her blind son was also going deaf, on top of everything else? It was simply more than she could bear.

But bear it we did. Malki and I made our way to Long Island for Yossi to be tested at the Helen Keller National Center for Deaf-Blind Youths and Adults. The results confirmed that Yossi was profoundly deaf. He was three and a half years old and none of us – not we, his parents, nor the professionals who worked with him – had realized. He had so many issues that we'd assumed his failure to listen was because he didn't understand. He used to sing along with us and say the *Shema Yisrael* prayer, which means, ironically, "Hear, O

Israel." Yes, his vocalizations were odd, but who had thought it was because his hearing was deteriorating? Malki had assumed that he was mimicking the odd sounds of his younger brother Yochanan.

Were he someone else's child, my attitude would have been: "What neglectful parents!" But this was my child, a child whose every need we responded to, day and night. Yet no one had known. It took even Barbara, with her special expertise, a long time to figure it out.

So Yossi now had hearing aids to go with his glasses. We didn't notice much difference in his hearing, but given that he always wanted them and always wore them, he was clearly deriving some benefit.

Nonetheless, he was a frustrated child, and he poured out his frustration on the household. He couldn't communicate and was hyperactive and full of energy he couldn't let out. Even so, the boys shared a bedroom with Yossi and thrived amid much joy. Yossi was part of everything, but life with him wasn't easy.

During the years ahead, we occasionally witnessed the marriages of parents of children with disabilities stagger under the immense pressures and sometimes fail. Malki and I, however, were blessed in being able to face things together. Within weeks of Yossi's injury, still in our early to mid-twenties, we had our third child. We wanted a large family and consciously decided that despite the challenges, we would welcome our children, with G-d's help, while we were young. Three more came in quick succession: Avi nineteen months after Yochanan, Simcha twelve months after Avi to the day, and Shlomo twenty-two months after that. And that seemed to be that, until almost seventeen years later when we were blessed with Sara.

We remained intact as a family despite Yossi's overwhelming needs, in no small measure because of Malki's boundless love for our children coupled with our joint flexibility. We understood that staying together is all about whether you can give up on your own goals and dreams, realize life has changed forever, and make new choices. My sister helped me discard my yardstick for measuring

Yossi, a yardstick on which he never could have measured up. With Yossi, and in fact with our other children, we recognized that in raising children successfully it's not about our journey as parents, but about each child's own personal journey.

* * *

From time to time former teachers from Israel would be in Brooklyn for personal reasons and would take the opportunity to visit Malki, and invariably they felt obligated to offer advice.

Exemplifying their well-meaning counsel was "the Rebbetzin," an older woman, well-known in Orthodox Jerusalem circles, and someone Malki knew well and respected. Her visit with Malki was warm and meaningful until she turned to the problems we faced raising a young family along with Yossi's crushing multiple challenges.

"This is commendable," she said, "but it's not fair to yourselves or to your healthy children." Voicing what many others no doubt thought, she continued, "You can't live this way. You should consider moving this child out of the house, so you can all get on with your lives."

Malki listened courteously. When the Rebbetzin finished, she responded in Yiddish: "Rebbetzin, do you know what your problem is?" "No," replied the surprised visitor. "Well, I'll tell you," said Malki calmly. "You have no faith in G-d." Boom! It was like telling Bill Gates he's broke. The Rebbetzin was speechless. Without faith, what did she have? Malki continued, "The good L-rd gave Yossi to me. Yossi is my heavenly gift and not something I'll ever run from. You are asking me to cut off part of my body; which part do you suggest?" The shocked Rebbetzin began to apologize, but Malki stopped her. "Wait twenty minutes until Yossi comes home and meet the child whose life course you want to decide."

The school minivan honked its horn, and Malki ran down the front stairs to meet it. She made her way back much more slowly with Yossi clumsily negotiating each step. The Rebbetzin stood at the top of the staircase, watching. There had been a birthday party at school that day and Yossi was dressed in cute black shorts with matching suspenders, a white shirt, knee socks, and patent leather shoes. His little black yarmulke, *peyot*, glasses, and hearing aids made him look all the more distinguished. He and Malki entered the house where they hugged and kissed as usual – their only means of communicating. The Rebbetzin was weeping and asking Malki to forgive her. Following all she'd heard about our son, this was something she hadn't imagined. The visit ended cordially with the Rebbetzin the wiser.

Not long thereafter, the kids were playing on the swings in our backyard, and Malki was observing them from inside through the large glass doors of the porch. The rays of the late afternoon sun shone on her as she gently rocked the baby carriage via her foot on its wheel, with Yossi on her lap occupying her hands. Powerful emotions rose from within as Malki sensed her helplessness in trying to cope.

Sobbing quietly from the depths of her soul, she took a deep breath, paused, and made a solemn pact with the Almighty. "You gave me my beloved Yossi and I will care for him until my final breath, but I promise You this: If You ever decide to help my Yossi, I will dedicate my life to helping so many other mothers of children with disabilities whom I know are crying with me for their children."

In the span of a few years, Malki had lost her beloved mother and watched her healthy son gravely harmed, but her faith never wavered. "Every action is guided from heaven," she often said. "I've always believed that G-d is with me. I've always felt G-d's hand in mine, each and every step of the way."

And thus she had the strength to pour her love into our six young children, care for Yossi, reject any suggestion of institutionalizing him – and make her pact with G-d, her constant companion.

Chapter 9

Medics, Mystics, and Mealtimes

Of course we didn't sit back waiting for G-d's intervention. Our odyssey to find someone who could help Yossi continued unabated.

There was the "amazing" pediatrician to whom we were referred, whose hands were white because he washed them with a bleach solution every few minutes. Amazing maybe; OCD certainly. He described Yossi's gait "as if he has a grapefruit between his legs," and referred us to his uncle, a well-known neurologist in New Rochelle, using his influence to get us an appointment at the uncle's home the following Sunday morning.

Once again out came the road maps, and I carefully plotted our journey along unfamiliar highways. What may be a simple drive for most people was anything but for a newcomer to New York, driving with a hyperactive, blind, and deaf three-year-old. The doctor was very pleasant, talked about encephalitis, or swelling of the brain, as a possible vaccine reaction, and had nothing practical to suggest.

The search continued and we took Yossi to another leading neurologist, Dr. Myles Behrens. Upon learning that Yossi had been examined by Dr. H., whom he knew, he asked for a written report of her findings. He also referred us to Columbia-Presbyterian for a neuro-pediatric assessment with Dr. Arnold Gold, the granddaddy of neurology in New York.

Dr. Gold was a most impressive individual and examined Yossi very carefully and asked many questions. He sat us down and suggested we hospitalize Yossi for three days for a battery of neurological tests to clarify his condition. I was excited by this opportunity. A world expert wanted to examine my son and finally find out what was wrong. Not so Malki. There was a pause and then she deferentially asked, "Doctor, after the three days of tests, do you think you'll be able to help my son?" There was an even greater pause before Dr. Gold replied: "I can't say whether I'll be able to help him, but I'll gather important data about what he has." Malki then asked, "And doctor, who'll be doing these tests, you or your students?" Another pause and then: "Well naturally, my associates, some of whom are my students, will be involved – but I'll be guiding them." Malki said, "Thank you doctor," and Dr. Gold was taken aback, realizing that she apparently didn't intend to do the tests.

I guess most people are like me and would say, "Gee, thanks, that's great." Not Malki. What was her objection? I asked her as soon as we left. Her reply was, as usual, succinct. "My Yossi will not be his guinea pig. Yossi may be a fascinating case for research, but he said openly he doesn't think he'll be able to help him. So what will I have, his research on my shelf? Can you imagine how many times they're going to stick Yossi with needles and the different ways they'll traumatize him without him understanding what is happening? And for what? The doctor doesn't know if he can help him, but my fear is that it may damage him. Forget it."

Malki's words were hard for me to accept. I strongly felt this was an opportunity we couldn't afford to miss. We would finally know what there was to know about Yossi's condition and could then plan accordingly. How could we possibly not follow through? My respect for the medical profession was innate and ran deep. Most of my uncles and cousins were doctors, my lawyer-dad being the family exception. When a doctor spoke, my reflex was to agree. Malki had respect but would not allow Yossi to be their pincushion.

Shortly thereafter, Uncle Hershel and Aunt Edie visited on a Sunday afternoon. He incidentally shared that, of late, he had been treating a most interesting patient, an elderly hasidic woman who was the wife of Rabbi Schneerson. "Rabbi Schneerson?" I asked. "As in the Lubavitcher Rebbe?" "Yes," he replied. I was amazed at what I was hearing. "So what makes her interesting?" I asked, and he proceeded to explain that she was not only refined and cultured, but also brilliant, and there was just something special about her. I told Uncle Hershel that I would love to get a blessing from her husband for Yossi, and he immediately said, "No problem. Next time Mrs. Schneerson comes for an appointment, I will ask."

About a month later, Uncle Hershel called. "Mrs. Schneerson was in earlier and I told her that my nephew would appreciate a blessing from her husband for his sick child. She said she would call me later, and she just did. You are to be there at 3:00 p.m. tomorrow to meet him." I couldn't believe it. I was not a card-carrying member of the Lubavitch hasidic community and had never visited the famous Lubavitch headquarters at 770 Eastern Parkway in Brooklyn, but I had untold respect for the Rebbe's greatness in all areas of Jewish life. He was one of a kind in his brilliance and in his love for his fellow Jew and fellow man.

I shared the news with an emissary of the Rebbe whom I knew and he laughed. "Kalman, your uncle may mean well, but the Rebbe is not accepting even his closest people at this time due to a medical issue of his own."

I felt that we had to at least go through the motions, so the following day I came home from work early and Malki, Yossi, and I made our way to 770.

The street out front was packed with cars and there was no parking so I told Malki to just stay there double-parked for a few minutes while I went in to size up the situation. I entered and found a Rabbi Klein, one of the Rebbe's secretaries, in a little reception office. I took a deep breath and said in Yiddish, "The Rebbetzin has invited us to have a private meeting with the Rebbe at this time." I was ready for hearty laughter. How totally shocked I was when Rabbi Klein responded in Yiddish, "We are aware. The Rebbe has advised us of your coming. We will *daven minha* (pray the afternoon prayer) together with the Rebbe and he will then receive you." I kindly thanked him and sprinted out to Malki, fumbling for words and sharing with her what had transpired, telling her that I'd go inside with Yossi and she should park the car quickly and then come in too.

There were some one hundred young men and rabbis present for the fifteen-minute afternoon prayer with the Rebbe. Immediately afterward, we were escorted after him through an adjacent door. We found ourselves standing in a wood-paneled room with a winding wooden staircase in one corner. The Rebbe welcomed us with a pleasant smile and we entered into conversation. I shared the background of Yossi's problems, and a couple of minutes into our discussion I mentioned that he was a direct descendant of King David via his mother. The Rebbe fixed a gaze on Malki and neither blinked nor broke his gaze. It was eerie and uncanny. Malki could not look away and break the gaze. Clearly, I was irrelevant and could equally have been on a telephone call outside in the hall.

We spoke about important issues. Most notably we asked the Rebbe for his guidance as to whether we should go forward with Dr. Arnold Gold's suggestion of hospitalizing Yossi for tests. The Rebbe went on at length and explained that according to Jewish law, we should share this question with two leading medical authorities and ask their opinion. If both concur, he said, then we are obligated to follow their advice. If they do not concur then my Uncle Hershel should guide us.

Finally, after seemingly endless minutes, the Rebbe broke his gaze and gave Yossi a nickel in his hand. Yossi took three steps and threw it down. We were so embarrassed, but the Rebbe calmly gave Yossi another nickel and told us, "Don't be concerned, this is a healthy quality in the child." After fifteen minutes of being in the presence of this giant, the conversation concluded with the Rebbe asking me to please give his warmest regards to my Uncle, Dr. Samuels. He made it perfectly clear as to why we had received such extraordinary attention: it was in gratitude for my Uncle's care.

Malki never quite recovered from what she described as his "blue eyes, deep like the sea." Years later I noted in the writings of Chabad that when one of their Rebbes stared at an individual, however briefly, it was considered an event of significance, and that the stare was given for a reason, often to give the person the spiritual strength to deal with future challenges. What then can I say about the Rebbe's extended gaze? In light of unfolding events it was seemingly a gift to enhance Malki's own vision.

I now turned to Uncle Hershel and asked him to identify two additional medical authorities with whom we could share our question as to whether we should hospitalize Yossi at Columbia-Presbyterian for the battery of tests as I believed, or whether I would have to buckle under. Hershel checked it out and referred us to two neuro-ophthalmologists. They each did a thorough checkup of Yossi in their offices with the latest equipment and both gave similar diagnoses involving vertical nystagmus and atrophy of the optic nerve along with meningitis. As for our key question, one said to definitely go ahead with the guru Dr. Arnold Gold's plan, but incredibly the other agreed with Malki. He did not have much hope that hospitalizing Yossi would yield information that would be helpful to him and had to admit that the trauma of such a frail child is not something to be taken lightly. I questioned him and tried to minimize the impact of his comments, but to my surprise he turned to me and said quietly, "Mr. Samuels, you have an unusually bright wife and her unconventional wisdom is worthy of being listened to." Voilà, Malki had her solid backing. It didn't help me, however, and while Malki appreciated my predicament, it was clearly not happening.

* * *

Even as we turned to doctors and rebbes, Malki heard about the impact of diet on children. She inquired further and was advised to make three key changes in Yossi's diet: no white flour, no white sugar, and no processed oil. Given the amount of time, money, and energy we were prepared to expend on helping our son, this seemed manageable. Malki decided it would be a family project and cleared the kitchen of all foods containing the forbidden ingredients, which turned out to be almost everything. She piled them into our car for Bella, the Russian Jewish immigrant who helped us, to take home that afternoon. Bella kept repeating in Yiddish, "*Malketza, du host heatz? Bist meshuga gevoren?*" (Little Malka, do you have a fever? Have you gone crazy?)

Our kitchen cabinets were replenished with products from a health-food store, where Malki found whole-wheat bread, cold-pressed olive oil, and an array of other wholesome foods. She went to great effort to prepare delicious meals and the kids and I loved them. We also excluded meat, chicken, and even fish, which made the Sabbath meals especially challenging, but Malki cooked up a storm of vegetables, healthy pastas, and many more nutritious foods.

Some six weeks later, Barbara from the Lighthouse called. "Malki, you know I see myself as your partner in helping Yossi, so I'm more than a little surprised that you haven't shared with me what you're giving him." Malki replied, "Of course we're partners, Barbara! What on earth are you talking about?" "C'mon Malki, don't play games," said Barbara. "Yossi's behavior these past weeks has totally changed! He's calmer, more attentive, and far less hyper. You're obviously giving him a new medication and haven't told me. I'm the one working with him, and I should know what it is." "Barbara," responded Malki, "I'm not giving him any medication. I've simply taken sugar and white flour out of his diet." Barbara scoffed, "Don't give me that, Malki! He's taking medication, and for whatever reason you're embarrassed to tell me." Malki laughed. "Barbara, believe what you want. If I was giving him medication, I'd have no problem telling you, but the fact is I'm not. The changes I have made are strictly dietary."

I don't think Barbara ever really believed Malki. In the years ahead, I met many other professionals who made light of the effects of a changed diet. We continued with the food changes for about a year and none of our children were ill during that entire time. Like anything else in life, though, a strict diet is a commitment, and slowly we slipped. The kids went back to their lollipops; what synagogue doesn't have a "lollipop man" who reaches into his deep pockets and brings a smile to a child's face? With that slippage, the colds and flus returned. I found myself back at our pediatrician with three little ones in tow. "So where've you been this past year?" he asked, and without waiting for my answer said, "I guess you tried out other doctors and realized that I wasn't so bad, after all." "Actually we haven't been anywhere else, but have been on a strict healthy diet," I shared. Slowly, he edged his glasses down his nose and, peering over them, said, "You really expect me to believe that? Please!" He examined each child and prescribed antibiotics all around.

* * *

Yossi still walked awkwardly. He would fall after running a short distance, his leg movements were irregular, and he rode his tricycle with difficulty. Hence, the next suggestion from another friend to visit a wonderful chiropractor she knew. I froze. "A chiropractor? They're quacks!" "No," she replied. "Donny Epstein is an amazing professional." In private, I told Malki, "Forget it. If you think we should see an orthopedist, we have the best one for free right here in Brooklyn – Uncle Herschel. But chiropractors are just quacks."

A week later, I was with Malki and Yossi in a busy waiting room on Brooklyn's Quentin Road at the clearly successful chiropractic clinic of Dr. Donny Epstein. Donny was young, very warm, and full of life and energy. He listened attentively to our story and then said: "OK, let's get to work." First he had Yossi sit, and then lie down, all the while gently moving his hands along our child's head, neck, spine, and legs. He noted that his nose was swollen and blocked, a result of the knocks from his convulsions and falls, forcing him to breathe through his mouth. For the next half-hour, he did all kinds of noninvasive "quacky" things, but amazingly, Yossi seemed to enjoy every minute and allowed Donny to work with him. Following the examination, with Yossi on my lap, Donny showed us an illuminated image of the human spine and introduced us to chiropractic methodology and philosophy. It was hard to admit, but I was impressed.

We went back weekly. At home some six weeks later, Malki called out to me urgently. "Kalman! Kalman, come here now!" I froze with alarm. "Look, just look at Yossi's nose," she insisted. "He's breathing through it!" I looked at the magical sight. His nose was indeed healing. We had no doubt that this was Donny's doing. Yossi's gait had also improved markedly, as had his tricycle riding. I, for one, was happy to eat my hat – but not so Uncle Herschel. He and my beloved Aunt Edie visited us on Sunday. As we watched the kids playing out front, they couldn't help but notice the extraordinary changes in Yossi. I shared my story about Donny Epstein. Uncle Herschel, turning to go back into the house, said with utter dismissal, "You can't effect those changes externally"; in simple English, "Oh please don't feed me that nonsense." I turned to Edie and asked her whether Herschel could see the improvement. She smiled and replied, "Of course he sees it, as do I. Your Uncle Herschel is a very wise man, but he's an orthopedist, and you can't expect him to admit that this change results from chiropractic treatment."

* * *

After two good years at the Lighthouse, it was time for Yossi to move on. His new school was the Hebrew Institute for the Deaf, in Bensonhurst, Brooklyn, which was much closer to our home. It was a well-run Jewish school but could not compete with the resources and professionalism of the Lighthouse. The principal, Laura Nadoolman, was a tough, no-nonsense educator. Malki received a call from her in which she asked very formally: "Mrs. Samuels, where are Joseph's glasses?" Taken aback, Malki replied, "They're broken for the umpteenth time and I haven't had them fixed yet." Mrs. Nadoolman continued, "I expect you're wondering why I'm making this call." Malki was doing precisely that. "It's because when Joseph has his glasses he may not see much, but he has a sense of where he is. Without them, he's out of it, totally at a loss. I want those glasses back on him as soon as possible!"

Malki phoned me to share this conversation and we confirmed that a mother's love and instinct about what her child needs are often right on target.

Chapter 10

The Letter from Dr. H.

Life was hectic. Our fifth child, Simcha, had arrived the previous summer on July 20, 1980, one year to the day after Avi. Our children were enrolled in school and pre-school.

Financially, things began to improve. I managed to enter the world of computer consulting by taking over a six-month project at Chase Manhattan when someone else left it in the middle. With that experience under my belt, I applied for a job at the enormous insurance company Equitable Life, and they hired me as a consultant, not even asking how many years I had been in the field. There I served as a programmer and analyst responsible for software updates for a Wang product used in over 170 branches of the company throughout the United States. It turned out to be a dream job. The people were nice and the consulting fees generous. I was valued, received regular raises, and had the satisfaction of managing a product on a national scale. I worked as much overtime as I wanted and even came in early for four hours on Sunday mornings, after which I would take Malki and the kids out for fun afternoons.

Sometime after I began at Equitable, a familiar figure appeared: my first boss from the consulting firm who had claimed that he was told that I wasn't churning out the latkes quickly enough. "May I speak with you privately?" he asked. We came into my cubicle. His company had gone bust, he told me, and he was interviewing at Equitable for a position. Would I put in a good word for him? I somehow kept my jaw from dropping and tactfully refrained from asking whether he was wearing the shirt he'd put away. As soon as he left I called Malki, who was not the least surprised. Fortunately, I was not asked for a recommendation, and he was not hired.

My work at Equitable put me in constant telephone contact with staff at its branches across the country – Cindy Lou in Alabama, Mary Jane in Texas, and many others. We became good phone-pals, and when they came to our head office in Manhattan I met with them. It was comical to see them walk down the hallway toward me and to see their faces full of surprise as they realized that the guy they were meeting didn't match their impression from over the phone. They'd never imagined that the helpful Canadian voice belonged to someone with a full beard, a large skullcap, white shirt, black pants, and four sets of biblical fringes, *tzitzit*, dangling at his sides. Within thirty seconds, they'd regain composure, we'd sit down to work, and life was as normal. For Cindy Lou, though, it took a few more surprised minutes, and she felt the need to explain: "Well, y'all will just have to forgive me for my surprise. I just could never have imagined you might look this way, 'cuz I never did see anyone looking quite like you. Ya know what I mean?" I did in fact understand what she meant; it was what others were thinking. We had a good laugh and I took it in stride.

* * *

Yossi was now four and a half and our family life was suddenly knocked into a new orbit. Dr. Myles Behrens received the letter

75

he had requested from Dr. H. with the summary of her November 1977 findings about Yossi. It was a pack of brazen lies from beginning to end, misrepresenting our son's developmental milestones and denying the positive report of Dr. Neiman, the well-baby clinic pediatrician who had examined Yossi immediately prior to his vaccination and given him a clean bill of health.

For us, it was a letter rather than a straw that broke the camel's back. In the three and a half years since Yossi's catastrophic injury, we had been so stretched by trying to help him as well as caring for our other children that there had been neither time nor energy to delve into exactly what had happened and address the incident itself. With the falsehoods of Dr. H.'s report, we at last began to put together the pieces and grasp the enormity of the crime committed against Yossi.

I wrote to Israel's Health Ministry. From its director-general, Dr. Tibor Schwartz, there was no response. That which came from its director of public health services stated:

> The pertussis vaccine does cause neurological reactions in some very, very small proportion of cases in many countries. But the public health tragedy of whooping cough is a far greater danger and the pertussis vaccine is considered to be essential to the health of children. Our department naturally investigated the matter and found no specific cause for the reaction. In consulting Connaught Laboratories [the manufacturers of the vaccine], no cause for the reactions could be determined.

With the Israel's Health Ministry doors slammed shut, I next wrote to Dr. David Robinson of the World Health Organization's Expanded Program on Immunization. He passed on my letter to Dr. Tibor Schwartz, who then wrote me, expressed regret about Yossi, and claimed he had never heard of him or me.

There was only one way I could understand these letters: those in Israel's Health Ministry charged with the public's well-being were banding together to deny and cover up what had transpired. My son was alive, injured, and in need of lifelong assistance. I wanted justice and I wanted the future of my injured son secured. I began looking for a lawyer.

The first issue was where to take legal action. The pertussis component of the vaccine, we ascertained, had been produced by the Canadian pharmaceutical giant Connaught Laboratories, but had been mixed with the diphtheria and tetanus components at the Rafa Pharmaceuticals laboratories in Israel. The vaccination was given in Israel. A lawsuit, I learned, could therefore only be filed in Israel, and thus I needed an Israeli lawyer. As I did with all serious matters at that time, I turned to my dearest friend, Rabbi Aaron Fischer, and asked him: "How do I find an Israeli attorney?"

"I think I may have just the man for you," he said. His brother Yisachar, he explained, had a successful law firm in Tel Aviv, and Yisachar's son Avi was a young lawyer there just beginning his career. "He's a brilliant young man who's already achieved distinction in his studies," Aaron told me. "He'd be perfect for this. I'll ask him to do it."

The first of what grew to a library of letters from Avi arrived two weeks later. He would, he wrote, check whether our claim would stand up in court in Israel, and if there was sufficient hard evidence to back it. Pending positive answers, he would file suit on our behalf.

So, now we had a lawyer, albeit an inexperienced one. At Avi's request, I wrote a comprehensive account of Yossi's story and ours. This was in pre-home-computer times and my work at Equitable filled my days, so for a week, I took pen and paper and composed it in the wee hours of the morning. I added copies of all the medical documents in our possession and then put it in the mail.

Several weeks later, in September 1981, Avi and I first came face-to-face. It was a cold and rainy day in Manhattan and I took an early lunch break to meet with him in the lobby of a large building a few blocks from Equitable. He was a robust, impressive young man, a major in the IDF tank reserves, who spoke good English and was clearly very bright. He pulled no punches. It wouldn't be easy, he told me, but he believed we had a case, and he was willing to act for us. I asked about fees. The way it works in cases like this, he explained, is that the client is responsible for incidental costs and the lawyer receives a percentage of the amount awarded by the court. I realized that Avi was prepared to invest enormous amounts of time and effort with no guarantee of ever being paid for it.

"Our first task," he explained, "is to understand exactly what happened to Yossi and how it happened." This was challenging enough: Israel in the late 1970s was a very different place from what it is today: there was little access to information, government bodies weren't obliged to open their records, and as a young country, there was a veil of secrecy over public health matters. There was no internet, no Google, and it was a time when medical professionals still stood shoulder to shoulder to protect their colleagues, no matter what their errors or transgressions.

But the second task was more challenging still: we would have to prove legal causation. This, he explained, meant that we'd have to prove a relationship between the first event, the cause, i.e., the vaccination, and the second event, the effect, i.e., the injury, and demonstrate that the first event was responsible for the second. The burden of proof was on us. All we had to show was our dear son with his multiple disabilities, who, according to Dr. H.'s lying letter, had been born that way. It was for us to prove that his disabilities resulted from his vaccination.

Avi and I set to work on the tedious legal process of discovery. "Our chances of success at this stage were zero," he recalls.

"I took the case because I never doubted your account of what had happened to Yossi. Today, a case like this would be brought as a class action – which would make economic sense, as well. But the paltry number of actions brought by other families with infants injured by the tainted batch of vaccine had all been several years earlier, within months of the problem, and all of them had been dismissed by the courts. We were on our own."

Not only were we on our own, we were taking on wealthy and powerful opponents. Those responsible for destroying Yossi's sight and hearing included the pharmaceutical conglomerates in Canada and Israel that had produced and mixed the defective vaccine, the City of Jerusalem in whose well-baby clinic it had been administered, and the government of Israel whose Health Ministry had approved it. Avi laid the groundwork with great care. Over the months ahead, he sought endless clarifications and explanations, which I dutifully produced, as well as reams of medical documents, some of which I had and many of which I had to get. It all took time. Even in New York in the early 1980s, there were few PCs and faxes in private homes, and not even very many in offices.

But between the two of us Avi and I began to turn up evidence. There were three memos from the Health Ministry addressed "to all public health centers" in Israel, which had been sent over a five-week period. The first was dated October 30, 1977, two weeks after Yossi's vaccination and, in bitter irony, the day of his first birthday. It read:

Re: Triple Vaccine Batch 7834

In light of complications of encephalopathy following use of this DPT batch during the past five months, we hereby order that you immediately halt all use of the aforementioned batch. Further details will be provided after the matter has been investigated.

Dr. Tibor Schwartz
Director-General, Ministry of Health

The next came five days later, on November 4:

Re: The triple vaccine

Pursuant to the notification of October 30 instructing you to halt all use of batch 7834 of the triple vaccine, you are now instructed to halt all use of batch 7862, in addition. This is because of the number of children suffering neurological reactions after being immunized from this batch. Even though at this stage it is difficult to establish any direct causal relationship between administration of the vaccine and neurological reaction, the possibility must be considered. The above-mentioned cases are under investigation and you will be informed of the outcome.

Dr. Tibor Schwartz
Director-General, Ministry of Health

Finally, a month later, on December 5, 1977, came the third:

Re: Cessation of the triple vaccine

In light of continued neurological reactions following administration of the DPT vaccine, it has been decided to halt administration of all triple vaccine until further notice.

To be totally clear: children scheduled for the triple vaccine should not receive any part of it – neither the pertussis component, nor those for diphtheria and tetanus.

Dr. Ted Tulchinsky
Director of Public Health Services, Ministry of Health

It took almost two years, until early 1983, to finish compiling the exhaustive paperwork we needed for the trial – in the midst of which we welcomed our sixth child, Shlomo, early one Sunday morning in May 1982. When Malki suddenly went into labor before midnight, there was no one to call at that hour to care for five young children, so I had no choice but to stay home and watch Malki walk painfully out the front door alone to get in a taxi and head to the hospital. The ob-gyn was surprised and asked if anyone was coming to be with her. "It's just you and me, Doc!" she replied. Six hours later, the doctor called me to say, "Congratulations, your wife has given birth to a boy!"

One month later, on June 6, Avi Fischer was called up to fight in the First Lebanon War as deputy commander of a tank brigade, and disappeared for several months. Upon his return, the preliminary paperwork we had compiled to expose what the faulty vaccine had done to Yossi was finally complete. Now, Avi explained, it was time for Yossi to be assessed by two leading neurologists in Israel. Their findings would be the deciding factor as to whether we'd litigate.

Malki and I agonized over whether the whole family would make the trip. All of us going meant two weeks absent from Equitable, traveling with six youngsters under the age of eight, and finding the money to pay for it. Malki going with Yossi meant her coping with everything alone and me juggling work and the care of five young children.

In April 1983, it was Malki and Yossi who flew to Tel Aviv. Yossi was now six and a half and Avi had scheduled appointments for him with two internationally known Israeli neurologists, Professor Shaul Harel in Herzliya and Dr. Pinchas Lerman in Tel Aviv.

Dr. Harel was an impressive man in his mid-forties, with a kind face and manner. He took a lengthy history from Malki, then turned to Yossi and handed him a toy. Yossi was not in a cooperative mood and didn't react. The doctor gave him another toy, but again Yossi showed no interest. Malki felt very uncomfortable and frustrated, knowing how animated Yossi usually is and how he's only too ready to interact. Most doctors would have given up on him at that point and concluded that he was nonresponsive, but luckily not Shaul Harel. He kept on trying until he had Yossi's attention, and eventually Yossi began acting like his usual lively self.

Dr. Harel's assessment lasted over an hour, conducted through play and myriad educational toys and devices. As the meeting progressed, he became visibly excited about this blind and deaf child, who, despite his overwhelming disabilities, was demonstrably alert and highly intelligent. The neurologist emphasized in his report that few professionals would assess Yossi accurately because of the rush to the next patient, and it was only because he'd taken time to establish a strong rapport that he'd been able to see the child's potential. He would be happy to testify on Yossi's behalf, the doctor later told Avi, as he believed it probable that the DPT vaccine was the cause of Yossi's disabilities.

The appointment with Dr. Pinchas Lerman was equally positive. An older man, Dr. Lerman was one of Israel's granddaddies of neurology. His assessment of Yossi resembled that of Shaul Harel, and he, too, believed the DPT vaccine to be the culprit. While there could never be absolute certainty, neither doctor doubted that Yossi's was a classic case of a post-vaccination reaction. Dr. Lerman, too, was willing to testify.

With two leading Israeli neurologists willing to stand up for Yossi in court, as well as all the paperwork we had compiled, Avi was now ready. In October 1983, he filed suit against the respected neurologist Dr. H.; Connaught Laboratories and Rafa, the Canadian and Israeli pharmaceutical companies that had manufactured and mixed the vaccine; the City of Jerusalem, which provides health services including immunizations for infants through its well-baby clinics; and the State of Israel, whose Health Ministry is responsible for ensuring the health of Israel's population, either directly or via medical institutions – among them, the well-baby clinics.

We were cognizant of the challenge ahead but there was no choice, both for the sake of Yossi's future and because silence would have made us complicit in the cover-up perpetrated by those responsible for the faulty vaccine and its appalling outcome.

Chapter 11

Coming Home

Having spent quality time with her older sister Sossy and her many friends in Jerusalem, as well as having found two leading neurologists willing to stand up for Yossi in court, Malki had a wonderful trip. She was reminded of how carefree life was in Israeli neighborhoods. Young children played outside their homes unsupervised, something impossible in Brooklyn. Our children were never allowed to play in front of the house without one of us there. When Nechama's school bus picked her up each morning five houses down at the corner of our block, I was always there to see her onto it, and Malki was always there to meet her when she came home. It wasn't safe for her to walk or wait alone.

Malki called me from Jerusalem. "Kalman, are you ready? We're coming home! We are coming back to live in Israel. It's where we can best help Yossi in the long term." I took a deep breath and said, "That's wonderful, but why don't we talk about it when you get back to New York?" I'd worked long and hard and was finally making real money, we were just beginning to feel settled, and I wasn't going to uproot myself and the family so fast.

But Malki's mind was made up. "We left Israel for a reason and that reason was Yossi," she reminded me. "It was helpful as we now know what we're dealing with, and he's made progress, but I see nothing in his future in the US that makes me want to stay. Despite everything, I want our children growing up in Israel, and that's where I want to live my life, too. I know we're settled in the US, but we'll get settled in Israel."

The taxi that Malki and Yossi took home from JFK had a Hebrew-speaking driver. Malki sang Israel's praises to him, until he stopped her with: "Let me tell you a story to give you some perspective, OK?" Without waiting for Malki's agreement, he continued, "A man I'll call Simon died and his soul went to heaven. Because he'd lived a decent life, he was allowed to choose where he'd spend eternity, in heaven or in hell. 'Well,' said Simon, 'that's hard when I don't know what either one is like.' It was agreed he could spend a week in each place before deciding. During his seven days in heaven, he watched old men sway, pray, and study Torah, each saying something wiser and more brilliant than the next. He was bored silly. An angel then brought him to hell's gateway, where he saw people eating, drinking, and living the desires and fantasies that escaped them during their lifetime. The week passed as in an instant.

Brought again before the Eternal Judge, Simon paused thoughtfully and made his choice. He would cast his lot with hell. Whisked back, he was surrounded by fiery angels, prodding at him with burning pitchforks. 'What is this place?' he screamed. 'This isn't the hell I was shown!' 'Correct,' replied a terrifying angel. 'The first week, you were our guest, but now you're here to stay as one of our own. Welcome!' As he was jabbed with pitchforks, Simon shrieked his despair."

The cabby continued, "This, lady, is the reality. I'm Israeli. I grew up in Israel and I served in the army. You lived in Israel as a youngster and then as a young couple in your honeymoon years. But going back to settle there with your family as 'one of us'? Don't say I didn't warn you!"

The Israeli driver's cautionary tale did nothing to dampen Malki's fervor. "I want to move back," she told me upon arriving home. I smiled good-naturedly and listened patiently, waiting for her enthusiasm to subside. I laughed at the cabby's story, said how true it was, and pointed out that while it's great to dream we must be realistic. I recalled our difficulties settling in New York and reminded her that I was at last earning enough to support the family, pay for help, and put the children in good educational frameworks. It would be somewhere between lunacy and suicide to pick ourselves up, move back, and start again, I protested. I reminded Malki of the talmudic expression that "all beginnings are difficult," and added, "May G-d help us that we not be beginners our entire lives."

I wasn't making headway. I tried again. "Your cabby's story is true of any immigrant situation, just as it was true of our coming to New York. A short visit is heaven, but when you try to be a permanent part of things, it can be hell. We've had our share of hell these past four years, and at last life is getting a little easier. If we up and go back to Israel now, we'll go through this same hell again," I restated.

There was silence. I took a deep breath and changed my direction. "Malki dear, if this is what you want, I'm willing to do it for you, and you'll never hear from me 'I told you so.'"

Malki cried from sheer joy. Going back to Israel at this juncture wasn't a rational decision. It was an act of faith – and as an act of faith, I sincerely hoped that G-d would help us.

As we began planning our return to Israel, I hid my ambivalence from my colleagues at Equitable. "Are you sure you know what you're doing?" my bosses asked. When I assured them I did, they organized a farewell lunch in Central Park with the entire staff. My associates were kind and funny, and prepared me a farewell gift.

I'd shared my cubicle with a fellow from Queens, whose wife ran a successful business called *Color Me Beautiful*. Its philosophy was that every person belongs to a particular season and should dress according to that season's color palette. This had been a popular topic among the staff – and at the park that day, I was given my personalized palette with strips of fabric laid out to show which colors best suited me. Wouldn't you know – I was winter, and my colors were black and white!

An associate, cognizant of both her and my significant consulting fees, asked me in front of everyone whether I had a job lined up in Israel. "No, not as yet," I told her, to which she emphatically replied: "In that case, I think you're absolutely *meshuga* (crazy)!" She drew hearty laughs and a chorus of "Me toos!" When the laughter died down, she said sincerely, "You have a big family. What are you going to do about work?"

"When I left the Holy Land to come to New York four and a half years ago, I had no job, and the good L-rd provided for us very nicely – most recently with you great folks," I replied. "So now that we're going back to the Holy Land, I'm confident that the same good L-rd will provide for us there, too." There was no further laughter. I thought to myself: If I could only tell you the truth! I came here knowing nothing about computers, did a four-month course, worked for a year, set myself up as a consultant, and got a great gig with Equitable Life after only two years in the field. Do I need to give the good L-rd advice?

Planning our return to Israel was more difficult than I could ever have imagined, and it quickly became clear that there was no way I could find a job until I got there. A few weeks before our August departure date, I ran into my computer-course guidance counselor. When she heard we were leaving and I had no job waiting in Israel, she was incredulous. "How can you be so irresponsible!" she admonished me. I reminded her that I'd always planned to be back in Israel within five years, so clearly

I had to keep my word. She smiled. I knew what that meant. What a *meshugene*!

Amid the flurry of our preparations, I decided we should take a personal computer back with us. Compared to the huge, cumbersome mainframe computers of the time, and the sizable Wang mini that I worked with, the PC lived up to its name. IBM had just come out with its first PC and I was able to get hold of one of the first PCs with 256K of memory on its motherboard. Better yet, I was able to buy an add-in card with an additional 256K, giving me a colossal 512k – or half a megabyte of memory. Coupled with a full-color graphics adapter, the first graphics card and first color-display card for the IBM PC monitor, this was one hot computer. To complete the package, I splurged on an Epson dot-matrix printer that knocked out documents at 180 characters a minute – yes, 180 characters per minute, not per second! The package cost $4,500, which was then a great deal of money, but I was determined to arrive in Israel with the very best professional tools.

Three months after our decision to return home, we arrived at JFK for our flight totally exhausted, hauling six little children and twenty-one large suitcases. Yossi did not let up for a moment. The El AL flight seemed never-ending, and there was not a moment when either Malki or I could shut our eyes. Yossi was noisy and rambunctious, running awkwardly up and down the aisle. An irritated fellow passenger called the flight attendant to demand that either we or he be moved. It was an unpleasant scene and we apologized but could do little. No one changed seats, but the passenger's ire was manifest all the way to Israel.

Tel Aviv was hot and humid on that August day and the airport formalities took an eternity. All twenty-one suitcases were loaded, largely by me, onto a big van. By the time we arrived in Jerusalem an hour later, and lugged all of our worldly belongings up two flights of stairs to the three-and-a-half-bedroom apartment we'd rented, I was beyond exhaustion, and with all the suitcases, there was little room left for us people. We noticed that the children's clothes were becoming smeared with white paint from the poorly finished walls and there was no way to stop them from accidentally brushing up against them. Finally we got the kids to sleep, and Malki and I collapsed – but of course, in the Promised Land.

I couldn't shake off the exhaustion, and the reason became clear when I was diagnosed with hepatitis. Infectious and extremely weak, I wasn't able to look for a job or even contribute much at home for two months. Each morning, Malki prepared natural apple and carrot juices and stood over me to make sure I drank them. My condition lingered. Malki did not. She bravely reinvented herself as a real estate agent, a field she had no experience in. After getting the kids on their school bus and making sure I was comfortable each morning, she set off in weather that had by then turned very cold and rainy to sell apartments in a new Jerusalem suburb called Har Nof, meaning mountain view, then under construction. It was most challenging and somewhat perilous, but she was determined, and successful, and it was there that she found the apartment that we bought for our family.

Yossi needed a school, and we began to investigate options. Given that he was blind and deaf, we were naturally referred to a school that catered to this population. It would provide the reliable routine and consistent, predictable schedule that is so essential to deaf-blind children, we were told. But we were disheartened by the totally nonfunctional level of its students and unhappy with its physical conditions. Malki was quick to remind me that the one thing Yossi needed was stimulation, and this was not an environment that would provide it.

So, despite the insistence of the English-speaking social worker that this was the only option, Malki said to me quietly but emphatically, "Over my dead body," and we were back to square one.

We were then referred to a school for the blind, but they balked. "Sorry," they said, "we teach the blind but we are unable to teach the deaf." We were referred to a school for the deaf, but they too balked. "Sorry, we teach the deaf but are unable to teach the blind." It quickly became clear that finding a school for Yossi, a little boy who didn't fit in any of the boxes, would be a long and arduous process. No one wanted the burden of a child who couldn't be independent in a classroom situation, unable to see or hear what was going on around him.

What a difference one person can make. After tremendous frustration and many lost battles, we finally got an appointment with Israel's educational supervisor for the blind, a dynamic woman named Chana Kadmon. She understood we wouldn't settle for anything inappropriate, and to her great credit, she recognized Yossi's raw intelligence. Chana mobilized the educational system, and despite opposition from within, she created a class for Yossi at the school for the deaf in Jerusalem's Kiryat Yovel neighborhood. Here he had his own teacher, Chana Hasid, and received the highly individualized program he needed. Once he overcame the initial opposition to his presence in the school, Yossi found his place.

The effects of my hepatitis continued to linger, but I was now well enough to begin looking for work. A wonderful position came to my attention, managing the development of a computer product for a large Tel Aviv insurance company. The pay was excellent, and after my years at Equitable it was right up my alley. The downside was that the workday there ran from 8:00 a.m. to 6:00 p.m., which would mean leaving our Jerusalem home before seven each morning and returning well after seven each evening. With our young family and Yossi's needs, this would be tough on us all.

While I was debating whether to accept it, I saw a want ad in the newspaper for, of all things, a Wang programmer. Wang? In Israel? This was truly my field. I called at once and was asked to fax my résumé. The phone call summoning me for an interview came from the United States–Israel Binational Science Foundation, which was, I learned, Israel's largest scientific research-granting agency, promoting and supporting collaborative research projects between the US and Israel in a wide range of basic and applied scientific disciplines. Their office was in Rehavia, an upscale Jerusalem neighborhood fifteen minutes from home.

My interviewer was Dr. Bill Rosen, who, to my surprise, was an American scientist spending three years in Israel as the visiting associate director of the foundation. Fortunately, Bill was impressed with my training and skills – which was critical for someone like me who stuck out like a sore thumb in this secular, scientific work environment. Bill, I subsequently learned, called everyone I had ever worked for in New York, inquiring about my abilities and character. My second interview was with Binational's Israeli director. Ari was very pleasant but had a negative bias when it came to the ultra-Orthodox lifestyle.

The foundation worked in conjunction with a counterpart in Washington, DC, an affiliate of the National Institutes of Health, and was buying their extensive software, which ran on Wang computers. The American head of computer operations was coming to Israel for two weeks to install it and get it up and running. They needed someone at the Israel end to help him, to learn the programs, and to be on call for several hours a month to deal with problems and future modifications. They offered me the job for a handsome hourly consulting fee.

I discussed it with Malki. Despite the commute and the twelve-hour days, I leaned toward the Tel Aviv position because after the initial two weeks at the foundation, all I'd have would be five or six hours a month. Malki differed, saying, "The job in Tel Aviv is a nonstarter because of the hours; the one at the foundation sounds good." "How can five hours a month be fine?" I retorted, but as usual, Malki saw things more clearly. "I really don't understand you, Kalman," she said. "You're the one who works in computers. Don't you see they have no idea what they're talking about? You'll be working as many hours as you want in no time. Call and tell them yes."

The consultant arrived from Washington in late December 1983 to install the system, and from then on, for almost two decades, I steadily worked long days. As I had told my colleagues in Central Park, the good L-rd, who had provided me with meaningful and profitable employment in New York, now saw to it that I had work in the Holy Land too.

Chapter 12

A Seat at the Table

Yossi quickly made himself known in his new school. "The first time I saw him, I took fright!" remembers special education teacher Shoshana Weinstock. "He was a child who didn't speak, didn't know sign language, couldn't spell, and was always running about, always looking for company!"

In addition to her daytime teaching hours at the school, Shoshana also taught sign language classes there in the evenings, which parents of new pupils were required to attend. With our six young children – one of them, Yossi – it was impossible for us to get a babysitter, but we were blessed with an angel in the form of Malki's sister Sossy – as well as her husband Yakov, and their dear children, who provided our children with another unconditional loving home. We went to the school for our first lesson with Shoshana and listened attentively as she introduced herself and her subject: "I am deaf from the age of five following meningitis, and with your help, I am going to teach you sign language and how to communicate with your child." Although she spoke Hebrew well, her intonation contours were sometimes incorrect, and we had to listen carefully to catch all she said. She was a vibrant educator and Malki did her best to give her full attention, but after a long day with the kids she often found herself dozing off.

Malki approached Shoshana after class. Shoshana apologized, saying she was in a hurry and couldn't stay to talk. Malki offered her a ride to wherever she needed to go, suggesting we talk en route. Where she needed to go, she explained, was the Hadassah Medical Center to see her husband, Yosef, who sadly was losing his battle with cancer, she shared. As we drove, Shoshana told us that her Yosef, too, was deaf. Until his illness, he had worked for the Bank of Israel. She, Yosef, and their three daughters lived close to us, it turned out, on a parallel street. We were devastated to hear about her husband.

Malki asked Shoshana if she could possibly teach Yossi privately after school, since she lived nearby. Shoshana agreed to think about it but did not get back to us.

In the ensuing weeks, Yosef Weinstock's condition deteriorated, and he died three months after that car ride. Shoshana contacted us soon afterward to say she was prepared to work with Yossi. She shared that her initial reluctance was because she had seen his intense energy level at school and didn't have the strength for that during her husband's illness. With the loss of her Yosef, she felt that bringing Yossi into her life would be a comfort.

We began taking eight-year-old Yossi to Shoshana twice a week for hour-long sessions. In the course of one such lesson, Shoshana suddenly appeared at our house with Yossi, knocking loudly at our door, breathless with excitement. "He got it! He got it!" she cried. "His life has changed forever!"

Malki and I had no idea what she was talking about. We looked at his hands to see what he had "got." "No! No!" Shoshana shouted. "He *got* it! He understands that I'm signing letters in his palm. His entire world has just opened."

Yossi was beaming, but we still didn't take in what Shoshana was telling us. She sat us down along with all our children and began exultantly to explain. "We were sitting at the table in my house and I was finger spelling the five symbols that spell the word 'table' [*shulhan* in Hebrew] into the palm of his hand, while his other hand rested on the table." She continued excitedly, "I have done this for the past few lessons but Yossi didn't respond. Today," she said, "a smile suddenly lit up his face and he began to touch the table deliberately, and we both knew that he'd understood I was spelling *shulhan*. We did it over and over and he smiled again and again, touching the table every time. He has a new life. I can teach him all twenty-two letters of the Hebrew alphabet and give him language."

We were all sobbing as Shoshana began to demonstrate on the palms of Yossi's sister and brothers how to spell *shulhan* and how to sign the other letters. She told them: "You, too, are going to learn the letters, and you'll at last be able speak to your brother."

With everything we had done and with all our hope and faith, we never imagined reaching this moment. Like Helen Keller and Anne Sullivan, Yossi and Shoshana had shone light into the dark and silent void in which our son had languished for seven of his eight years. Shoshana had shattered the barrier between Yossi and the world. Yossi finally had a seat at the table. By teaching him that everything has a name and that there's a way to communicate that name through letters signed into the palm of his hand, she opened his door to language, and Yossi would at last be able to make known his needs, his thoughts, and his feelings.

With astonishing speed, he picked up the other seventeen letters, learned how to combine letters into words, and words into concepts. None of us understood how he did it. He was unstoppable, touching things with one hand and moving his forefinger over his cheek to sign, "What's this called?" with the other. Glass, plate, fork, knife; his siblings' names, Nechama, Yochanan, Avi,

Simcha, Shlomo; us, Malki, Kalman, Mom, Dad. He was a child possessed, demanding a name for everything. His school made him a dictionary in which every new word was entered. It was a time of excitement. I vividly recall when he learned his tenth word, his fortieth, when he got to a hundred words.

Now that Yossi had grasped language, a gifted young speech therapist at his school stepped forward. Osnat Ben Tsur undertook to do the seemingly impossible: to teach Yossi to speak Hebrew. Her daunting task was to explain what sound is and how to vocalize letters and words to a child who could neither see nor hear.

She all but crawled with her fingers into Yossi's mouth to teach him each consonant and each vowel. Yossi initially recoiled and bit her fingers. She persisted. Yossi placed his hands on her face and neck, fingering her lips and the vibrations around her mouth and throat, as he struggled to pronounce the symbols and sounds finger spelled into his palm. Some were tougher to teach than others, and Osnat came up with ingenious solutions. To teach the "p" sound she took a lighted candle, and every time Yossi blew it out using the newly learned "p" phoneme he received hugs and encouragement. For the next two years Osnat and her team worked with Yossi, and he learned to speak Hebrew synthetically. It was complicated. Consonants were signed in his palm and Hebrew vowel symbols were signed on the inside of his wrist. He then had to put them together, which he did through endless practice over time. With intense focus, he spoke syllables slowly and deliberately, and while his manner of speech took some getting used to, it was amazing how quickly the attentive listener picked it up. Yossi could communicate, and for Malki and me this was nothing short of a miracle.

The two-month summer break from school arrived. Shoshana decided that despite Yossi's motor coordination difficulties, she was going to teach him braille during the vacation – letters consisting of combinations of six raised dots, which the blind read via their fingertips. There was heated opposition to this within the deaf school, a sense that Shoshana didn't know when to stop. Despite the school's opposition, we gave Shoshana the go-ahead. Unbeknownst to us she had taken private lessons in braille, and to the school's enormous surprise, Yossi returned from summer vacation reading braille and writing it using a six-key braille machine.

Shoshana took on the role of the miracle worker, Anne Sullivan, and Yossi became the Helen Keller of Israel. Shoshana changed Yossi's life, and with it, the lives of our family. Our connection to Shoshana is so deep and enduring. "I am who I am because G-d has been good to me," said this woman who lost her hearing to meningitis at age five, and lost her beloved husband when she was still a young woman and young mother. "He has placed me in life where I ought to be, and no sadness can make me despair."

With Shoshana's help and his own quick mind, Yossi developed an extensive vocabulary, and teaching him more words became the mission of the capable staff at the school for the deaf. Many words have signs. France is a triangle made with the index fingers and thumbs touching, an Eiffel Tower. Egypt is a triangle formed over the head, symbolizing a pharaonic headdress. Others must be spelled out. And for those words that have no signs, Yossi created his own. Each of his siblings got a sign, and Yossi's own sign was his open forefinger and thumb on the bottom of his chin.

"He speaks a thousand languages," Malki always said. "Everyone he talks to – in school, at home, round the neighborhood – signs to him, but inevitably we all have our own slightly different versions of the signs in his palm. And he understands us all. He 'talks' for hours with his friends who rattle off letter after letter with no spaces between words and no punctuation. Yossi breaks it down into words and sentences in real time. His memory is phenomenal; he remembers everything."

We saw the impact of language on Yossi and understood that it is an essential need and the key to his future, and we recognized that for this alone, our return to Israel had been critically important. He wanted to know everything. Virtually overnight he changed from a solitary being who craved human interaction into a youngster fully engaged with others. Malki and I, and his siblings, couldn't fingerspell in his palm fast enough for him. We took turns naming objects and reading to him.

Soon, the frustrated, frenzied little boy we'd known had become a typical mischievous kid. One evening, after Yossi had been settled down to sleep, I found him out of bed at his desk, typing braille. "What are you writing?" I asked him. It turned out to be an entire roll call of everyone he knew – family, friends, teachers, neighbors. I put him back to bed, but five minutes later found him adding to his braille list. When he realized he'd been caught again, he giggled and said, "Just joking," and went happily into bed.

A few days later, I found him helping himself to another piece of cake after he'd already had more than his share. When I asked him what he was doing, he gave a shamefaced grin and signed in Hebrew: "I'm stealing." I laughed and he got his cake.

His memory was prodigious. When the weather turned cold and rainy, we got out the kids' windbreakers for the first time in months. Yossi had no sooner touched his, when he said: "Bubby and Zaidy!" (Grandma and Grandpa). I'd forgotten that my parents had given them the jackets over a year ago, but Yossi hadn't. When he knocked his mouth and a baby tooth went flying, he insisted on going to "Gary the dentist." It had been over two years since he had last visited Gary.

With his fierce intelligence, Yossi soaked up words, ideas, and thoughts, important and trivial, complex and simple, religious and secular. For me, witnessing his spiritual development gave me special pleasure. My sister Marilyn had brought home to me the fact that my son would never be the Torah scholar I dreamed of, but now he could become an educated Jew. He had a braille *siddur* (daily prayer book) which he took with him to synagogue, repeating the prayers at his own pace and enjoying every moment.

He queried me as to whether the Almighty listened to his prayers. When I assured him He did, he asked: "G-d isn't deaf?" "No," I told him, to which he responded with a playful smile, "Does He at least wear hearing aids?" I laughed as I realized that everyone creates G-d in his own image.

Yossi also showed us that he grasped concepts of our faith. He was learning about the Jewish dietary laws, although his teacher at the deaf school was concerned that the subject may be over his head. "There are kosher and nonkosher animals," she explained. "Even kosher animals aren't fit to eat unless they're slaughtered according to Jewish law, by a *shohet*, a religious man who has studied the laws." She then had Yossi separate a dozen toy animals into kosher and nonkosher. He was happily and correctly doing so, when he suddenly stopped and ran out of the room, returning minutes later with a knife in his hand. His teacher had no idea where he'd found it, but his intention was clear: he'd come to slaughter the toy animals. "But you're not allowed to," she pointed out. "You're not a *shohet*!" Yossi disagreed. "Why not?" He said. "I'm religious, I'm studying the laws, and I have a knife." He had clearly grasped the concepts involved.

Chapter 13
Payback Time

We were in the midst of Yossi's legal case, with no end in sight, but Malki had other things on her mind. The children were asleep and the quiet in the house was welcome as she sat me down in our living room, and, speaking with emotion, she reminded me of her prayers and the promise she had made to the Almighty during those dark early days in New York: "If You ever decide to help my Yossi, I will dedicate my life to helping so many other mothers of children with disabilities whom I know are crying with me for their children."

"G-d has answered my prayers," she said. "Now it's payback time, and I know exactly what I want to do. I want to create a center that will provide parents and families with what we never had – a program that will care for their challenged children after school each day, giving the child therapy and a good time, and giving the family a chance to live a normal life. And I need your help."

Overwhelmed as I already was with the court case, my computer work at Binational, and our family, I sat back, took a deep breath, and said: "Malki, there's no question that G-d has helped us, and in a very unexpected way. And of course I remember your promise. But I'm not the guy who can make this happen. I have six young kids, with Yossi equivalent to ten, I work full time at odd hours, and I don't know how to move this forward."

Malki said no more. Her silence morphed into eloquent tears. "OK, I will try," I said. "Let me hear how you want to do this," and, after a pause, Malki laid out her vision.

"I want to create an after-school program that will ensure that children with disabilities are not wandering the streets and their mothers are not sitting and crying alone like I did. We've faced so many challenges with Yossi, at home and with the system. It is so important to support the parents as well as the children. I want to build something that will provide quality of life for the entire family, and the only question that will ultimately be asked is: 'How did we ever manage without this?'"

I pledged to Malki that I would do all that could to help her keep her promise, and I meant it, but that certainly didn't mean that I had any idea how I would do it. One thing, however, was crystal clear to me. Whatever else was needed to create such a program, nothing would happen without funding. If I were to help Malki keep her promise, I'd have to find someone to buy into her dream.

So I began to inquire as to who might help and began to write letters to many North American Jewish philanthropists whose names I was given. Surprise, surprise, there were no replies. Over time I understood that reading a letter from a father of a child with disabilities whom they didn't know, asking them to help his wife establish a new program for other children with disabilities, was simply not enough to pique their interest. It was heartbreaking to me and to Malki that we were not able to move her dream forward.

Chapter 14

Settling In

My concerns about the difficulties we would face in returning to Israel played out in full. We overcame challenges, but from the outset, getting settled had certainly not been easy.

When we entered our new apartment in Har Nof, the neighborhood was still under construction. The roads weren't yet paved and there was no electricity in our building when we moved in among the first residents. A kind soul in the completed apartment building next door allowed us to run wires from our roof to his and down into his electrical box, so although it was unstable we had electricity.

The next priority was a phone – a necessity rather than a luxury, with Yossi's issues. Dream on. Mobile phones were still a decade away, digital phone systems were only beginning to be used in Israel, and the average wait for a landline was counted in years. In a new neighborhood with its infrastructure still incomplete, we may as well have been reaching for the stars.

But ... I had a brilliant idea! I'd get a high-powered portable phone with a large antenna, set it up on the roof of our building, and with its range of six miles, it would cover Jerusalem. Sarah, a New York friend who was coming to visit, agreed to bring the phone and its seven-foot-high antenna. To my great dismay, upon arrival she was stopped at the airport, and in short order the customs officers confiscated the phone and antenna. Poor Sarah! It took her quite a while to convince them that she was simply a good friend helping out a family who had a child with disabilities. Eventually, she was allowed to go, but not so the phone or its antenna. Obtaining their release took me several trips to the airport and payment of a "reduced" fine of 100 percent of the phone's value. Worse yet, despite many hours working with a professional setting up the receiver on the roof, the contraption never worked.

I knew that we had to have a phone and was determined to get one, so I networked intensively and eventually was introduced to a well-placed technician in the phone company who took Yossi's predicament to heart and wanted to help. In short order, we became one of the first homes in the neighborhood with a telephone. Its impact on our life was immense, and unbeknownst to us at the time, my new friend in the phone company would have yet greater impact on our lives in the future.

I was happy at Binational and my colleagues quickly became friends. The associate director, Bill, was always jovial, looking heavenward and greeting me each morning with: "How is *She* today?" We enjoyed one other's company. The Israeli director, Ari, was kind, took good care of me, and was always concerned about my family, but his disdain for ultra-Orthodoxy remained. When the staff gathered in his office for a toast before Jewish festivals, there was always a caustic remark about Judaism. Malki had urged me long ago to stay away from discussing politics, family, and religion at work, so I always caught the barbs he threw with humor.

On one occasion, Ari started in on a harangue and joked that while I was a returnee to religion, he was a returnee to questioning and atheism. I ignored him for a while, but suddenly and most unexpectedly, I couldn't control myself and blurted out: "Ari, I don't know what you can say you returned from in order to begin your questioning, since you were never religious, or what process you may have undergone, but I can tell you that I did go through a process, and a very trying one at that. For six months, at age eighteen, I painfully questioned every premise I had in life, and slowly became observant. It was a tormenting, soul-searching experience that went on not only day by day but hour by hour. At times I could scarcely bear the burden of this self-inflicted spiritual and mental anguish. But I thought it through, became religiously observant, and moved on. I sincerely doubt that you ever underwent such a process in returning to your questioning of religion."

There was dead silence. No one knew what to say. At last, Ari answered with a civil, "Perhaps I wasn't aware of the intensity and seriousness with which you undertook your religious beliefs," and left it at that.

Interestingly, rather than damaging our relationship, it improved it, as Ari now held me in greater respect. That respect grew the day that Ezer Weizman visited as minister of science and technology, some years before he became Israel's seventh president. He spent the first hour with Ari and Bill in Ari's office. When they emerged, I was expected to show the minister our computer system and explain how it worked. The minister approached the large, partitioned, climate-controlled area which housed the Wang minicomputer. He carefully took in the scene, including me, dressed as usual in the garb of an ultra-Orthodox Jew.

The minister paused and inquired, "What do you do here?" Deadpan, I replied, "Our director is very concerned that our computer system should function properly, so he pays me to stand here from sunrise to sunset and pray for it." Mr. Weizman broke into hearty laughter, caught himself, and began apologizing profusely. Ari almost died of embarrassment, but seeing that the minister took it well, he tried to relax and even forced a smile. I then gave him an overview of our hardware and software, and while he wasn't a computer expert, I could see that he fully grasped the subject at hand. He then turned to the issue of prejudging people based on appearances and talked at length about the problem in the Israel Defense Forces, where he had commanded the Israeli Air Force for eight years. Somehow we got onto medical issues and spoke about my son Yossi and his son Shaul, who had suffered a grievous head wound from an Egyptian sniper's bullet in 1970. We rapidly bonded.

Those early choices about where to work and where to live proved to be good ones. Over time, Ari gave me complete flexibility with my working hours, and Har Nof suited our needs well.

It was a safe neighborhood consisting of young families with many children. As Yossi acquired language, he also acquired friends. Naturally fun and gregarious, with an inner charm that attracts people, he was a magnet for the neighborhood children. In synagogue, I chose a long bench at the back so there would be room for my five boys and for friends who wanted to sit with Yossi. After school, Yossi and his friends would meet outside to play. When Yossi returned late one afternoon from a three-day school trip to Eilat, his first question was: "Where are my friends?" "You'll see them tomorrow," I told him. That wasn't good enough. "What do you mean tomorrow?" he exclaimed. "They can't have forgotten I was coming back this evening!" By the time he'd showered and changed, a friend turned up and the two reunited as if they'd been apart for years.

Playing outside with his pals one day, Yossi touched a parked car, and gestured: "What kind of car is this?" The boys checked and told him that it was a Ford. Yossi made his way further down the block to the next car and asked again what kind and was told

Peugeot. Several cars later, Yossi didn't ask, but rather told them that this was a Ford. They checked and confirmed that indeed it was. Surprised, they asked Yossi how he knew, and his response was, "The door handles are the same." And so began a new pastime. Yossi's friends would take him to cars parked up and down the street. He had to be told a make and model only once to remember it and could then identify it ever after. They graduated to parking lots, and we eventually took Yossi to dealerships in Jerusalem and later in Tel Aviv, where the managers kindly made an exception and allowed him to sit in the vehicles on display and touch all the parts, providing a real hands-on experience. We bought Yossi a monthly array of car magazines that we read with him, and through these he learned about every car, every model, and every engine size.

The following is my journal entry from that time:

> Yesterday evening, after maariv [evening prayers], a twelve-year-old neighbor asked me if it's true that Yossi can recognize the make of a car by its door handles. On our way home, he led Yossi to the first in a line of several parked cars. "What make is this?" he asked. Yossi touched its door handle and identified it as a Volvo. He then made his way down the sidewalk, giving a glancing touch to each car's door handle, and named the make of each one: Citroen, Opel, Fiat, Peugot, Ford van, Subaru, and another Citroen. All were correct, except for the last. "Look again," I told him. He brushed the door handle of the last car again and, highly embarrassed, corrected himself to Peugeot. I later learned that Citroen and Peugeot are manufactured in the same French plant and their door handles are similar.

Car keys remained of great interest to Yossi. One day I received a phone call from the famous pioneering Israeli psychologist, Professor Reuven Feuerstein, with whom we had consulted years earlier in New York when Yossi was four. At the time, Reuven was intrigued and excited by what he saw in Yossi and told us that "with the right education, this little heart-stealer can become a second Helen Keller." Given Yossi's condition, that seemed wishful thinking.

Now Reuven demanded, "Where's your son? I need you to bring him over right now! I have a film crew with me visiting from Britain and they must meet him." I brought Yossi over, and as we waited around, he began to hold court. Examining the lead cameraman's large keychain, Yossi stated, "You drive a Volkswagen?" Reluctantly he replied, "Sorry, but no I don't." Yossi repeated himself, adamantly insisting that he does in fact drive a Volkswagen van and showed him the key.

The cameraman suddenly caught himself and stammered, "Oh, you've got my London keys. Yes, my car at home is in fact a Volkswagen." Reuven was amazed and delighted and gave Yossi a big hug.

Despite his multiple disabilities, Yossi was no pushover. From my journal:

> After *shul* [synagogue] last night, Yossi started up the stairs that lead to the street when he encountered R. R is a challenged neighborhood kid, who's now reached five feet eight inches, and probably weighs 150 lbs. Undeterred, Yossi shoved his way past. R didn't like that, and shoved him back. Well, that wasn't smart. Yossi waited until they reached the level sidewalk and then went at R with his fists and feet, catching him completely off guard. A half-hour later, R turned up at our house and rambled on for a good ten minutes until I realized what he'd come for. To my surprise, he'd been sent by his father to apologize for having started up with Yossi. I gave him a Popsicle and we created a new neighborhood alliance: R with the Samuels'. Any problems and he calls them; any problems from them and

he calls me. Even Yossi accepted his apology graciously and understands that R is now a friend.

And Yossi developed his own means of protecting himself.

Yesterday evening, Shoshana took Yossi to a course she's teaching to sixty special education teachers. She had Yossi tell them how he was injured. He related his story about being a healthy baby and receiving a shot from a nurse and becoming blind and deaf. The women began weeping, so Shoshana quickly changed the subject, asking Yossi what he had in his pockets. "Take everything out and tell us about it," she said. Among the contents was a toothpick. "Why do you have a toothpick?" he was asked. His answer was to the point: "When someone bothers me, I stick 'em with it." The whole place erupted in laughter, salty tears running into open mouths.

Chapter 15

Parallel Lives

Through the 1980s, we lived two parallel lives. One was consumed by the lawsuit we filed on Yossi's behalf against those who had supplied, mixed, and delivered the faulty DPT vaccine that had so grievously injured our son. The other was our changed world after Yossi breached his barriers of darkness and silence.

He now spoke Hebrew, albeit with an accent, and we could say anything we wanted to one another, via fingerspelling, braille, and speech. Between those at home, in school, and among Yossi's many friends who learned to fingerspell, there was always someone who could interpret for anyone without these skills.

Our son's extraordinary breakthrough and subsequent progress didn't go unnoticed. When Israel's president, Chaim Herzog, visited the school for the deaf, Yossi was among the children introduced to him. Photos of Yossi and the president appeared in newspapers, and Israeli television's version of *Sixty Minutes* aired a segment about Yossi. He was often referred to as "the Helen Keller of Israel." Helen Keller had visited Israel for two weeks in May and June 1952, and like Yossi she met the president, then Chaim Weizmann.

Shoshana Weinstock, still on staff at the school for the deaf, told us about a meeting held to discuss "this wonder child." It was, she says, "the longest and most high-powered meeting I've ever known at the school," and was attended by Yossi's teacher Shoshana, Israel's national director of education for the blind Chana Kadmon, Israel's national director of education for the deaf, as well as the school's principal, Osnat the speech therapist, and others. Yossi, apparently, was at the top of his game, showing them how he talked, read braille, and did arithmetic. Shoshana cried when she told Malki, Malki cried when she heard, and I teared up when Malki phoned to tell me.

From my journal:

Yesterday, I came home from *shul* on Shabbat morning and sat down on the sofa, still wearing my *tallit*. Suddenly, the muscles in my already sore back went into an agonizing spasm. I was now lying half on, half off the couch, and couldn't move. The boys all came running in and Yochanan who was ten and Avi nine, began whimpering at the sight of me. Malki rushed over and somehow got me onto the floor where I could at least lie straight. I was in immense pain and she gave me a strong pain killer, but the sight of all those troubled little eyes watching me made it worse. Yossi, who'd immediately sensed the commotion, was deep in worry. He asked Malki whether G-d was going to take me, and then asked would I get up if the Messiah came. I realized yet again how deeply I love this pure little soul.

He brought a small chair, positioned himself by my head and sat, elbows on knees, chin on palms, and meditated on the situation. The other children drifted off after a while, but Yossi stayed on, the epitome of concern. I was almost asleep when I felt him carefully cover me with a sheet. He folded my arms on my stomach, placed my feet straight, arranged my beard and covered me from head to toe.... When I woke an hour later, I found him still next to me.

Yossi understood his disabilities, and when he wasn't too busy and reflected on them, he was saddened. One morning I noticed that he wasn't wearing his braille watch and I asked him why. "It's getting fixed," he answered, "but when it comes back I'm going to throw it away." "Why?" I asked. "Because Yossi doesn't want to be a blind boy in the deaf school," he answered. Yossi no longer wanted to be at the school for the deaf, and he made that clear to all. Several months later he got his wish and he moved to the Jerusalem School for the Blind where he felt so much better about himself. Socially, the fact that he was also deaf among the blind didn't seem to bother him as much.

With Yossi there was never a dull moment.

Yossi came home from his new school with an impish grin, and declared: "Yossi is blind!" He began a wobbly walk with his eyes squinted tightly shut and his face molded into the exact expression seen on many of the blind children. Malki and I couldn't help but laugh at this kid, who, unable to see, had read the faces of his blind schoolmates through touch, and reproduced them so precisely. Of course, we stopped his parody at once, telling him it wasn't nice and, in any case, he's not totally blind, as he is sensitive to light and darkness. But it was hard stopping him. It made his siblings laugh, and everyone loves to be a clown!

Yossi drew a picture some time ago and has been asking me to hang it in his room ever since. He says he wants his room full of art. Although I promised I would,

I haven't gotten around to doing so. Last night, Yossi wouldn't go to sleep until I promised him: "I'll put your picture up tomorrow." When he got home from school next day, Yossi went straight to his bedroom – to discover the picture still wasn't up. Malki found him sobbing bitterly. "What's wrong?" she asked. "Yossi's hurt that Daddy forgot to hang his picture," he choked. He was devastated not because the picture wasn't up, but because I had a onetime slip.

Yossi was approaching thirteen and his bar mitzva, the time when a boy becomes a full-fledged member of the Jewish community and takes on the responsibilities that go with that. Our first thought was to hold the party celebrating his bar mitzva at a restaurant, but, realizing that many people felt involved in his life, we decided it should be at a larger venue so that everyone who wanted to could be part of it. We invited family, friends, teachers, and others who loved Yossi and had helped him to learn to function and communicate with the seeing and hearing world.

We wanted to get Yossi new glasses for the event, so we visited the ophthalmologist to whom we'd taken him once before. "I remember being here," Yossi said, as the doctor looked at his almost-two-year-old medical card. Yossi tapped me and said: "Ben Tzion," and tapped me again when I didn't respond. "No," I told him, "this is Dr. Silverstone." "Oh," said Yossi. "Is it a different doctor from last time?" I told him it was the same doctor. Another tap from Yossi, who said again: "Ben Tzion! Ben Tzion!" At this point I turned to the doctor and asked him if his first name happened to be Ben Tzion." Malki and I almost fell off our chairs when he said it was. Yossi then demanded that the consultation proceed exactly as the previous one had – drops in his eyes, not once but twice, and a small gift at the end. The gift this time was a red wristwatch. "Why's he giving me this?" Yossi asked. "It's not a braille watch. I can't see it."

Yossi proudly wore his new glasses to synagogue on the morning of his bar mitzva, when, as with all Jewish boys reaching this milestone, he was called up to the reading of the Torah. He was dressed in a beautiful suit that Malki had picked out for him. Just as he was to be called, Yossi murmured to himself, *Hazak me'od*! – Hebrew for "[Be] very strong." The entire synagogue fell uncharacteristically silent as he came up to the Torah scroll.

He boomed out the blessings deliberately and precisely, each word loud and clear. I put my hands on his back to steady him as he stood, but he shucked them off and straightened his *tallit* (prayer shawl). His eyes never left the Torah scroll throughout the reading. At my cue, he recited the blessing after the Torah reading, and then allowed the sweetest smile of satisfaction to spread from ear to ear. The entire congregation began singing the traditional *siman tov u'mazal tov* song of congratulations in Hebrew. It is traditional to shower the honoree with candies, and candies came pelting down on Yossi and me from every side, most of all from where the women sat. At first, I covered him with my *tallit* but then took it away and allowed him to enjoy every sweet moment.

At Yossi's request, I had sent an invitation to his Saturday night bar mitzva party to President Chaim Herzog and received his response:

```
מדינת ישראל
دولــة اســرائيل
STATE OF ISRAEL

ديوان رئيس الدولة
OFFICE OF THE PRESIDENT                          לשכת נשיא המדינה

                    Jerusalem, 15th November, 1989
                              143/LL


    Mr. Sholom Yosef Samuels



    Dear Mr. Samuels,

    President Herzog would like you to know how pleased
    he was to hear from you about the unique Bar
    Mitzvah party arranged on November 4 for those who
    helped you to develop so remarkably despite the
    great physical obstacles you have to overcome.

    The President remembers with pleasure the
    opportunity he had to meet with you at the school
    for the deaf in Kiryat Yovel. He regrets that his
    calendar is so crowded that he could not arrange to
    be with you on the special occasion - but he is
    sure it was a memorable evening and he sends you
    very best wishes for further achievements in the
    years ahead.

                          Sincerely,


                          Shulamit Nardi
                    Assistant to the President
```

The president didn't join us, but hundreds of others did, among them my parents who flew in from Vancouver. It was an overwhelmingly joyous event with intense dancing and a beaming Yossi sitting on many different shoulders. In the corner, my eye caught a diminutive figure quietly weeping. It was the Rebbetzin who had visited Malki in New York years before, as a self-appointed emissary of the "Institutionalize Yossi" lobby.

Chapter 16

In Search of Payback

The years were flying by, and Malki and I realized that her dream was not materializing. I called my sister Marilyn and shared our frustration. "Sit down with Malki," Marilyn suggested, "and describe her dream in no more than three pages. Send it to me and I'll show it to several charitable foundations that I work with; maybe they will take an interest." And so Malki and I sat down and hammered out her vision and our mission.

A Proposal for a New Outreach Program in Israel
August 1988

Purpose

Outreach program designed to assist families with handicapped children and of limited financial means to cope with their daily struggle. At times when other parents are enjoying their children and relaxing, these families are under constant stress, 365 days each year.

Need

A family with a severely handicapped child, regardless of the cause, has a problem that affects both parents and siblings. The nature of those problems is varied and numerous and often is capable of destroying the family unit.

An outreach program designed to supply volunteers to enter the home and help the family occupy the child in ways which will be described releases tremendous pressure from all concerned. The end result is parents who can better cope with their other responsibilities and children who can hope for a little peace of mind and possibly a little attention from their parents.

It is difficult to express adequately in words the plight of such a family or the need for such an organization, but I must at least make the attempt. As an ordained rabbi, I view circumstances and chains of events as being meaningful and not simply happenstance. Both my personal situation and my acquaintance with yourselves can together, I believe, lead to a phenomenal new public service, as I will explain.

I am the father of six children aged 6 through 13. My second child, Yosef, was injured by a routine triple vaccine (DTP) at the age of 11 months in Israel in 1977. As a result he slowly lost his vision and hearing, of course speech never developed properly and he was extremely hyperactive. We as parents did our utmost to assist the child. We moved to New York in 1979 where we spent almost five years in search of medical help and in 1983 we returned to our first love, Israel, when all options were exhausted. In the course of getting the child placed in school in Israel, after great difficulties we succeeded in arranging a program from 8:00 a.m. to 12 noon. At 12:15, the child arrived home and for the remaining daylight hours, my wife, myself or both of us were totally tied down to the child. Since there was

another program available in the blind school a few afternoons a week, we did our utmost to have the child accepted.
We were advised that if we would attend a psychological
session with a therapist once a week, every effort would be
made to accept the child. Having no choice we agreed. It
meant my missing an additional few hours a week of work
as a computer consultant and losing badly needed finances,
and it meant my wife having to hash through painful problems. After a number of weeks of "coping sessions," I told
the psychologist point blank, "If you want to help us, we do
not need these sessions. After all your advice about how to
cope, I still have to run to make up the lost bucks and my
wife has to run home to be on time to receive Yosef and then
sit with hands tied the regular six hours. If you are serious
and sincere, for goodness sake, arrange the afternoon program for the child and we will then indeed be able to cope
better." The child ultimately was accepted a few afternoons
a week and then and only then was the prospect of coping
a reality. Then and only then could we sit down and think,
gee, how could we possibly improve the situation? Advice
is sometimes cheap and even quite painful when the individual cannot help himself.

Today, thank G-d, my little boy is a bright 12-year-old,
considered a second Helen Keller, and he is well cared for,
so I have no personal need in this outreach program. But
my experiences in raising a special child and witnessing the
suffering of countless others, has clarified the vital need of
such families. Many simply do not make it.

Shortly after our return to Israel in 1983 we moved to
a new neighborhood on the outskirts of Jerusalem, called
Har Nof, where many residents are new immigrants from
English-speaking countries. To my great shock and sorrow, there was almost no apartment building on our little

block without a severely handicapped child. The problems include a semi-retarded epileptic, CP, Down syndrome, various stages of mental retardation, disability from birth, deaf children – and all this in a 200-yard radius, a small fraction of a large neighborhood. Every day at 1:00 p.m., my wife hears the school bus honk its horn and our neighbor Mrs. A steps out to pick up her severely retarded seven-year-old daughter who is still in diapers. Knowing full well that Mrs. A has other small children and cannot afford help, my wife often breaks down and cries while picturing just how Mrs. A will push through the remainder of the day.

The B family has a five-year-old boy who has lost his hearing. With several other young children at home and the father struggling to make a living, they are very pressured and do not handle their situation well. The child is bright, but since he has schooling only three mornings a week, the father has enrolled him in a school for the retarded during the other two mornings. I have personally spoken to the father and explained that placing a bright deaf child among retarded children is very damaging and that he should keep him at home if need be. His reply was that they cannot function and there is no choice. Here again, the long days with no organized activity or help are draining this young family to the breaking point.

C is a mildly retarded 15-year-old who at age 11, 12, and 13 was our neighbor and found at our home love and care and frequently visited. C arrived from his educational framework every day at 1:00 p.m. and from that hour until nightfall he would roam the streets either playing with or terrorizing children of all ages. He comes from a good American family but the poor mother was helpless when it came to occupying an energetic 12-year-old for hours at a time. Superficial attempts of neighbors to calm him down often landed them foreign objects on their porches and windows. We found that the child loved to draw, and he often spent hours creating masterpieces for us which we would either accept as gifts or purchase from him in order to give him an excuse to go buy himself sweets in the corner store. Again, a child and family that desperately needed organized activity.

The case histories are numerous and varied but they share a common ground: a little bit of thoughtful assistance can go a long way to saving entire families. The proposed services are as critical and beneficial to each family member as oxygen is to a suffocating man.

Therefore it is essential that an organization be founded to assist in relieving the burden of families with severely handicapped children by:

- having a professional staff to identify the nature of problems and their best solutions
- having a local community activity center designed for these children
- organizing volunteers to occupy these children during the long afternoons and holiday periods when the families are literally climbing a straight wall

Implementation

The program could initially be implemented on a pilot basis in a selected neighborhood utilizing local volunteers who may even know the families. This could then be used as a model to implement it in additional neighborhoods and communities. The goal is ultimately to service the entire country but to retain the personal touch of a local organization. The bulk of the workforce is volunteer. Some kind of neighborhood center would be required but these facilities could be rented initially. These handicapped children, who are often either pitied or viewed as extra-terrestrials, will begin to be a visible entity in community life. The "normal" children are willing and even anxious to be involved and such activity will contribute greatly to their own development and ultimately to a more sensitive, aware community and society.

There is a famous organization in Israel that loans medical equipment. It now has a multimillion dollar budget and about 85 centers around the country. The young man who began it all some fourteen years ago was a neighbor of mine. He started with one small location in our neighborhood; it proved successful, they began a new branch in a second neighborhood until they stretched throughout the country. I foresee going after a similar pattern and ultimately serving every community in the country – and all with the joy of a vibrant volunteer army.

Staff

The staffing needs will depend on the initial scope of the project and it is premature to discuss them at this time. The key to success will be our ability to mobilize volunteers. An office must be established with the necessary facilities to efficiently operate.

The project must be started with adequate funding of approximately $100,000 with the goal being that the project will ultimately merit wide recognition and financial support. I currently am in charge of computer operations for the United States–Israel Binational Science Foundation, a one hundred million dollar joint research-granting agency, and I am confident that with G-d's help, once this organization builds a successful track record, it will be able to raise the required budget on its own and will prove to be a true credit to all involved.

The only question that will then be asked will be, how did we manage without it until now?

With special permission from Binational, I sent the document to Marilyn using their amazing bitnet, the slow-moving ancestor of internet. Marilyn shared it with her foundation contacts, who were generous in their admiration for our vision, but unprepared to commit funding.

One philanthropic family with an interest in the field of disabilities sent a social worker to Israel to work with the municipality and rank projects which they were interested in supporting. We were among those who met with him at a session attended by several professionals. One professional, a woman who ran a Jerusalem preschool program for challenged youngsters, was particularly outspoken in her support of our proposal, emphasizing it would answer vital needs. The North American social worker's final report did include Malki's vision, but regrettably, he placed it far down on his priority list.

Time was moving on. Malki was heartbroken that we couldn't make this happen.

Chapter 17

Into the Legal Labyrinth

Even as we rejoiced in Yossi's communication breakthrough, we were stumbling through a treacherous labyrinth with the long, drawn out, very costly, and very painful court battle against Goliath.

Our suit, filed in September 1983, six years after Yossi's fateful vaccination, was, incredibly, delayed until May 1987. Only then was our case heard in court. There were no laws of freedom of information, and getting each legal document was a major and time-consuming feat in itself. The case was further delayed because court sessions were scheduled several months apart. When there was a date, it was often canceled at the last moment because one of the opposing lawyers was called up for military reserve duty or was to be out of the country – and yes, the judge allowed it. This was calculated to break us.

Israel was still a young country, and not one in which citizens often sued their government. We were challenging giants, and from the very first court session, there was little doubt about what lay ahead. We were "trouble-making ants," our lawyer Avi Fischer was told, "a nuisance to Israel's government-run health system."

The suit had taken the government by surprise, but they quickly organized to bring down what they saw as little more than a nuisance claim. But the claim was comprehensive and cogent, so instead of having the government's own legal staff fight it, they took the unusual step of hiring Israel's premier tort lawyers. Speaking of the case years later, Avi recounted, "One of them had been my lecturer in torts at university not long before. They were all big guns on Israel's legal scene, all highly experienced, all twenty to thirty years older than me, and all with offices, staffs, and legal assistants. This was my first (and last) such case, and I found myself up against Israel's national league of tort lawyers! Making it still worse was what I felt to be the judge's condescending attempt to be kind to me. 'My best regards to your father, Avi,' he said at the first meeting in his chambers. 'He's a first-class lawyer and a good friend.'"

The judge may have attempted kindness, but that wasn't a word in the vocabulary of the defense team. Eight pages angrily denying any and all responsibility for Yossi's injury met the claim that Avi filed on our behalf. It began:

> The minor's illness is either congenital, a degenerative brain disease, or the result of encephalitis and has no connection with the vaccine. At any rate, his condition is improving. While the vaccine's possible complications are known and documented worldwide, they are very rare and are agreed to be a far lesser risk than that posed by the illnesses it prevents. Epidemiological surveys conducted in Israel and abroad show that mass immunization with the triple vaccine has significantly brought down incidence of the three diseases. The withdrawal of the vaccine batch, which the plaintiffs claim was contaminated, was in no way related to what happened to the minor. There is no reasonable or relevant connection

between the administration of the vaccine and the minor's condition. The minor was given the standard dose. Had it been the cause of his condition, the symptoms would have appeared earlier than they did. If he had a sensitivity to the vaccine, this could not have been predicted. The plaintiffs are not medically qualified to claim any link between the vaccine and the damage to the minor. In any event, the State of Israel cannot be held liable, because there was no negligence. It is unnecessary to warn families about the vaccine because it is not dangerous, and its complications are extremely rare. The vaccine batch from which the minor was vaccinated was manufactured, imported, mixed, and stored according to regulations, in every particular. There was no need to halt its administration, because it is statistically expected that it will have negative effects in a very few instances. The minor's parents tacitly consented to the vaccination. The Samuels family did not relocate to the US to seek help for the minor. All such medical and educational services are available in Israel. They left Israel because they hadn't settled well and were struggling financially. Because there is no connection between the vaccine and the minor's condition, no compensation is due to the family for their move to the US. The fact that they have now returned and found a suitable framework for the minor demonstrates that their move was unnecessary and an overreaction. Nor should they be compensated for a car. Public transportation is adequate. The opinions of the neurologists Shaul Harel and Pinchas Lerman are incorrect. The claim of the Samuels family is baseless, exaggerated, and totally disproportionate. They have run up their costs heedlessly, doing nothing to minimize their expenses. Their claim is frivolous. It should be thrown out of court and the Samuels family should be liable for the time and costs of the defense team.

And that was only the opening shot! From the judge, the spoken and unspoken message transmitted to Avi was that he'd never be able to prove causality, and the case was therefore unwinnable.

When asked why he didn't recognize this and drop the case, Avi replied, "The prevailing attitude is: 'They have a mentally challenged child. Unfortunately, people have such children, especially in ultra-Orthodox circles where families keep having babies to a late age.' They are not moved by Yossi's plight. It is because of this apathy, because of Kalman and Malki's unswerving insistence that their child was born healthy, and because they are clearly pursuing justice above all, that I will not waver in my desire to represent them. At worst, we'll lose the case, but it is a case that has to be fought." Avi was indeed young and idealistic, and he too sought justice.

Up against major law firms, and with very little money or manpower available, much of the legwork fell to me – digging out, tracking down, and collecting facts and documents that Avi was to use so successfully in court. My flexible working hours at the foundation were a blessing. In those pre-email, pre-internet days, I wrote letters, sent faxes, made phone calls, extracted records from hospitals, and wheedled files from the legal system. I read the medical reports in search of damning contradictions and pored over the professional literature about vaccine reactions. I spent days on end in libraries, searching through police archives chasing down different sources. I drafted comprehensive cross-examinations of witnesses.

On one occasion, I traced a file we urgently needed to a document repository in a court in Jerusalem's Old City. When a senior judge refused to hand it over without a written legal request, I went back into the street, took out pen and paper, and wrote a one-page request, making it sound as learned and legalistic as I could. I waited some time for the judge to exit his chambers, and with some surprise at both the way I looked and what he read, he said, "Well done!" and immediately signed the request. Fifteen minutes later, the document was in my hand. I had come a long way and Avi was impressed.

I read the classic medical textbooks on vaccination injury to prepare for out-of-context citations, and contacted the authors of those books in Israel and abroad. The names of these world experts, their sympathetic opinions, and their willingness to testify for Yossi made an impact. Dr. John H. Menkes, who established UCLA's pediatric neurology program and wrote a classic textbook, *Child Neurology*, which was published in seven editions, was a willing source of help and advice and agreed to testify. And Dr. Wolfgang Ehrengut, a professor of medicine at the Institute for Vaccinology and Virology in Hamburg, West Germany, shared his study of bias in evaluating central nervous system complications following pertussis immunization, including convulsions and high fever, which can lead to brain damage and death.

Many of these biases were unfortunately familiar to us: adverse post-immunization reactions unreported by the health system, frequency of adverse reactions unreported by the vaccine producers, inaccurate statistics, and others – all clearly showing that central nervous system complications after pertussis immunization are underestimated and perhaps occur in more than acceptably small numbers.

While Israel's health authorities remained resolute in their refusal to admit to anything, winds of change were beginning to waft, if not yet blow, around Connaught Labs in Canada, where the pertussis component of Yossi's vaccine had been manufactured. On July 13, 1987, the *Vancouver Sun* reported that Connaught had discontinued sales of the pertussis vaccine in the US because of costly lawsuits. On April 18, 1988, Canada's *Globe and Mail* featured an Alberta study which had found a dramatic increase in adverse reactions to the Connaught-manufactured pertussis vaccine. And, two months after that, under the headline KIDS HURT BY VACCINE TO GET AID, the *Edmonton Journal* described a national program being set up in Alberta to compensate families of children injured by the vaccine. It noted:

> In the past eight years, three or four Alberta children have suffered permanent brain damage after receiving the vaccine. There is general consensus among health professionals across the country that compensation is necessary.

Israel's health professionals thought differently.

The seemingly endless court case was still dragging on. It was time for Yossi to be reexamined by the two neurologists who had first seen him in 1983. Their stated opinion – that Yossi's disabilities resulted from the contaminated vaccine and not, as the defense would later claim, from an inborn degenerative nerve disease, and their willingness to testify to this – had been key to our decision to litigate, and it was soon time for them to take the witness stand.

The following journal entries recount our visits to those two neurologists at that time:

> Late yesterday we went to Prof. Shaul Harel so he could see Yossi again before testifying. Malki drove in the unbearable 40-degree [Celsius] heat because of my back. Of course, my directions got us lost in Tel Aviv and it was hectic. Anyway, we arrived only a few minutes late – and ended up waiting forty minutes. Yossi set up shop in the waiting-room, taking out his brailler and putting it on the glass coffee table. Luckily, I was alert and caught a falling vase just in time. Yuval, the legal intern, had arrived before us, and with me as his liaison Yossi now engaged him in conversation. "Right, you were at my house last

week with Sarah? I was sick. You shave, don't you? And you have curly hair?" Lifting my yarmulke to expose my bald head, he proudly announced to everyone present: "My father doesn't have curly hair!"

Yossi performed for Dr. Harel as only Yossi can, and the neurologist was rendered speechless by the changes in him. There was nothing the doctor asked of him that Yossi didn't do well. He demonstrated his braille reading with a resounding *Shema Yisrael*, Hear O Israel, his hand, of course, covering his eyes in accordance with Jewish custom. He typed out an entire Purim song on his brailler to give to the doctor. As he was about to pull it from the machine, he realized he hadn't printed a solid line along the bottom to indicate The End, and duly corrected his "mistake." I asked Dr. Harel about the defense's assertion that Yossi had a degenerative nerve disease. He said it was impossible due to Yossi's extraordinary development. All in all, it was a most worthwhile visit.

Yesterday we gave Professor Pinchas Lerman his opportunity to see Yossi again. We picked Yossi up at the School for the Blind after his swimming lesson, and headed west toward Tel Aviv. Malki changed Yossi in the car into clean pants, a white shirt, and clean white socks – a matter of principle with her from the time that Yossi was tiny, so that he'd feel good about himself, and those working with him would feel drawn to him. As with Dr. Harel, Yossi put on quite the show, did everything asked of him and then some. To see whether Yossi could find the door, the doctor asked me to tell him to go to the waiting-room. Well, I told Yossi to go and bring the doctor a newspaper, only one, from the other room. He went directly to the door, brought the newspaper, and handed it to the doctor. What the sharp-eyed doctor also noticed was that when he came back into the room, Yossi turned the key in the door, locking us in and sliding the key behind a small vase on a nearby shelf. When we left an hour later, Yossi went straight to his hiding place, retrieved the key, and unlocked the door.

To say the least, the doctor was impressed. He said Yossi's progress was awesome, and there was no question of degenerative nerve disease. He also told us that Dr. H., whom he knew professionally, was furious that he was submitting a medical opinion that differed from hers, and she would no longer speak to him.

Opposing counsel were not only condescending toward us, they were also callous beyond measure. Lodged in my memory is a question that one of their lawyers asked Dr. Lerman: "Doctor, how much compensation money are we discussing anyway? Just how long can this child be expected to live?" And when, at that, Malki broke into a storm of weeping, he said dismissively: "Your Honor, I didn't ask this woman to be in court."

Dr. Lerman responded thoughtfully and deliberately, "Well, let us see. His general health is excellent, he's a nonsmoker, and he's blind and deaf, so he won't be crossing busy streets alone. He doesn't have to cope with the ongoing pressures of everyday life, so there's no reason why his lifespan shouldn't be as long as any other healthy person, and he could comfortably live into his eighties." Opposing counsel was livid and dropped this line of questioning.

The legal case took over our lives. With the "incidental costs," for which I was responsible, and the many days and half-days I took off from work for research and court hearings, financial worries weighed in ever more heavily. Their tactic was clear – delay until we collapse and give up due to the unbearable pressures. I struggled and often prayed for the ability to see the case through.

At the time, I wrote in my journal about the extreme pressure we were experiencing:

Wednesday, February 1, 1989. This morning I received a beautiful fax from Dad who told me that they are behind us all the way and not to even consider expenses. It was such a positive, warm fax that I teared up while reading it to Malki. We are so alone, and to know that Mom and Dad are there with us brings great strength because this pressure simply destroys us. We feel that we are existing, not living. This is the goal of the defense – to break us and make us lose our initiative to fight, as they have done to so many other families. They have time on their side, and they know they'll wear us down to a breaking-point, when we'll either give up or settle for some minimal compromise. They know too well the price a family has to pay in order to sue. The pressure is immense and the outcome always seems further away.

The constant legal delays and incessant pressure were depleting our endurance.

Chapter 18

Goliath Stumbles

On Sunday, July 16, 1989, my blind and deaf twelve-and-a-half-year-old son took the stand, finally putting a human face on all the years of contention. By then, the case had been making its way through the courts for six years and filled over a thousand pages of court records, and Yossi's emotional testimony was about to fill even more.

We left Jerusalem at 7:30 that morning for the hearing in Tel Aviv – a very tense Malki, a scarcely less tense me, Yossi, and Shoshana Weinstock, who was battling the flu. Yossi was dressed immaculately in an ironed short-sleeved shirt, a tie, dark pants, hearing aids, his vibration sensor with its wire down his arm, and of course, his white cane. The courtroom fell silent as he entered, tapping as he went. As usual, we sat waiting for the judge. Israel has no jury system. During the wait, Avi suddenly decided on a switch in tactics: he would question Yossi on the stand, rather than have him make a statement.

When the judge entered, the lawyer for Rafa Pharmaceuticals immediately stood up and protested, "He's not qualified to be a witness, Your Honor." Fortunately, the judge simply replied: "We'll hear him anyway," and instructed his assistant to record Yossi's testimony meticulously.

Yossi answered the questions put to him like a pro, speaking slowly and quite clearly, from the first more basic questions, including, "What's your name?" "How old are you?" and "When is your bar mitzva?" through the later questions that required more thought, including the very last: "What do you want most in life?" to which he responded: "To see my father and mother." It was so powerful, and defense counsel strategically declined cross-examination. We were delighted.

Bringing Yossi into court had been a hard decision, but we'd all felt it was important for the judge to meet him, and see beyond the years of legal wrangling to the actual child and the terrible damage done to him. And while the defense appeared unmoved by a child robbed of his sight and hearing by an indifferent and negligent bureaucracy, Yossi's impact on the judge – a religiously observant grandfather near retirement – was acute. Avi told me the next day that Yossi's court appearance was the highpoint of his career – not something said lightly by a lawyer who, by then, had spent many days in court representing a long list of eminent clients.

Malki had been so anxious that she'd considered not attending the session at all, afraid to see Yossi bullied or belittled by the judge or the lawyers. Avi, in his gentle way, had persuaded her to come, saying he needed her there to support Yossi, and that so close to the end of the legal marathon, this was no time to quit. She agreed and came in spite of the emotional toll it might take on her.

It was not only against Yossi that the defense fought. They attempted to block every one of our key witnesses with ever-changing legalistic arguments. One such witness was the prestigious Hebrew University biostatistician Professor Zvi Gilula. From their perspective, they were right to do so because the evidence he gave was devastating – both in itself and because it gave the lie to a report submitted to the court by the defense two years earlier.

On January 29, 1987, Professor Chaim Grichter, director of the Health Ministry's Central Laboratory at the time in question, had testified in detail that of over 600,000 DPT vaccinations given in Israel between the years 1977 and 1981,

> the cases of encephalitis following DPT reported to me
> are as follows:
>
> 1977   4
> 1978   2
> 1979   none reported
> 1980   1
> 1981   1

Professor Gilula's figures were very different. During 1977, he told the court, there was a significantly greater proportion of brain-damaged children in Israel than any year before or since, for no apparent reason, and that requires some serious explanation. Professor Gilula backed up his findings and didn't flinch in the face of the fierce cross-examinations. The judge seemed to internalize his testimony and recognize that it was in fact from June to December 1977 that the flawed vaccine had been administered in Israel's well-baby clinics nationwide.

At the end of the day, the crux of the legal case was clearly in the hands of the medical experts. Each side fielded two expert neurologists. Ours were Shaul Harel and Pinchas Lerman, and they both held up well through extensive and grueling cross-examination. Each had seen Yossi in 1983 when Malki had brought him from New York and then again several years later, in advance of their court appearances. The first visits were before Yossi's communication breakthrough with Shoshana Weinstock, and the second visits were after the breakthrough. Both were astonished and elated at his progress, and both testified that Yossi's disabilities resulted from the vaccine. The two men were shunned by their medical colleagues for this "betrayal." Dr. Lerman, close to the end of his career, had knowingly put a great deal of his prestige on the line. Professor Harel, a child Holocaust survivor, overcame the disapprobation and went on to establish Israel's Institute for Child Development and Pediatric Neurology and to chair Israel's Pediatric Neurology Society.

While their testimonies were a very important contribution to our case, those of the experts appearing for the defense helped us as much, if not more. For the defense and for themselves personally, the court appearances of the two "neurological experts" brought by the defense were an unmitigated disaster. Not only could neither offer a plausible alternative explanation for what had happened to Yossi, but both damaged their own integrity by showing extreme bias. One, a pediatric neurologist, was repeatedly tripped up by Avi on his selective and slanted quoting of experts. He finally lost all credibility when he asserted categorically that vaccines NEVER cause damage.

It was Dr. H., however, whose lying letter to American neurologist Myles Behrens had started us down this path, who did more than anyone to rattle the defense. She had initially been named as one of five defendants when we filed suit in 1983, along with the Canadian and Israeli drug companies, the Israeli health authorities and the City of Jerusalem. We later dropped the claim against her for technical reasons, but her Hebrew medical report, which she now presented to the court as her professional opinion, was in fact identical to the report that she had submitted as a defendant, six years earlier. Incredibly, the report she'd initially given to absolve herself from blame was now being introduced as unbiased expert opinion.

At the top of her profession in Israel and beyond at this time, with no one more aware of this than she was, she strode confidently to the stand and answered the defense lawyer's questions in a tone that made it clear her expertise was unassailable. She crisply repeated the lies of her letter and her report, stating that Yossi's development had been severely delayed prior to the vaccination, and his problems were thus clearly inborn.

"We're discussing a child who presents a picture of very slow gradual degeneration of different channels of the nervous system, beginning with the optic nerves in infancy, audio nerves in young childhood, and the coordination system and balance in recent years," she pontificated. "This illness has no connection with a dose of vaccine, this or any other."

Dr. H. then brazenly unleashed her venomous lies on Malki and me as well. "The parents did not come to receive the answer," she fabricated, "and in spite of the fact that in these circumstances I phoned them of my own volition, they did not return to my clinic to receive the results for the completion of the examination, and they angrily received my attempts at communication." Having tried so helplessly to get information at that time from this doctor only to have her snub me, I was now dumbfounded by her audacity.

She officiously concluded: "The extended development of symptoms in the illness of Joseph Samuels removes from the realm of possibility that the vaccine given at the age of eleven months was the cause of this development. These symptoms, in the development of the illness, point to a slow-spreading degenerative illness."

Dr. H. could not produce even one original document to support her claims, while we had a dozen notarized medical documents, from the well-baby clinic pediatrician onward, that refuted them.

Avi, whose competence in the courtroom was uncanny, was ready to attack. He had a concealed weapon in his arsenal. Some months earlier, he had been secretly approached by a bereaved father who was a former policeman. He shared that his child had died as a result of Dr. H.'s mismanagement, but that the aftermath of this tragedy had gone beyond human error and into the realm of the criminal. He discovered that the neurologist had altered the medical file to absolve herself of all liability. He brought charges against her – but she'd been lucky. The facts were sufficient to lead to a criminal conviction but the judge ruled that there was not clear proof that she had criminal intent. The policeman gave Avi all of the court documents.

At the beginning of Avi's cross-examination, Dr. H. was, if possible, yet more arrogant. "She talked down to me as if I were an office boy," Avi later recalled. "I was relishing what was ahead, but I didn't expect the reaction that came."

"Dr. H.," Avi said, "I must ask you – and I do apologize for this question – but have you ever been on trial for forging medical documents?" This celebrated medical authority was caught completely off guard and turned in an instant into a screaming harridan. She glared at Avi, and screamed: "I WISH YOU WERE DEAD!" And with that, her entire lying testimony began to crumble.

By late 1989, we'd established, against all odds, a case too powerful to be easily thrown out. The Tel Aviv district court judge had seemingly been convinced by our claim – but the defense wouldn't give up. Admitting responsibility would, they knew, cause a countrywide scandal and lead to a flood of compensation claims. It was now clear that the health authorities had known the vaccine was problematic as early as June 1977, but they hadn't withdrawn it. It had remained in use, with their knowledge, for a further six months and injected into infant after infant. Yossi, in fact, had been one of the last. Had responsible steps been taken in a timely manner, he and so many others would have been spared.

Even when the government belatedly decided to halt DTP immunization countrywide, it acted with no visible urgency. Given the terrible and irreversible neurological damage it was inflicting on helpless infants, you'd expect an emergency recall of all contaminated vaccine batches, with health ministry vehicles driving from clinic to clinic to collect them. You would, however, be disappointed. The government didn't want any kind of panic or, worse, to create circumstances that would lead to future claims against it. So there was no vaccine collection; no newspaper, radio, or TV announcements; no Health Ministry calls to well-baby clinics ordering immediate cessation. What the authorities did do was send out a memo to all vaccination centers by regular mail on December 5, 1977. Mail takes several days. Another day or two – or certainly a few critical hours – would surely have elapsed until the letter was opened, because nothing on the envelope marked it as urgent. Twelve days later, on December 17, there was a newspaper announcement that DPT vaccination in Israel had been suspended.

"DPT immunization was halted for at least two months," Avi shared, "and when it was restarted, the diphtheria and typhoid (DT) components were administered separately from the pertussis (P). What clearer indication can there be that they knew? Had this happened today, it would rightly have been a huge public outrage, marking the end of the careers of those responsible. But then, it could still be hushed up."

Clearer indication did, in fact, come in a document that the Health Ministry desperately tried to keep secret. It was some twenty-five pages of minutes from a high-level Health Ministry meeting where a broad array of experts testified, which ministry director-general Tibor Schwartz tried to pass off as "a routine academic get-together." As the minutes show, however, the meeting was far from routine. It was about "the DPT problem" and how to handle it – and Schwartz eventually admitted this, under Avi's relentless cross-examination.

Chapter 19

Diamonds Are Forever

The phone rang at our home on Friday afternoon, in late January, 1990. It was Mom, and while she did her best to remain composed, the news was worrying. Dad had been rushed to the hospital with an expanding aorta. Open-heart surgery was scheduled for Monday morning.

"I'll come at once," I told her. "No," she replied. "There's no need. It'll be all right." We ended our conversation, and I hung up and turned to Malki. Before I even opened my mouth, she said, "You're getting on a plane right after Shabbat." With the eleven-hour flight to Montreal or Toronto and five and a half hours more to Vancouver, I would get there at noon on Sunday, in good time for the surgery. "You're panicking," I told her. "Mom said there was no need." Malki insisted that I call an anesthesiologist friend from the Hadassah Medical Center to ask him about expanding aortas. He was unequivocal in his answer. "It's serious business," he said. Malki asked him, "If it was your father, G-d forbid, what would you be doing?" "I would be flying to see him before surgery," he replied.

I booked a Saturday night flight to Montreal. "Have you got the three-page proposal?" Malki asked, as I threw things into my carry-on bag. "I'll be spending my time with Dad," I said, "so why would I take that?" "Take it," she said firmly. "You never know who you might meet."

I landed in Vancouver on Sunday morning and went straight to the hospital, where I found Marilyn, who'd come in from Calgary, and Uncle Herschel, who'd flown in from New York. That was when I realized that things were very serious. Dad gave me a bear hug that lasted a full minute, kissed me, and said, "I'm so glad you're here." I told him not to worry, that we'd see this thing through together with flying colors and that Malki and the kids were waiting for his next visit to Jerusalem.

Confident though we were in the surgeons, we took out extra insurance in the form of a special blessing. The local Chabad *shaliah* (representative) in Vancouver, Rabbi Yitzhak Weinberg, heard from me that Herschel had treated the Lubavitcher Rebbe's wife nine years earlier, and he urged me to ask my uncle to write the Rebbe and ask for a get-well blessing. I was surprised Herschel agreed because he wasn't a great believer in the power of blessings. Perhaps he viewed it like chicken soup in that it *"voudn't hoit."* Without identifying himself as the Rebbetzin's former orthopedist, he quickly jotted down on plain paper:

Dear Rabbi Schneerson,

I am currently in Vancouver, Canada, where my brother is about to undergo life-threatening surgery to repair his expanding aorta. I ask you for your blessing for a full recovery.

Sincerely,
Herschel Samuels, MD

Rabbi Weinberg faxed the request to New York. I sat with Dad until it was time for *minha*, afternoon prayers, for which I went to the Schara Tzedeck synagogue six blocks away. Back at the hospital an hour later, I was beset by the nurses. "Mr. Samuels, *where* have you been? There's someone who keeps calling, looking for you." On cue, the phone rang.

It was an excited Rabbi Weinberg, also asking me where I'd been, though he didn't wait for an answer. "You've no idea what's happened!" he said. "You know the Rebbe is inundated with requests from all over the world and his answers normally take weeks at best. Even an emergency takes days. But there was a response to your uncle's fax in just TWO HOURS! And not by fax, but by PHONE, and from none other than the Rebbe's personal secretary, Rabbi Leibel Groner! Rabbi Groner asked me, 'Who in the world is this Herschel Samuels?'"

The Rebbe, it seemed, had recognized Uncle Herschel's name, stopped the review of faxes, and immediately handwritten on the fax, "Blessing for a greater recovery than can be foreseen." He instructed that it be sent back at once. Dad's surgery the next day was successful and he lived another eight rewarding years.

The Rebbe's blessing and Dad's recovery turned out to be only two of the remarkable events which marked that trip. Another was my running into the Diamond family. Each day I joined some twenty men at synagogue for the morning and evening prayers. Among them, I ran into old family friends – Jack Diamond, a contemporary of my parents, and his sons, Gordon and Charles. Jack's wife Sadie had died several weeks earlier, and they were there to recite the traditional mourner's Kaddish prayer, which is recited in ancient Aramaic.

Jack was a pillar of the Vancouver community. An old-time immigrant from Poland, whose family was largely wiped out by a pogrom, he came to Canada with nothing in his pocket and not a word of English. He peddled potatoes, swept floors, worked as a butcher, eventually bought his own meat-packing plant, and from there built an enormous business called Pacific Meats. From ages eight to twelve, I'd proudly worn a Little League uniform emblazoned with the team name, "Pacific Meats." One of Jack's great loves was horses. He owned the local racetrack and was the father of horse racing in Canada. A man of vision and an extraordinary philanthropist, there wasn't a major communal institution in Vancouver's Jewish or non-Jewish communities to which Jack hadn't contributed in some way. His contributions had been recognized with prizes, honorary doctorates, and the country's highest public service award, the Order of Canada. Of his two sons, I'd known Gordon better even though he was some fourteen years my senior, and meeting again after so many years, we fell into schmoozing before and after each service. Given that I was there praying for my sick parent and he was there struggling to recite Kaddish for his deceased parent, we had a lot to schmooze about.

Two days before I was to leave Vancouver, I called Malki. I told her I'd seen Gordon Diamond in *shul* each day and we'd become quite close, but I was hesitant whether I should tell him about our dream for children with disabilities and their families and ask for his help.

"Of course you should!" she said. "What's he going to do? Give you a *patsch* (spanking)?" How much, I ventured, should I ask for? She didn't miss a beat: "Double *hai* – $36,000 – because that's what we need to get started." It was a major request, but I knew as well as Malki that renting space and hiring two staffers for the first year would indeed cost at least $36,000.

The next morning, I summoned my courage, and as we walked out of *shul* I said to Gordon, "This isn't easy for me, but before I leave tomorrow, I want to ask you something. My wife and I have a dream that is described on these pages. Would you mind reading it and let me know later what you think? "Sure, no problem," he responded, holding out his hand for the proposal.

Gordon brought it with him to *minha* later that day. "Kalman," he said, "this is a bottomless pit. You're going to be coming to me for money every year, and I just can't do it." I assured him that all I wanted was help to get the project up and running and I wouldn't be coming to him again for funding, until such time as he told me to.

During the fifteen-minute break between the afternoon and evening prayers, an agitated Gordon stepped outside. I followed him. "This Kaddish business is really getting to me," he confided. "I struggle with the words every time I say it, and spending this much time at synagogue is time-consuming. I can manage this first month, but the rabbi's expecting me to do it for a year. I really can't, Kalman. It's cutting into my aerobics."

I paused, dug deep, and replied carefully: "Gordon, let me tell you something. And please, understand me clearly, because I don't want you ever to say that a rabbi told you to skip Kaddish. But look, an army has different battalions – tanks, air force, infantry, intelligence, reconnaissance, and all the others. If you take the world's greatest pilot and put him in a tank, he'll be next to useless. I hear you struggling with Kaddish. To be honest, it's painful listening to you trying to get out the words to honor your mother and nurture her *neshama*, her soul. And yes, you should say it during this year, but Gordon, if you really want to help your mother's *neshama* fly, climb into the fighter jet: give the *charity* that will launch this essential center for children with disabilities. This is your expertise, your strength. Help Malki and me get started and I promise you here in this *shul* that I'll never come back to you for money, unless you tell me otherwise. We need you in order to begin making our dream reality, because only then can I go to others for help."

"You're workin' me, you're just workin' me," Gordon retorted gruffly. And then: "Kalman, know this. If I help, I don't want your center to be named for my mother because then for sure you're gonna be coming back and workin' me some more." "Gordon," I said, "if you get us off the ground, you'll be starting a snowball in which everything that follows will be to your credit and that of your mother's *neshama*. She doesn't need the naming." "How much are we talking about?" Gordon asked. I struggled, but got it out. "Double *hai*, Gordon, $36,000 – US."

"*Yisgadal veyiskadash*," Jack and Charles intoned the opening words of the Kaddish prayer as the break ended. Gordon hurried back inside. I followed, but my mind wasn't on the prayers that afternoon. As Gordon left with Jack and Charles, he said: "I'll see you in the morning. Leave things with me and I'll talk to [my wife] Leslie." With that, he was out the door. I stayed put, and in the five minutes it took the *shamash* (synagogue caretaker) to put away the prayer books and lock up, I prayed my little heart out, beseeching the Almighty for His continued help.

Vancouver time is ten hours behind Jerusalem, so I waited until 11:00 p.m. to call Malki, when it was 9:00 a.m. her time and I knew the kids would all be in school. I anxiously shared my exchange with Gordon. "Relax," she replied. "If it's meant to be, he'll do it, so stop worrying. G-d can manage it without your nerves. Just get a good night's sleep." That proved easier said than done.

Next morning, Gordon was in *shul* as usual, donning his *tefillin*. It seemed like forever until the service ended, and we walked out together. "Listen," he said. "I've talked this through with Leslie and we've decided to give you seed funding. "This is not about agriculture," I responded. Gordon grimaced and clarified. "We are going to help you with the first funds, but there are three conditions: First, I want you and only you to manage this. I've had too much of giving money to people for organizations, only to discover they've delegated and things fell apart. Here, there will be no delegating. I know your family and trust you, and you will personally run this. Second, you'll undertake to do only what you've written in your proposal. If you think you're going to save the world, don't take my money. And third, of course, you'll have to get me a Canadian tax receipt."

With tears in my eyes, I hugged and kissed him right then and there, acutely aware of the significance of the moment. "Gordon," I blurted out, "without your generosity, Malki and I would still be dreaming. The snowball you've set in motion is going to be bigger than you or I can ever imagine. And yes, you have just sent your mother's soul into orbit." As we walked slowly through the morning mist across the street to his car, he said, "Leslie and I will give you $50,000 Canadian. That's about $43,000 US. Before you go back to Israel, phone Leslie and thank her because she was the key. Kalman, your coming here was good for your Dad, good for you, and good for me. Goodbye, have a safe trip. I love ya, pal." And with that, he drove away.

I stayed on the sidewalk for a long moment, numb, overwhelmed and humbled by my role as conduit. Then I raced to my parents' house to call Malki. Even as she expressed her great excitement and gratitude, Malki, being Malki, couldn't hold herself back from asking, "*Nu*, so was it such a bad thing that you took the papers with you?"

My next phone call was to Leslie. Graciously, she assured me they were proud to partner with us and looked forward to hearing about the wonderful things we'd be doing to help people in need.

Dad had come home from the hospital the day before and was thankfully well on his way to recovery. He and Mom were elated with the news, and Dad said it would give him added strength to heal. We ate our regular breakfast together, the one I'd known since I was a kid: half a pink grapefruit with each segment loosened with a special grapefruit knife, two slices of toast, two poached eggs, and, for the adults, a cup of unsweetened percolated black coffee. The radio was on as usual, even though no one was listening, making conversation difficult – which may, in fact, have been contributory to my parents' long and happy marriage! I finished packing and took a cab to the airport.

Chapter 20

Peace of Mind

Things were now moving rapidly. As soon as I got back to Israel in February, we began looking for premises to rent – even as the court case for Yossi continued.

I remembered the well-known professional who had advised the US social worker two months earlier that our suggested afterschool program should be supported, and I now called her on the phone. "Remember how disappointed we were when the North American philanthropists decided not to fund it?" I began. "Well, you're not going to believe this, but my dad was ill and I went to Vancouver to be with him, and while I was there I ran into a friend with whom I shared Malki's dream and he's given us the money to get it off the ground. Isn't that amazing?"

My excitement was greeted with silence. Then she said: "Oh no, I am planning to do that program myself, so you can't go ahead with it now." I was dumbfounded. "But, yours is a morning program," I eventually managed. "Yes, I'll be carrying on with that, too," she said. Utterly shocked, I simply responded, "Listen, there are a lot of kids out there who need this kind of help – more than either of us can handle. So don't worry. If the day comes when we both want to help the same child, I'll gladly back off and let you do it."

I hung up and tried to process the conversation. Only two months earlier, this respected professional had encouraged us to launch our program – but as it edged toward reality, she felt clearly threatened by a new player on the block. Malki and I decided then and there to do what we believed was necessary, without worrying about those who may be pressured by our presence in the field. To no one's surprise, the professional never opened such a program.

In synagogue on my first Sabbath back from Vancouver, I shared with Zev, a lawyer friend who sat in front of me, that we were at last moving ahead with our program. "Have you given it a name and legally registered it?" he asked. The thought hadn't crossed my mind. "We just want to help people," I said. "Why do we need to be legally registered as an organization?" He smiled and suggested that we talk about it after the Sabbath.

It proved to be an instructive conversation. I learned that you can't simply use charitable funds to do good things for people; there are liabilities and you must do it through a legal entity with a unique name. Fortunately, Zev happened to be going to the Registry the next day. "Think of a few names for your organization," he said. "Give them to me in the morning and I'll check to see which are available."

Malki and I sat down to think. I came up with what I thought were great suggestions, but she rejected them, one after the other. She suggested a few that I nixed. Then her face lit up. "I have it. *Shalva*," she said excitedly. "Terrific," I replied. "You're naming it for a popular Israeli breakfast cereal?" "No, no," she said. "It's the perfect name. The Hebrew, *shalva*, means 'peace of mind' or 'serenity' in English. It's simple, it's gentle, and it describes exactly what we want to provide." The four Hebrew letters that spell *Shalva* also stand for *Shihrur Lamishpaha Velayeled Hamugbal* – Freedom for the Family and the Disabled Child.

I gave the name to Zev. To his surprise, it was available. He registered it and began working on the legal paperwork necessary for creating Shalva. To my surprise, I later noticed that in the proposal I had sent to my sister Marilyn almost two years earlier, I had written, "The end result is parents who can better cope with their other responsibilities, and children who can hope for a little *peace of mind.*"

We found it very meaningful to learn that the word *shalva* appears but once in the entire Bible, in Psalms 122:7 – "May there be peace within your walls, serenity (*shalva*) in your palaces" – with the following verse, verse 8, stating our mission: "For the sake of my brothers and friends, I speak peace unto you."

Chapter 21

Justice, Law, and the Daylight Between

W e'd made progress in court, but the case still dragged on. It seemed as if it would dominate the rest of our lives – lives we felt growing shorter with each pressured day – when suddenly, it took a sudden and unexpected turn. On Wednesday, April 4, 1990, Avi called me.

"Kalman," he said, "there's been a development. The judge called all the lawyers into his chambers and told us, 'Gentlemen, the morning is yours, but at this time, in keeping with the law, I want to suggest that you consider a compromise. We have before us a serious claim which now spreads over more than a thousand pages of court records. And as you're surely aware, Mr. Fischer, no such case has ever been won in this country. If my ruling were to be in your favor, it would be a land-mark precedent, and creating a legal precedent is extremely difficult. In short, I would like to get the ball rolling and ask you, Mr. Fischer, to quote an amount for which your clients would settle.'"

Avi respectfully had refused to quote a figure. "I told the judge I must consult with you, and he's agreed to wait until later this morning for an answer," he told me. "Kalman, find a copy of our original claim, get paper, pen, and calculator, and let's get busy." At last, it seemed, light glimmered ahead. Avi and I analyzed the data and he now had a clear idea of how he would approach the matter.

At noon, the judge called the lawyers back into his chambers. Avi began with a summary of how much our family had suffered and the costs we'd already shouldered. He emphasized that personal gain had never been a factor in our lawsuit and that we had never wished to damage the system. We had taken legal action only in order to receive compensation that would help us support our son through adulthood, to win acknowledgment of responsibility, and to ensure that nothing like this could ever happen in Israel again. He then named the settlement figure we had calculated. The defense counter-offered a greatly reduced sum and demanded a blanket pledge of absolute secrecy on the court case.

"Does anyone," asked the judge, "want to hear my opinion?" The three defense lawyers immediately declined, all but drowning out Avi's "Yes, Your Honor." The judge gave his view, regardless. Double or triple the amount requested would be insufficient compensation, he said, but, given the challenging legal restraints, he suggested his own figure. The defense lawyers hit the roof and left the half-hour meeting fuming about "the *hutzpa* of that interfering judge."

The sum offered covered the extensive debts we'd incurred through the legal proceedings but did not adequately provide for Yossi's future. We had carried on the fight all these years in order to ensure a quality life for our child – and we'd failed. I was devastated.

We had until May 10 – thirty-six days – to decide whether to accept or refuse the settlement. They were days of anguish.

The following are excerpts from my journal, written during those excruciatingly trying days:

Sunday, April 29, 1990. I have been ill the past few days, lacking strength and only wanting to sleep. I finally came down with a sore throat and a flu. I know that my exhaustion is due to the stress of having to internalize the ramifications of accepting the judge's compromise. I am having great difficulty. If we accept, I have done little for the future of the child. I will be copping out in that I am not forcing the judge to make a ruling which, if in our favor, could revolutionize the treatment of DTP injury cases in this country. But as Dad says, once the judge has intervened, there's little to be accomplished by further challenging him other than alienate him. As I write this, the past years flash through my mind and I simply can't believe it. Dad said it wisely on Thursday: "If they were to offer you double the current sum, would it be sufficient to provide for Yossi's future? Of course not! If so, the issue is not a little more money but a great deal more, which isn't realistic. So why spend another five gut-wrenching years at this? Your victory lies in their urgency to settle. Get out now and start life again."

Tuesday, May 1, 1990. I told Avi that I don't want to delay settlement nor do I know exactly how to handle this, but to please understand that with the amount they want to give, we have done little for Yossi's future. They've already destroyed our lives, at least they should care for our child after our passing. I told him to please fight for everything he can now, because after May 10, there may not be another chance. If he wishes to blame me, I said, he is more than welcome to do so, but in my opinion, even the judge will understand my fears. Extraordinary settlements have been paid in different fields for claims more frivolous and with less legitimacy than ours.

> *Sunday, May 6, 1990.* As usual it comes down to the major decision: Do we fight to the end and break the DTP claims barrier here in Israel once and for all, sacrificing our personal lives? Or do we compromise, resume living our personal lives, and thus hand the pharma establishment their ultimate victory. Oh G-d, please guide us down the right path so that we can live our lives and live with ourselves.

Avi filled me in on what happened when the lawyers reconvened in the judge's chambers on May 10 to decide on the settlement. Avi began. "Your Honor, my client is very angry about the amount offered, but during the trial, we developed a deep trust in you, and I've used my full authority to help him realize that a court-brokered compromise shouldn't be refused. He's not happy, but he has agreed to the offer. I know what the defense thinks, but I am convinced that it is in their best interest to accept the settlement Your Honor has suggested, since if we were to continue to fight this case in court, I'm certain we would win."

The judge turned to the defense lawyers and asked, "Who exactly is the problem here?" "Your Honor," replied one, "we've checked the figures in England, and Your Honor is offering far more than is paid out there." The judge replied: "Please take note that I am a citizen of Israel, not England, and although our law is based on English law, I am not obligated to accept every detail. At any rate, you should think very carefully before refusing."

The settlement would make the moral victory ours, but that didn't relieve the distress. And there was something else I knew, as well – Malki could no longer fight. She may have been a mother of a child with severe disabilities but that had never been of interest to anyone. The legal process was brutal and seemingly inhuman. "If you want to go on for years and battle to the end," she said, "be my guest, but I can't anymore – give me my *gett* [Jewish divorce certificate] now and let me walk away from it." I was more than broken but knew deep in my heart that she was right, and at the end of the day we had to extricate ourselves, settle, and make a new start on life. We instructed Avi to accept the offer on two conditions: First, the confidentiality clause would concern solely the amount paid; everything else in the court record would be in the public domain. We hadn't invested almost a decade to give the defense the sweet taste of closing the court records forever. Second, the full sum was to be paid immediately, without preconditions and bureaucratic delays.

For Avi, like us, the settlement left a sour taste. "I have no music playing in my heart," was the way he phrased it, but he stressed that we had, nonetheless, won a major victory. No such sum had ever been paid out in a case like this. Our alternative, he said, was to continue the crusade for many more years, including an appeal to the Supreme Court with its heavy demands on our nerves and our pockets. Even if it was decided in our favor, the judges would likely deduct from the settlement the future disability payments to Yossi over his lifetime, leaving him with far less, and that assumed that the Supreme Court would rule against government and Big Pharma."

Avi's words made sense. He had established a monumental case, demonstrating that Yossi was healthy prior to his vaccination, damaged immediately after it, and the medical authorities had been grossly negligent. Amidst my tears, I knew that I must focus not on what we had been through, but rather on what we had accomplished.

On May 24, 1990, the judge and lawyers met again regarding the settlement. The defense hollered about the two conditions we had stipulated and tried in every possible way to water them down. It quickly became clear to them that the judge had had quite enough of them and they huffily accepted the two conditions and signed the settlement on behalf of their clients.

Avi stayed on afterward, as the judge seemed inclined to talk. "I have never encountered such devotion and care as the Samuels family has demonstrated. At first," the judge continued, "I didn't believe that the faulty DTP vaccine could have caused such dreadful damage, but as the case progressed, I learned it was possible and, in this case, probable. I had, however, a legal difficulty in that this was an unprecedented action, and creating legal precedents is never easy. That was why I had so definitively preferred a settlement. I know full well that the amount agreed upon is insignificant in relation to the child's problems, but I hope it will at least ease their burden to some degree."

Avi also spoke with the chief defense counsel. His view remained that the case was in no way related to DPT – but if ever there was a case that the plaintiffs had a chance of winning, this was it. That was why they had decided to settle, even though the sum was so disproportionate to anything they'd paid out in the past. "You must be celebrating!" he told Avi. "No," Avi replied, "none of us is celebrating."

Avi was very kind and spent considerable time with us that final day. He was especially supportive of Malki, who was very down, realizing that it was now over without providing adequately for Yossi's needs. I asked Avi, "If you thought that this might be the way it would end, why did we ever begin?" Avi paused and thoughtfully replied, "I didn't know, and despite the personal price we paid during the case, we'd feel far worse had we never fought it, had we never struggled for the child and simply let government and Big Pharma off the hook. Clearly, it will take us all time to get over these long years of litigation and put our lives back together again, but we will surely do so."

Of the many children damaged or who died due to the faulty vaccine, the Health Ministry accepted responsibility for twelve. Yossi was not among them.

That was where the story seemed to end – but it had, in fact, one more chapter, as I discovered later. In 1992, two years after we settled, a new minister of health took office in Israel. Among Haim Ramon's goals was enforcing blanket vaccination of Israel's population. And this, he realized, could be achieved only if the government took full and explicit responsibility not only for ensuring immunization but also for protecting any children inadvertently harmed by it.

He established a taskforce on vaccine-related injury, whose work resulted in a no-fault compensation program designed to spare the families of injured children the heavy court costs, and protects government and vaccine manufacturers against lawsuits. Under the newly introduced legislation, passed in order to execute the "Insurance Law for Vaccine Victims – 1989," if specified symptoms appear twenty-four to seventy-two hours post-vaccination, the government takes responsibility without proof of causality. All families pay a small insurance fee for each vaccination, which creates a fund from which families of injured children are compensated.

"These laws were based on Yossi's case," said Avi. "Although the trial garnered little general publicity, it was hotly debated in the Health Ministry. They realized that unless they made themselves accountable for vaccination problems, they would never get enough of the population to comply. Yossi's is one of only a handful of legal cases that has changed the law of the land. Let us hope that the newly established protocols will indeed work to help those injured. And even if over the test of time it becomes clear that the execution of this law is lacking and such families continue to face the same challenges as we did, it is nevertheless an important step toward the establishment's recognition of the problem."

With the trial finally behind us, friends and colleagues were asking me, "What will you do with your time?" That was a question to which there was an easy answer. In just seventeen days, we were at last to make good on Malki's pact with the Almighty. The task was enormous and I didn't anticipate being bored.

Chapter 22

Opening Doors

Finding premises for Shalva had proved to be our greatest problem. It was essential, we believed, to locate Shalva in a residential neighborhood, but few people were willing to live next door to a center for kids with disabilities. We were beginning to despair when I ran into a neighbor who had been renting the apartment adjacent to ours in Har Nof. Out of the blue, he told me, "We are moving to Jerusalem's Old City in six weeks and want to say goodbye and thank you for being such good neighbors." "What's happening with your apartment?" I asked, and like music to my ears, he replied: "The owner's looking for new tenants." I shared that we planned to open a new center for children with disabilities and are interested in renting it.

He gave me the owner's phone number and said, "It may not be easy but I am confident that you will get it." As I shook hands and told him we'd miss them and wished them well, all I could think of was getting in touch immediately with their landlord in the US. The apartment they were vacating was, like ours, a garden duplex on the entrance-level of the same seven-story apartment building.

I contacted the owner. He was not enthusiastic about renting to an organization, especially one for children, with the inevitable wear and tear that would involve, but over time he softened up. I assured the owner that we would return the apartment in even better shape than we received it – and the deal was done. Oddly, no one else had been interested in it. Some twenty-five years later, I learned why, when I ran into our former neighbors. "From the moment I heard you wanted it for your new project, I told everyone who came to see the place that it wasn't a good apartment, it has a lot of problems, and they really wouldn't want to rent it. I held them all off to make sure that you would get it," he said with a big smile.

On Sunday, June 10, 1990, Shalva opened its doors to six neighborhood children as an after-school program staffed by two professionals and half a dozen volunteers – among the latter, our own young children. Every detail was overseen by Malki with great thoroughness and infinite love. Every day, she collected the children from their homes in our family minivan, brought them to Shalva, cared for them through the afternoon, and, after a hot supper at 6:00 p.m., she took them home. It was her baby from soup to nuts.

The program was small, but running it occupied most of our waking hours. Added to that, we had our own six kids, and I continued as the computer professional at Binational. My evenings were spent at Shalva in a tiny corner of the owner's library, which we were not allowed to move. We set up a small desk with my PC and printer and I began to keep records and write letters. On the wall directly in front of me, Malki placed one image: a framed photo of a herd of horses galloping and raising dust, pushing forward behind the galloping lead mare. In response to my question as to why this picture, she explained, "Do you see the horse in the front?" "Yes," I answered in a puzzled tone. "Well, that horse is you. And do you see the horses running after him?" "Yes," I replied again. "Well, those horses are the Shalva children. You must understand that whenever you speak to someone about Shalva, you are not alone. The Shalva children are always there with you, so be strong and remember who you are fighting for." Malki's message served me well and that photo remained with me. On many occasions upon entering an important meeting with a donor, I paused and invited the kids to join me.

Word about Shalva was spreading, and our phone and doorbell began ringing at all hours. People were pleading with us: "I have a son/daughter/niece/nephew/neighbor with disabilities. The family is falling apart under the strain and your program will save us/them. You must take the child at once."

And Malki took them, one after the other – kids with cerebral palsy, developmental delays, Down syndrome, autism, along with others. They were of all ages and backgrounds. Day after day, without a break, like clockwork, Malki got behind the minivan wheel, picked up the kids, brought them to Shalva, and then, with her dedicated volunteer, our fourteen-year-old Nechama, drove them home. Clear in our memory was our experience at the New York Lighthouse, which charged no fees so as never to differentiate between a paying and a nonpaying family; all the children were equal. This had meant the world to us, so we made it Shalva's policy too: no fees and children were accepted solely on a first-come, first-serve basis.

Malki and I knew day by day and hour by hour what it takes to raise a child with disabilities and what it implies for a marriage and a family. We were keenly aware that such families are overwhelmed with protecting and defending their children, comforting and loving them, cherishing and teaching – even as they often mourn the healthy child they didn't have. Every minute lasts an hour, every day lasts a year, and the round-the-clock care demands so much physical and emotional energy that many parents simply break. We knew that we were not going to sit back with our arms folded. We were going to give them the kind of programs that, had they been available for us, would have changed the quality of our lives when Yossi was young.

We were amateurs, but as Malki wryly pointed out, experts built the *Titanic* while amateurs managed to build Noah's ark. Naturally, we recognized that professional expertise was vital in order to adequately meet the needs of each child, but we amateurs too were going to give it all we got.

We turned to Shimona Horev, a special education teacher who had worked in the afternoon program at the School for the Blind that Yossi attended, to help establish the initial after-school program, together with her colleague Tali Ohion. Each day had its own agenda of games, cookery, drama, puppet-theater, and other activities. It was all fun stuff, but all meticulously structured to help our youngsters prepare for life: improve their social skills, advance their motor coordination, and promote their emotional well-being – in short, to make Shalva's kids feel fulfilled and good about themselves, and to maximize their development, while giving their families critical time off.

In those early days, Shalva was very much an extension of our own home. Physically, it was right next door. Malki was chef and driver. She made nutritious and delicious suppers for the youngsters to eat before they went home. And she placed the name Shalva in Hebrew and in English on the two front doors of our ten-seat family van. It was soon a familiar sight as she drove the children home, with one of our own kids helping her as escort. When I returned home at the end of my work day, if I wanted to see my family, I generally knew where to find them.

For our own children, Shalva was part of the air they breathed. They dropped in whenever they wanted, and they very much wanted to. They grew up with Yossi and knew how it had impacted our family. They understood how it felt to have other kids pick on him, and on them. Shalva was part of their collective journey, and in a very deep way they understood what we wanted Shalva to be and to do.

Nechama, our eldest, then in her mid-teens, was especially attached to a little girl whose paralysis was so extensive that she could only blink her eyes. She would rest her stiff little body contentedly in Nechama's arms while she read her stories. Her favorite was *Where Does the Butterfly Go When It Rains?* She would blink and blink again as Nechama read it to her. Our twelve-year-old Avi would bring his guitar, gathering children and young volunteers round him, with everyone singing, clapping, nodding, tapping – or blinking – while he sang and played.

Housed in an apartment that Malki made homey in look and feel, located in a quiet suburb, Shalva quickly became a neighborhood address. Local youngsters flocked to Shalva to volunteer. They were generous, imaginative, and energetic, and also very necessary. Some of the children we cared for had to be watched every moment – like the little girl who tried to eat everything in reach, down to the sand in the sandbox.

Dovi Rebibo was one of the first of many volunteers who followed, about whom Shimona commented, "He is one of the most remarkable kids I've ever met. I first saw him staring over the low stone wall into the yard where our kids played. Lots of children did that, because Malki made sure the Shalva youngsters had the best playthings – toy cars and the like. But Dovi, who was no more than eleven at the time, kept coming back. One day, he saw me looking at him, and asked, 'Can I help?' I answered, 'Come inside and let's talk about it.' He came in and proved almost at once that he could help a great deal. He had smarts and passion, and he connected effortlessly with the kids. Young as he was, he could play with four or five kids at a time, keeping a watchful eye on all of them. Far beyond his years, Dovi was someone on whom I could rely."

Like so many, he grew up with Shalva, not only in age, but in understanding and experience. He continued volunteering throughout high school – which, as far as he was concerned, was simply a distraction that took time away from being at Shalva.

Inducted into the IDF where he became an officer in the tough Golani infantry brigade, he would come to Shalva on every furlough, often straight from his unit, in uniform and boots, his M16 over his shoulder, before going home to his family. "Shalva kids are the best people," he would say. "No fights, no ego, so sincere. It's always hard to leave them."

On June 10, 1991, we celebrated Shalva's first birthday, with the number of children steadily growing. Israel's schools and childcare frameworks would be closing for the long, hot month of August, but our doors stayed open. Once again, Malki and I knew what it meant to have a child with disabilities at home with no framework during the summer, which in addition to the obvious difficulties, included the risk of halting or even undoing the child's hard-earned progress throughout the year.

In Malki's view, day camp at Shalva was obviously needed but it was not enough. "Our kids should have sleepaway camp like every other child," she said, even as I voiced profound misgivings. "Why should Shalva children be any different?" she contended. "Why shouldn't they experience that kind of fun? And it'll be more than fun. It'll help them develop self-confidence, social skills, and independence, and give their parents a full eight days for themselves and their other kids."

Shimona, I learned, had a sister who lives on Kibbutz Shaalvim – about twenty miles from Jerusalem – and that was where Malki reserved rooms for the upcoming camp, which would give the Shalva kids a week of fun, and their families precious time to relax. The kibbutz mobilized to help, offering to take the kids for tractor rides, to see the animals, and much more – but I was petrified. The responsibility was enormous, and I kept thinking about all that could go wrong. I asked myself just what am I doing? We had kids with sensitive syndromes and disabilities and the staff ratio would have to be one to one. But we planned well, and it was a resounding success.

Chapter 23

Intestinal Fortitude

While it had once seemed to me that Gordon and Leslie's generous gift would last forever, it was becoming ever clearer that we needed more money, and we needed it soon. I was figuring out this new world, hurdle by hurdle, exercising what in sports we referred to as "intestinal fortitude," or the will to get the job done at all costs. With the help of my dad in Canada and good friends in the USA, we created Canadian Friends of Shalva and American Friends of Shalva with the tax-deductible status necessary for collecting charitable funds. But with my full-time work in computers, travel was challenging and it made sense to save my time and Shalva's money by approaching possible donors when they were vacationing in Israel. The High Holiday period was approaching and I had learned of several visitors from abroad who would be arriving at hotels in Jerusalem. I shared with Malki that I was planning to call them and ask if they would see me.

"You won't call them and you won't see them here," she said firmly. "They are in Israel on vacation. You'll go and see them in their offices." "You must be kidding," I objected. "They are a fifteen-minute drive from here and you are telling me to fly over oceans? You're tying my hands behind my back." But Malki stood her ground. "They're here on vacation with their families," she said calmly. "And you are not going to be a *schnorrer*. You'll see them at a time that is convenient for them, in their offices. Act like a *mensch* and people will respect you as a *mensch*!"

And so I applied for two weeks' vacation from Binational after the holiday of Sukkot in October. My plan was to go to New York and try to raise the funds that were vital for keeping our fledgling organization alive. I knew nobody and had no idea what I'd do when I got there, but I knew I had to go.

Sitting in front of me in synagogue over Sukkot was an elderly Hungarian Holocaust survivor, Mr. Yakabovich from Brooklyn, who came to Jerusalem each year for the High Holidays. I'd heard he was well-to-do, so I approached him one day after *shul*. "Mr. Yakabovich," I began awkwardly, "you know that my wife and I run an organization that helps children with disabilities. I'm going to be in New York next week looking for funds to keep it afloat. May I visit you when I'm there?" "Sure," he responded in his heavy European accent, "you can come see me." That was it.

At Ben Gurion Airport, I ran into Mendel, a hasidic man I'd known for years. "Where are you headed?" he asked in Yiddish. Upon hearing that I was bound for New York to raise money for a new organization I had established, he exclaimed, "Kalman, *bist di mishiga*? Kalman, are you nuts? Don't you know that two out of every three people on your flight are *schnorrers* headed to New York?" I didn't know, but as I said to Mendel, I saw only two choices: "Either I take my bags, go home, and close up shop, or I get on the plane with all the others and trust that G-d will show me my way." "Good luck," he wished me, with a sympathetic grin.

Next to me on the flight was an Israeli young man with a long, unkempt ponytail, a gold chain hanging over his plaid shirt, jeans, and cowboy boots. "Hello," I said amicably, but noted that he wasn't up for conversation. After ten hours of sitting side by side, breakfast was served and he said hello and asked me why I was going to New York. I outlined my story. Unexpectedly, he was interested, and plied me with question after question. Before landing, he turned, looked at me searchingly, and said, "Your story is fascinating and I want to help you. I know I look like a bum, but that's part of my business. I'm a salesman for a large diamond dealer on Forty-Seventh Street in Manhattan, and I'm usually on the road, selling diamonds in places where I don't want to look conspicuous. I'll be meeting with my boss later today and I'll arrange for you to meet him. He's a good man and I know your venture will move him." He gave me his card with instructions to call the office the next day and ask when I should come. I didn't know if he was for real, but I couldn't help feeling excitement. Someone was watching out for Shalva's children.

Two days later, I was in Manhattan's Diamond District on Forty-Seventh Street, meeting, as promised, with the young man's boss. My friend from the plane was nowhere to be seen. He was already back on the road, and our paths never crossed again. But he was right about his boss wanting to help Shalva. He heard my story, wrote a check for $1,000, and called other diamond dealers up and down the block. Each of them, too, donated to Shalva. I was overwhelmed.

Later that same day, I called Mr. Yakabovich at his office in Brooklyn. He took my call and told me to come in at noon the following day. I duly appeared at what turned out to be a busy real estate office that managed many apartment buildings. Shown into a small, undistinguished waiting-room crowded with Yiddish-speakers of clearly modest means, I told the tough, overtaxed receptionist that I wasn't there to complain or to rent an apartment. Rather, I was a friend of Mr. Yakabovich from Israel whom he'd invited to visit. She was clearly underwhelmed and I doubted she'd pass on my message. Twenty minutes later, I tried again, but was firmly told to sit back down. Mr. Yakabovich would see me when he was free.

After what seemed like a very long while, the door opened and I was ushered inside. Mr. Yakabovich was clearly a busy man and had little time to talk. He introduced me to his sons-in-law, Albert Kahn and Moishe Lieberman, and got straight to the point. What began rather brusquely developed into a warm exchange in which I shared who I was and what I was trying to do, and I was gratified to find them all genuinely engrossed. "You must meet our brother-in-law, Tommy," they said, and, with that, picked up the phone. "Great!" I was told a minute later. "Tommy wants to meet you. His office is in Flatbush, a fifteen-minute drive from here." And off I went.

Tommy Rosenthal was a tall Viennese gentleman, then approaching forty. He received me warmly, and once again, I introduced myself and told my story. "This is very moving," he said. "I'm going to make you a parlor meeting, two evenings from now." I confessed to having no idea what a parlor meeting was. He explained: "I'm going to fax invitations to friends to come to my house for coffee and cake. You're going to tell them about Shalva. And, hopefully, they'll get out their checkbooks. Let's say 8:00 p.m.? Come a little before then. Here's my address. See you then."

I left Tommy's office in a daze, amazed by the outpouring of goodness and goodwill. Two evenings later, I presented myself at his home and was introduced to his wife Judy and their children. Albert and Moishe were there with their wives, and – surprise, surprise – a beaming Mr. Yakabovich with a regal Mrs. Yakabovich. The dining room table groaned under platters of pastries, and the samovar steamed with aromatic coffee. The guests arrived and the room filled quickly. I told Shalva's story in the allotted fifteen minutes, and then chatted casually with the many guests who wanted to hear more. When the last had left, Tommy handed me a pile of checks.

I returned to Israel exhausted but with $6,100 in my pocket. Shalva would need more, but it was an enormous help. I had met wonderful people and was full of hope for Shalva's future.

* * *

Inroads had been made, but the bills kept piling up. Within six months, I was taking another week off from Binational for another visit to New York, but this time I was better prepared. On a shoe-string budget I created a short but moving video, which included testimonials from parents of Shalva children.

One of my first phone calls was to the Manhattan offices of the Jerusalem Foundation, the dynamic charity set up twenty-five years earlier by Jerusalem's legendary mayor Teddy Kollek. In their mission statement they described themselves as being "dedicated to preserving an open, equitable, and modern society in Jerusalem through an approach centered on community vitality, cultural life, and coexistence for all Jerusalem's residents," and so it sounded plausible that they might be interested in donating to Shalva – but I was nevertheless astonished when the woman at the other end of the phone immediately replied that she would be delighted to meet me the next day.

I spent most of the intervening twenty-four hours trying to locate and rent a portable video player to screen my masterpiece. After a frustrating and unsuccessful afternoon, I was eventually directed to a video store on Thirteenth Avenue in Boro Park, and upon arrival I learned that it had just closed for the day. Waiting outside when it opened the next morning, I was speedily equipped with a thirty-pound projection device comprising a full screen with a large slot at the bottom in which to insert the hefty video cassette. This was cutting-edge technology then and I was delighted, but it was too heavy to carry on the subway and so I had to rent a car.

My hostess at the Jerusalem Foundation warmly ushered me into her office where we had a lively conversation about the Foundation's wonderful work and, naturally, about Shalva. Truly moved by the video I'd brought, she said, "The work Shalva does is so very meaningful." Without giving me time to respond, she continued: "We have a large Young Leadership gathering tomorrow, and New York's attorney-general, Robert Abrams, is to deliver an address. His office has just told us he'll be forty minutes late, and I'm wondering if you would be willing to use that time to speak about your project and show your excellent video." Needing little convincing, I replied, "I will be delighted to do so and thank you for this opportunity." I left the foundation offices high as a kite.

The following day, I drove back into Manhattan in pouring rain and circled around frantically looking for the Republic Bank, where I had been told the event would take place, and then circled around some more to find parking. Arriving with no time to spare, I was led straight into the atrium where the foundation's Young Leadership program participants were assembled. Ignorant of what the Republic Bank and an atrium were, I was astonished at the beauty of both. The Republic Bank, I learned, was also known as the Safra National Bank of New York, and its vast pillared, chandeliered atrium was breathtaking. Scarcely less impressive were the two hundred or so young businesspeople who filled it that afternoon: aged twenty-five to forty-five, smartly dressed, milling around drinking cocktails and engaged in high-powered conversations. I quickly set up my video player, sweating under the pressure, as the participants were asked to sit down, were welcomed, and were told that the attorney-general was running late. I heard my name and heard the announcer say that the director of one of Jerusalem's important projects was here to introduce it to them.

I did my passionate best to share Yossi's story, Malki's promise, and the story of Shalva, all in fifteen minutes. I then showed the video and concluded by telling the audience how deeply I appreciated the Jerusalem Foundation and that I would be happy to discuss Shalva's work more extensively with anyone interested. To my surprise and great pleasure, I sat down to resounding applause.

A strapping young man in his late twenties approached me and introduced himself: "Hi, my name is Nathan Low. I'm deeply impressed with your work and want to help," he said. "Here's a check for $500 but don't count on it for next year because I don't know if I will be doing as well." Nathan and his wife Lisa became significant partners who contributed critically to Shalva's growth and development in many ways.

Chapter 24

Respite, Despite…

Shalva's programs continued to grow by leaps and bounds, with children now coming in from other parts of the city. Malki could no longer pick them all up nor drive them home, so the school bus dropped them off directly at Shalva and those families who lived farther away were responsible for picking them up at 6:00 p.m.

Malki decided it was time to introduce a new – and costly – program. The plan was that each weeknight, from Sunday through Thursday, a different group of youngsters would spend the night at Shalva. They would stay on after our afternoon program and sleep over, and we would work on life skills that the parents often didn't have time to get to. The following morning their school buses would pick them up from our center. After school, they would return to us for Shalva's regular after-school activities, eat dinner at Shalva, and then return to their homes at 6:30 p.m.

"Parents and siblings will have two days and one night each week," Malki explained, "thirty-six hours in which their focus does not have to be mostly on their child with a disability, as it inevitably often is. Imagine what this will mean to them!" she enthused. "Imagine what it would have meant to us when Yossi was young. Families will be able to do whatever works best for them, whether it's spending quality time at home, going out together, shopping, taking a class, going to appointments, or simply relaxing. With all the love and best intentions in the world, a child with disabilities greatly impacts the family, and this will give them a critical break."

Malki's concept differed from existing respite programs in which families could drop off their child at a center for a week, twice a year. In those programs, the youngsters are not familiar with the caregivers or the other children, and the caregivers are not familiar with the children, so while it gives parents a free week, their children may well have an uncomfortable experience. Malki's idea was like one night of camp every week, with familiar friends and staff who knew them well and could work systematically over time to help them develop crucial life skills.

"Great idea," was my lukewarm response. "But why in the world does it have to be every week? Once a month would still be fantastic and deeply appreciated – not to mention a whole lot cheaper. Why go to extremes?" "Because that's what's needed," Malki flatly responded. "You know as well as I do that once a month is a nice thing to do, but it's once a week, a substantial slice in time, that will spell the difference for the family and the child."

No one needed to explain to me that it was ridiculous to introduce a costly new program when we didn't have the funds. Equally, no one needed to tell me that this program was going to become reality.

Several days later found us shopping for bunk beds. Our quest was highly specific: three units, each with a different and colorful design to give it its own identity. After visiting several furniture stores, one proprietor showed Malki various options and she found one bunk bed that she liked. It came in three colors. She asked him to make the beds with alternating rows of the three colors in each one. Unable to dissuade her, he eventually agreed to produce what she wanted as a special order. Several weeks passed and we received the beds. They looked amazing and the children loved them. Upon visiting the store sometime later, the proprietor welcomed us with a broad smile, showing off his multi-colored bunk beds, and thanked Malki for designing his most successful line.

The overnight respite program was a resounding success. While it added a great deal of pressure in logistics, staffing, and funding, the youngsters had a ball and gained a great deal of skills, while their parents got a chance to recharge their physical and emotional batteries. Parents embraced their free time and unreservedly told us so. In one instance, a mother rushed through Shalva's front door one evening at around 7:00 p.m. and hurried past me and up the stairs to her daughter. I said hello, but she ignored me. Through the open front door, I saw her husband and several kids in the car. A minute later, she was running down the stairs again. "Kalman," she said, "I'm so sorry to be rude, but I've no time to talk right now. I had to drop something off for Ruthy – this is our family night at the movies." With that, she was out and back into the car, and off they went.

Initially, several mothers expressed a twinge of guilt about taking a break, but one mother wryly noted:

I hate my Wednesday guilt. Every Wednesday, as I prepare my beloved son for the day ahead and walk him through his morning routine, I try not to feel too pleased that it's Wednesday.

I pack up a bag with his lunch, as well as his pajamas, a change of clothing, and a toothbrush, while he hums his way through his breakfast of toast and fruit. He goes to Shalva five afternoons a week, coming home between 6:30 and 7:00 p.m., relaxed and happy, after a full day and a tasty dinner there. On Wednesdays, he also sleeps over at Shalva, tucked into his bunk bed, with a staffer nearby in case of nighttime needs. On Thursday morning, he is bused to school from Shalva, then returns back there for the afternoon program, after which he returns home on Thursday evening.

Not bad at all. Wednesday nights, my husband and I often go out for a late bite to eat or schedule stuff that isn't as easy to do the rest of the week when a sitter has to be booked if we both want to step out together. Sometimes we just relax, knowing we don't have to get up at 6:15 a.m. on Thursday. We have a weekly rotation such that each of us does the morning routine with him every other day. Mind you, it's not like it's so hard. After years of getting up early – in the summer heat and the dark, cold winter – our son is a pro and quite routinized to the system, but it's still an effort and, I confess, I hate it.

And then, that monster called parental guilt hits. I love my boy. I love his chipper good nature in the morning and his loving hugs at night before bed. But I confess, I also love Wednesdays, and most importantly, Thursday mornings – and am just grateful to Shalva for the parental respite. Getting a breather really helps break the parental doldrums. Guilt is just a bore – it doesn't really help anyone work through the real challenges of living with a child who has a disability. As I write this, it's Sunday. Deep breath... Wednesday will come soon.

Malki had been right. Once a week is what is needed for these parents who had so painfully readjusted their hopes, dreams, and expectations for their children and for themselves.

Chapter 25

I Want to Close Down Shalva

Yom Kippur, the Day of Atonement, was over and we'd just broken our twenty-five-hour fast with Malki's delicious meal. It was October 7, 1992, two years and four months since Shalva had opened. Tremulously, she turned to me and said, "I need some air. Let's go out front." This was unlike her. I assumed she was not feeling well and didn't want the kids to know. But my unease grew when the moment the front door was closed behind us, she erupted into bitter weeping.

"I'm so terribly, terribly sorry I've gotten you into this," she sobbed, her voice thick with tears. "I only wanted to do what was right. I always believed G-d would help us, but here we are with debts of $40,000! I can't let you carry this burden any more. You're my beloved husband, the devoted father of my children. I can't do this to you. I want to close down Shalva and we will find a way to repay our debts."

Shalva, Malki's vow brought to life, was a runaway success. Against all odds and practicalities, we'd managed to do everything pledged in the three pages of our "Proposal for a New Outreach Program in Israel" – everything, that is, except to finance its unforeseen growth.

I was stunned. "Malki," I said, "I agree we can't go on like this with money hemorrhaging away. I, too, am so very sorry – sorry I haven't been able to find the funds to keep Shalva going. But we can't give up yet. Let's wait three months until the year's end. I'll make another trip to New York. If G-d wants it to continue, it will, and if not, then we'll accept that it's time to cut our losses and get back to a normal life." Malki, calmer now, agreed. She dried her tears and we went back inside to our children.

Early the next morning, our phone rang and a man with a thick French accent asked to speak with me. He introduced himself as Yanky Landau. "I was given your name and number by a mutual friend who believes you have a contact at the phone company," he said. His father, he explained, was arriving from Belgium in three days, on the eve of the Sukkot holiday, and would be staying in his new apartment in a well-known Jerusalem hotel. "His phones must be installed before he comes," he said, "but the phone company literally laughed at me." The young man sounded desperate, the full weight of his father's phone needs on his shoulders.

There was something in his voice that moved me to help and so I said, "I am happy to try but I can't promise anything. What does he need exactly?" "Two phone lines with seven extensions," came the reply. I took a deep breath and told him I would get back to him.

I hadn't spoken to my contact in a while, but he was genuinely happy to hear from me and inquired about Yossi. "What can I do for you, my friend?" he asked. I apologized for bothering him and shared the request. He burst out laughing. "Your

friend is nuts. It's after Yom Kippur and three days before Sukkot, busier than between Christmas and New Year's in the USA.
Even if I wanted to help – and I do – it's just not feasible." There
was a pause and then, "You know what, I will give it a shot but
please, no expectations."

Three days later, on Sunday afternoon just hours before
Sukkot, a large and beautiful bouquet was delivered to our door.
"Malki!" I called. "You've been sent gorgeous flowers, and not by
me." She came out of the kitchen and opened the accompanying
card. "These aren't for me," she said, handing me the card. I read
it aloud.

> Dear Mr. Samuels, I want to thank you for enabling me to
> receive my telephones prior to my arrival today, and I wish
> you and your family a very happy holiday. Moucky Landau
> (Yanky's father)

I picked up the phone, called the hotel, and asked for Mr. Landau,
who , like his son, sounded very European. "Thank you so much
for the beautiful bouquet," I said. "It's the first time I've ever been
sent flowers and I'm not entirely sure whether that indicates that
I'm alive or dead!" He laughed and said, "I'd very much like to meet
you. Please call me during the holiday so we can get together." We
wished each other a *gut Yom Tov*, a happy holiday, and that was that.

In spite of Shalva's potential closure hanging over our heads,
the week of Sukkot was filled with joy and singing and it passed
quickly. With little more than an hour to the arrival of Simhat
Torah, the final festival day of the holiday, Malki suddenly called
out to me from the kitchen, "That fellow from Belgium told you
he wanted to meet you. Why didn't you call him?"

"Malki, you must be kidding!" I answered. "You've always
been so against my approaching foreign visitors for funds.
They're here on vacation, you say, and I mustn't bother them,

but rather go to their offices. So what's this about calling now?" Without bothering to relate to my words, Malki simply said, "The man asked you to call him. Pick up the phone and call him!" So I did.

"Thanks so much for getting in touch," he said. "Where are you? How long would it take you to get to the hotel for a quick visit before the holiday?" I couldn't believe what he was asking. I covered the receiver and whispered to Malki, "He wants me to come right now, but I can't. There's no time and I must help you get the house ready." Without hesitation, Malki responded, "Go! I can handle the house!"

I hurried to the hotel, arriving less than an hour before the holiday. Mr. Landau, or Moucky, as he asked me to call him, was waiting in the lobby. We went into the hotel's large *sukka*, (temporary dwelling used during the Sukkot festival) which was now empty, as the holiday was winding down. He was a warm and pleasant man, and we began schmoozing – playing Jewish geography, discussing my Vancouver roots and his in Brussels and later Antwerp. A charity collector came up to us with photos of poor children, asking for a generous donation. "I'm happy to help you," Moucky told him, "but I only have $20 on me at the moment. If you come back after the holiday, I'll give you more than that." He took the bill and said, "I believe only in what I see, and I now see your $20." He mumbled a thank-you and was off.

Moucky and I both chuckled. Then he became serious. "I've heard you do wonderful work with children with disabilities," he said. "Tell me about it." In the quarter hour available, I did the best I could. I hurried to leave and Moucky escorted me out. In the middle of the spacious lobby, he stopped and turned to me. "I'm very taken by what you do and I'd like to help. When can you come to Antwerp?" Thinking that he probably had in mind a visit later in the year, I responded, "Whenever you want. When do you suggest?" "Come next Sunday afternoon," he said. "I'll introduce you to some of my friends. We're diamond dealers and we'll raise some money."

On Sunday morning, I flew to Brussels, cabbed the twenty-seven miles to Antwerp, and arrived at Moucky's home in the late afternoon. I met his wife Charlotte and was shown my comfortable lodging. His good friend Soli Spira would join us the next day, Moucky shared. Interestingly, I had just met Soli briefly for the first time during the holiday.

Antwerp was an eye-opener. It seemed to be the last authentic Jewish *shtetl*, full of ultra-Orthodox and hasidic men and women dressed modestly and stylishly, with synagogues on seemingly every street, Jewish boutiques, brisk conversations in mixed Yiddish and French, and above all a feeling of upbeat warmth. The next morning, fortified with delicious coffee prepared by Moucky in a special percolator, we went to the local *shtiebel*, a small synagogue that surely resembled any Eastern European *shtiebel* of a century ago. On the way back, we picked up warm Danishes from the corner grocery and enjoyed them with another delicious coffee. Then it was down to the underground parking lot and into Moucky's Mercedes.

These cozy first impressions of Antwerp did nothing to prepare me for the *Diamantkwartier*, the diamond district, dubbed the Square Mile. Not far from Moucky's home, it comprised block after block of highly secured old buildings, each with an enormous number of offices all connected to the diamond trade. Moucky's office was spacious, well lit, and immaculate. His staff converged, each vying for his attention first thing that Monday morning. Two collectors were waiting for him. Moucky gave everyone their due attention, with smiles all around.

A half hour later, Soli arrived, an incredibly warm and positive man with a powerful personality. Moucky stood up from his desk and said, "OK, the day is short and we've a lot to do. Let's get started."

For the next four days, Moucky, Soli, and I went from one diamond dealer to the next, entering each office through tight security, where we were greeted with the traditional "*Salut!*" (Hello!) In each place, my two sponsors introduced me and Shalva to the dealer and explained why they were taking the unusual step of escorting me. They spoke in French, and while I didn't catch every word, I understood enough to follow the basic gist. After the introductions we switched to English or Yiddish, as the dealer questioned me, often very closely indeed, about Shalva. And then came the closing, which knocked me off my perch. They would ask: "*Qu'est que vous donnez? Cinq milles ou dix milles?*" (How much are you giving? Five thousand or ten thousand?) And to my amazement, one or the other sum was named, and $100 bills were counted out and casually passed over. The first dealer we approached gave $10,000, which Moucky saw as an excellent beginning, and, at the next, when the "*Cinq milles ou dix milles*" question was posed, he didn't fail to mention that the previous gift had been *dix milles*, ten thousand.

Moucky came to all but one of these incredible meetings. That which Soli and I attended alone was more than a little embarrassing. The diamond dealer, about forty-five years old, greeted us warmly and Soli began the pitch. The dealer was not interested and said so. Soli was somewhat hard of hearing and didn't pick that up. So Soli asked him once again how much he would like to contribute. Raising his voice, the dealer said he wouldn't be contributing, but the miscommunication continued as Soli smiled and asked, "How much did you say?" The dealer, by now flushed and angry, snapped at me in English: "Do you understand what the f--- I said, because your friend certainly doesn't!" "Yes," I said, "but Soli doesn't hear well." The irritated dealer, who knew Soli well, took him by the hand, threw an arm over his shoulders and led him to the door. I was so hurt for Soli, but he was unfazed. "I know he has the money," he said respectfully when we talked it through later, "but he has his own problems at the moment. At least we tried." Soli moved me greatly and left a deep impression.

A more successful meeting was with a younger man named Benny Steinmetz, who seemed to have even more office security than the others. He warmly welcomed Moucky and Soli, who clearly had great respect for him. They went through the routine in French, Benny handed over the cash, and then Moucky told me that he and Soli were leaving but I was to stay. They left me to answer a barrage of questions from Benny about my secular background and why someone who had grown up comfortably in Vancouver had left everything to lead a religious life in Israel. He was bright, insightful, and, to my surprise, was sincerely interested in my past and spent a lot of time on the subject before escorting me graciously out.

Thursday afternoon, as I was saying my goodbyes at Moucky's office, he shared that we had raised $100,000. Not only had the entire debt been cleared, but incredibly we now had $60,000 with which to move forward.

Upon arrival to Israel, Malki, met me in the reception area and was alarmed at my pallor. "It's nothing to worry about," I said. "I'll be fine. I'm simply overwhelmed by G-d's goodness and divine providence." Emotionally, I recounted what we both knew well. "Two weeks ago, we were going to close Shalva; today G-d has given Shalva a miraculous new lease on life."

Chapter 26
Growing Up with Yossi

Yossi was developing and now strove toward greater independence. He learned to take public transportation and traveled on a large bus home from school. A staff member called to tell us when he was on the bus, and we waited at the designated bus stop near our house. Yossi knew every curve in the road and rang the bell to get off right on time. Given that he had no way to communicate with fellow passengers or the driver, Malki made a clear sign that he hung from his neck with identifying information, where he was to get off, and how to contact us in case of emergency. She also created a rectangular plastic piece with the alphabet on it in raised letters that Yossi hung from his neck when traveling, and someone could place his fingers on the letters to spell words or Yossi could spell back.

This was a huge step toward Yossi feeling independent. Initially, without him knowing, a staff person was always on the bus with him until we were confident that he was capable and had the routes clear.

Despite or perhaps because of what life dealt him, Yossi has been intensely spiritual from a very young age. He is fully aware of his challenges and his inability to do many things, and while he sometimes expresses his complaints toward both those who were involved in injuring him, as well as toward G-d, these have never impinged on his deep faith nor impacted on his profound connection with the spiritual. Each morning, he straps on his *tefillin,* prays briefly from his braille prayer book, and then takes his time beseeching G-d with all his soul on behalf of those who need help – the sick, the lonely, the childless, the imprisoned, the Jewish people, all of humanity.

This has always been an essential part of who he is. Nor does he let the Almighty off easily. With his eyes closed, his lips moving, and his concentration absolute, he enters his own world, praying with nonstop intensity.

Yossi's spirituality and prayer didn't go unnoticed, and friends in need sometimes turned to him. A hasidic couple who Yossi knew and loved did not have children. Naftali and Rachel were both from large families and were aunt and uncle to dozens, but they were childless. During the eight years since their marriage, they'd done all they could on both the medical and spiritual planes, following the directives of doctors and fertility experts and seeking blessings from prominent rabbis, but there was no pregnancy. When Naftali was offered a teaching position in the US for September, they decided to distance themselves from the social pressures they faced and accept the job. Just before they departed, Naftali called and came to visit. "We have done all that we can and have come up short," he said with a heavy heart. "I want to ask Yossi to pray for us to have a child. He is a holy soul and perhaps his sincere prayers will be heard." Yossi took the request very seriously and every night before going to sleep, he placed his hand over the *mezuza* on his bedroom doorpost and recited the biblical verse "*Shema Yisrael* – Hear, O Israel, the L-rd our G-d, the L-rd is one" and then in a loud voice, implored over and over again, "Shalom Yosef requests from G-d to bless Naftali and Rachel with a child." We heard this every night with the same fervor and it became music to our ears.

Some six months later, Malki suddenly realized that Yossi had dropped Naftali and Rachel from his prayers. "Why?" she asked him. In a very matter-of-fact manner, Yossi replied, "Rachel is pregnant."

A couple of months later, I was surprised to receive a local phone call from Naftali. It was the night before Passover. "I know it's a really busy evening, but I am now here visiting and must come over to talk," he said. "Come whenever you want," I told him. As he entered our home the first words out of his mouth were, "I have something important to tell you that you won't believe." I smiled. "Why won't I believe it when *I* can tell *you*?" As if to challenge me, he said, "OK, so what is it?" "Yossi tells me that Rachel is pregnant." Naftali was shocked and asked how in the world he could know, and I shared the details. Naftali became very emotional and couldn't stop hugging Yossi. Three months later Naftali and Rachel gave birth to a long-awaited precious baby girl. More children followed.

Chapter 27

The Wachsmans

Esther and Yehuda Wachsman lived in the Ramot neighborhood of Jerusalem with their seven sons, a fifteen-minute drive from the Shalva Center. Their youngest, Raphael, with Down syndrome, attended our afternoon program. Given the distance, his school bus dropped him off and a family member picked him up at 6:00 p.m. This role was sometimes filled by his loving older brother Nachshon, who, whenever available, arrived in his soldier's uniform to pick up Raphael. Shalva was an intimate organization and we knew everybody involved very well.

On a quiet Tuesday evening in 1994, Israeli television broke the news that an Israeli soldier had been kidnapped by Hamas terrorists and ran footage of him with hands and feet bound to a chair while a terrorist wearing a *keffiyeh* and mask stood over him, holding the captive's identity card toward the camera. We didn't need the soldier's ID card to know who he was. It was Nachshon Wachsman, and we and our children were shaken to our core.

At gunpoint, the trussed nineteen-year-old duly recited: I've been kidnapped by Hamas. They want Sheikh Ahmed Yassin and two hundred others released from Israeli prisons. If their demands aren't met, they will execute me on Friday at 8:00 p.m.

Nachshon's parents didn't have the luxury of being shaken. As Nachshon's mother, Esther, later related, she and her husband, Yehuda, mobilized quickly and for the next four days, twenty-four hours a day, did everything in their power to save their son's life. They spoke to Prime Minister Yitzhak Rabin, who informed them that he would not negotiate with terrorists nor would he yield to blackmail. They announced that Nachshon held American citizenship, and US President Bill Clinton intervened. Both US Secretary of State Warren Christopher, who was in the area at the time, and Edward Abington, then the US consul general in Jerusalem, went to Gaza – where it was believed Nachshon was being held – and brought them messages from Yasser Arafat.

They appealed to world leaders everywhere and to Muslim religious leaders, all of whom stated on the various media channels that the captors must not harm the Wachsmans' son.

The world media camped in the street outside the Wachsman home, which had become a beehive of activity with the constant entry and departure of military and political leaders.

Malki turned to me and said, "Kalman, take a small suitcase, make your way through the crowds, and tell Esther that you are taking Raphael until Nachshon comes home." I drove to the house and negotiated my way inside with glances from those camped outside, everyone wondering who I might be. Upon seeing me, Esther cried, as did I. Quietly, I shared my message. She acknowledged that caring for Raphael had been so very difficult under the circumstances and turned to her husband Yehuda to prepare the bag and bring Raphael. Raphael smiled at me and we made our way out, hand in hand, through the crowds and into my car. Upon arrival, Raphael was royally welcomed by our entire family and immediately felt at home.

On Thursday night, twenty-four hours before the ultimatum, a prayer vigil was held at the Western Wall and, at the same time, prayer vigils were held throughout the world in synagogues, schools, community centers, street squares, and many more venues. People of good faith everywhere hoped and pleaded and prayed for Nachshon.

At the Western Wall, 100,000 people arrived with almost no advance notice. Hasidim in black frock coats and long side curls swayed and prayed and cried alongside young boys in jeans with ponytails and earrings. There was a total unity and solidarity of purpose – religious and secular, left wing and right wing, Sephardic and Ashkenazic, old and young, rich and poor, all came together as one, an occurrence almost unprecedented in our sadly fragmented society.

On Friday afternoon before the Sabbath, Esther addressed her moving words to Nachshon via the media and begged him to be strong, for our entire nation was with him. She asked that every woman light an extra Sabbath candle for him.

In our home as in so many other homes, we remained at the Sabbath table with our young children, watching the clock and reciting psalms in fervent prayer. As Sabbath observers in an Orthodox community, we didn't turn on TV or radio or receive newspapers during the Sabbath, and had no way of knowing what was transpiring, but at 10:00 p.m. on Friday night in the midst of our psalms, the unsettling silence was suddenly broken by frantic knocking on our door. As we opened it, a sobbing sixteen-year-old girl, a dear Shalva volunteer and neighbor, burst in screaming, "Nachshon has been murdered!" Pandemonium broke loose.

As Esther later wrote,

We sat rooted to our Sabbath table; my eyes were glued to the door, expecting Nachshon to walk in at any moment.

We were not aware of the fact that Israeli Intelligence had captured the driver of the car that had picked Nachshon up, and that he related that the terrorists had all worn *kippot*, that there were a Bible and *siddur* on the dashboard, hasidic music was playing on the tape deck, and an unsuspecting soldier got into the car.

We were also not aware that they [Israeli Intelligence] had discovered from their informant that Nachshon was being held in a village called Bir Nabbalah, under Israeli rule, located about ten minutes from our home. We were not aware that Prime Minister Rabin had made a decision to launch a military action to attempt to rescue our son.

At the hour of the ultimatum, 8:00 p.m. Friday night, General Yoram Yair, not Nachshon, walked through our door and brought us the terrible news. The military rescue attempt had failed – Nachshon had been killed and so had the commander of the rescue team, Captain Nir Poraz.

At the same time people had all returned to their synagogues, after their Sabbath meal, to recite psalms for Nachshon's rescue, including our sons. We called them home and together we all sat frozen, unbelieving, shocked, and devastated for the rest of the Sabbath.

On Saturday night at midnight we buried our son.

That same microcosm of our people who had come to pray for Nachshon's rescue at the Western Wall, came to Mount Herzl to attend Nachshon's funeral; many had never set foot in a military cemetery.

My husband asked the dean of Nachshon's yeshiva, who gave the eulogy, to please tell all present that G-d did listen to all of our prayers and that He collected all our tears. My husband's greatest concern when burying his son was that there would be a crisis of faith. And so he asked the rabbi to tell everyone that just as a father would always like to say "yes" to all of his children's requests, sometimes he has to say "no" though the child might not understand why. So too, our Father in Heaven heard our prayers, and although we don't understand why, His answer was "no."

The entire nation mourned with us. Thousands came to comfort us, though no one can comfort a bereaved parent. Israeli radio began each morning's broadcasts with the words "Good morning Israel, we are all with the Wachsman family." Food and drink were delivered nonstop to our home; bus and taxi drivers who brought people from all over the country who wished to express their condolences, left their vehicles and joined their passengers in our home. That unity, solidarity, caring, compassion, and love with which we were showered gave us strength and filled our hearts with love for our people.

On the seventh day, the *shiva* mourning period was ending and it was time for our family to get up and try to move on.

* * *

That morning, I received a call from a good friend who was vacationing in Israel. "Kalman, you are close to the Wachsmans. Please arrange for me to meet the mother now. She and her husband are noble souls who have sanctified G-d's name."

"The family is just getting up from *shiva*," I said, and now was not the time. But he urged me to call – and, when I did, Esther agreed to meet him, "but only because of you, Kalman," she said. "I would not do this for anyone else."

I picked him up and drove to the Wachsman home, where I found Esther weary, somber, and alone. He began, "Mrs. Wachsman, you and your husband are noble heroes of Israel," and then, taking me utterly by surprise, he continued, "Shalva has outgrown its duplex apartment and must work toward creating its own more spacious home. I ask you for your permission to name that new home 'Beit Nachshon,' the House of Nachshon."

Esther broke down. "I'm sure there'll be many memorials to Nachshon," she said, "but a Shalva–Beit Nachshon will always be the one that means the most. It will be a living memorial to one son, and a place in which another son and others like him will find a loving second home to help them develop and grow."

I was shocked. It was clear that Shalva would one day need its own building, but with his impetuous request from Esther, my friend had propelled us headlong onto a new path which had not yet even been discussed, let alone agreed upon. Of this, however, he seemed blithely unaware. As I drove him back to the hotel, he spoke instead about making a promotional video in which Esther would share a message about Beit Nachshon.

I was uncomfortable about approaching Esther with this new request at such a raw moment and was relieved when she readily agreed. Several days later, she recorded her heartfelt message in a moving four-minute clip that could seemingly melt a stone.

Chapter 28

"It's Obvious, Kalman!"

With its fifth birthday in sight, Shalva had become very crowded. Not only were we unable to accommodate dozens of families who turned to us, we were finding it increasingly difficult to give all we wanted to those already there.

For some time we had been considering options as to how to expand Shalva and rent a larger space, but we could not find anything appropriate, in no small measure because people did not want to rent to our children.

I turned to the Jerusalem Municipality, seeking an appropriate public facility for our kids. Their department of social welfare knew us well, and while there was no funding for us, they respected Shalva and the value of its programs. Shalva was making a name for itself; a year earlier Israel's President Ezer Weizman had honored Malki and me with the President's Award for Volunteerism at a major ceremony held in his official residence. He remembered me well from our meeting at the Binational Science Foundation. Mom and Dad flew in and over a celebratory dinner Dad said to me with great emotion, "You and Malki have brought me enormous joy, and if I die tomorrow, I will die a happy man." The good news is that he didn't.

I met with a senior person in the social welfare department and she spoke very positively about Shalva and shared that she in fact had a clean, spacious facility that had only recently become available and would work well for us. She called the person responsible, who had the key and would open it. Malki and I arrived and were shocked to see that it was a large bomb shelter. I stepped out of the car to look it over and discovered that the entrance to the space was two flights down massive concrete stairs. "It won't work for Shalva," Malki said. "If you want to put our kids underground, there are ways to do it, but not like this." When I later told the woman from the municipality, "Thanks, but no thanks," her response was: "Why are you making such a fuss? It's not as if kids like these will know the difference, and you will have the space to help them!" "Sorry," I said, "but kids like these deserve a space that gives them and their families dignity." She didn't understand, and we realized that we would have to do this ourselves.

* * *

One evening after a long day, Malki and I sat down for a coffee and, as we often did, were discussing pressing Shalva matters. She paused and said very matter-of-factly, "It's obvious, Kalman! We'll simply move out of our apartment and I will open up part of the fence dividing between the two yards. Then between the two adjacent garden duplexes, we will have the space needed."

This may have been obvious to Malki, but as far as I was concerned, people may move institutions out of their homes, but institutions do not, I firmly told her, displace the homes of those who established them. Her response was concise and irrefutable. "If you are not willing to put your money where your mouth is, why should anyone else?"

Three weeks later, shortly before the Passover holiday, in the spring of 1995, we saw a place that seemed suitable for us to rent. It was in Jerusalem's Kiryat Moshe neighborhood, close to Yossi's school – but it was not in Har Nof, where we'd lived for the past ten years, and where we and our children had our conveniences, friends, synagogue, and familiar shops.

The apartment was spacious, with a beautiful kitchen, and since Passover, with its extensive preparations, was now only ten days away, we were in a hurry to find something. We decided to take it and came in to sign the lease. The agent showed us a mirror-image apartment next door with a very small kitchen, and when we pointed out her mistake, we were told, "Oh, I am so sorry but I showed you the wrong apartment. That one is now taken and only this one is available."

We were horrified because the tiny kitchen could not meet our family's needs, but with nowhere else to go, we had no choice but to sign.

Moving week was hectic. We transported our family of eight and our furniture lock, stock, and barrel. We cleaned up our vacated home for Shalva, and then got to work putting our lives back together in our new apartment where, as well as settling in, we cleaned and readied it for Passover in line with the biblical commandment, "and no *hametz*, leavened bread, shall be in your possession."

Much like the rushed Exodus from Egypt, it somehow all got done. It was now the evening before the festival was to begin, and our exhausted family gathered for the ritual of *bedikat hametz*, the symbolic candlelight search for any forbidden leavened products in the home that might have been overlooked. It was a wonderful opportunity for us to bond as a family in our new home. My candle was in one hand, and the traditional spoon and feather for gathering up crumbs were in the other, when the phone rang – still an unfamiliar sound in our new apartment.

"Hi Kalman!" said a cheerful voice. "Gordon Diamond here. I'm in Israel, but only for a very short time. I really want to see you and Malki, and I'm free right now. Can you come pick me up at the King David Hotel and we'll have dinner? Sorry about the short notice, but there's no other slot."

"Hi Gordon, it is so wonderful to hear from you," I replied, and I was sincerely excited to hear from him, but I also knew that this was a time that I could not possibly go out. "One minute," I said, and placing my hand over the mouthpiece I quickly updated Malki. She didn't hesitate. "Tell him we're on our way." Malki was exhausted from the move and the Passover preparations, and in any case, we needed an hour or so for the *bedikat hametz* ceremony we'd been on the point of starting with the kids. "Malki, you must be kidding. We can't go anywhere for the next hour," I whispered. "Let's go," she replied, adding her familiar refrain, "Don't worry, I'll handle it; you will do *bedikat hametz* later."

We picked Gordon up and had a fine meal at a kosher Chinese restaurant. As always, we enjoyed being with him, and Gordon was most interested to hear how Shalva was doing. We shared that we'd just doubled its space and in the face of his continued questions we hesitatingly mentioned that we had created the additional space by moving out of our adjacent apartment. Gordon was very moved and wanted to see the enlarged Shalva, so after the meal, we drove to Har Nof and showed him the two apartments from the car. Gordon choked up. "I like what you've done. I respect the fact that you have moved out of your own home in order to help the children. When the time comes for Shalva to move into its own home, make sure you come to see me." It was after midnight by the time we dropped him off at the hotel, and later still by the time we finally got home and finished *bedikat hametz*. I lay down to sleep exhausted, with a joy-filled heart.

Immediately after the weeklong Passover holiday, we set out to create dedicated therapy areas for the Shalva children. Rooms were designed and equipped to promote motor development, teach functional skills, and stimulate the children.

The rooms came alive with bright primary colors everywhere – brilliant blues, vibrant reds, gleaming yellows, and lustrous greens – and the foam-covered equipment came in a wide assortment of appealing shapes.

We had practiced music therapy – a tried, tested, and highly successful therapeutic tool – at Shalva before the expansion, but now the initiative moved into its own space and was run by a professional as a more structured program, giving verbal and nonverbal children a channel of communication through which to express frustration, distress, joy, and many other emotions.

Yet another therapy from which the children benefited was the Snoezelen room, a multisensory resource that Shalva introduced to Jerusalem. Pronounced "snooze-ellen," the word is an acronym of the Dutch for explore and doze (*snuffelen* and *doezelen*) – which is as good a description as any for this multisensory environment. Entering it is like stepping into a giant cocoon. The air is scented, the lights are dim, and soft music plays. Optical fibers rhythmically stream changing patterns of light across white vinyl walls and across the ceiling. The floor is a sea of mattresses and waterbeds of different shapes and heights. Bubbles swell and subside inside glass tubes, and cushions and furry toy animals pulsate at the gentlest touch. This safe, accessible, almost magical landscape calms Shalva's children, and sometimes their stressed parents as well, in mind and body, while tempting them to explore using all available senses – to touch, taste, smell, listen, see, and move – at their own failure-free pace.

Both duplexes were now fully equipped and functional, and to the casual observer it would have seemed that the space had always been set up like that.

Months passed and I had little choice but to request two weeks off from work and make my way to Vancouver. Gordon and several others kindly agreed to see me. The night before my meeting with Gordon, I visited a dear mutual friend and shared that I would be seeing Gordon in the morning and that I wanted to ask him to help me toward creating Shalva's own center. "Do you think $250,000 is too much to ask from Gordon?" He answered with a question: "How much do you need?" "With real estate prices in Jerusalem being what they are, I believe that I will need about a million." "If that's what you need," he calmly said, "then that's what you should ask for. If you don't ask for it, how will you get it?" "I couldn't possibly ask for so much," I countered, and he responded, "Listen to me. Just share your need, and if Gordon wants to help at any level through his foundation, leave that to him."

He then asked to see the video of Esther that I'd brought with me. He was deeply moved and jumped from his seat. "That is incredible!" he shouted. "Forget about your meeting tomorrow. I am closely connected with the head of a national TV network that operates out of New York. I will speak to my friend and he will screen this, and I guarantee that you will have all the money you need quicker than you can imagine." I too was now excited. Who could have dreamed of such an opportunity?

Upon arrival at my parents' home, I called Malki to share the extraordinary news. Her baffling reaction was, "It's not happening." I was shell-shocked. "What on earth are you talking about?" I protested, but Malki was adamant. "I won't have us using Nachshon's tragedy like this to build a center in his name," she said. "And that's what you are doing and that is exactly how people will view it." I tried to make her understand that this wasn't using his tragedy, but rather helping us give something very important to his beloved brother and dozens of other children like him. But she wouldn't budge. Showing it privately to friends was one thing, she agreed, but to go public on television and use the video as a way to get funds was terribly inappropriate. To say that I grasped what she meant would be untrue. On the contrary, I felt robbed of a golden opportunity.

So, it was back to Plan A, and the next morning found me in Gordon's office. To my delight, his father Jack was there too.

Jack was indeed a tough, no-nonsense person who was best known for his incredible care and concern for others. His desire to give generously and his penchant for helping to develop and build communal institutions were unmatched.

I related the Wachsman story and showed the video. They were, of course, very moved. Then Jack, who was always direct, asked, "So how much do you want?" I swallowed hard and somehow managed to say, "Building and equipping the center will cost $1 million, so that's what I am asking you to consider." There was dead silence. A visibly angry Jack got to his feet, said to the room at large, "He's full of it!" and stormed out. Gordon quickly followed him. Left alone, I was beside myself. Jack was absolutely right; how could I possibly have said that? It was an agonizing twenty minutes before Gordon came back without Jack. "You should never have named a figure like that to my father," he said sternly. "But I apologize for what he said to you." There was a long pause. "We can't give you a million. How much do you want?" Somehow I again managed, "Would $750,000 be possible?" "No, that won't work – but we will give you a quarter of a million." With the Canadian dollar at 73 cents to one US dollar, I summoned the audacity to say, "Can we make that a quarter of a million US?" "Yes we can," said Gordon, "and if you want to know why, it's because you and your family gave up your own home to help the children. I respect that." Once again, I was left alone in the room. Gordon came back with a corporate check in his hand, made out for 350,000 Canadian dollars. "This is from my father and my family," he said.

I had never seen a check of that size and my Dad had never seen such a large charitable check. Always thoughtful with his words, Dad became emotional and said, "I am so proud of what you are dedicating your life to."

Naturally I called Malki to share the incredible news. We were excited and keenly aware that we were embarking on a challenging new phase of Shalva's development.

Chapter 29

Beit Nachshon

Having been warned about the complications and cost overruns involved in building from scratch, we began to search for an existing building that could be modified. We reached out to real estate agents who came back with many suggestions, and we visited numerous sites over the course of several months, some nicer than others, but found nothing of interest. The fact was that we had $250,000 and we learned that we would need several times that to make a meaningful move. It was very discouraging, and as time passed I was beginning to think that the most practical thing to do was to return Gordon's money.

I was considering another fund-raising trip when an unfinished four-story townhouse was brought to our attention. Only several blocks from our current location, it was on a quiet cul-de-sac at one end of the neighborhood with a magnificent view of the Judean Hills and valley below. It was little more than a concrete shell fronted by a littered courtyard. It was built into the side of the mountain, its entrance on the structure's highest level. The two floors below were of similar size, with an additional, far smaller floor beneath them that consisted of a small open space with a narrow hallway leading to a bomb shelter and then to the back door, outside of which there was a large pile of dirt slated to become a backyard. It encompassed some three thousand square feet and was designed to be a four-story family home.

Malki and I made our way down the narrow stairwell examining each floor until we reached the claustrophobic, windowless lowest level. I saw endless concrete and rock, but Malki saw something else entirely.

"Look, Kalman," she said, "on this floor I will place the kitchen, dining room, and auditorium." Her enthusiasm drowned out my mumbled "This floor is too small and anyway we can't possibly afford this place."

She was looking at the reinforced concrete walls, behind which stood the mountain, and she was telling me that this will be a beautiful large floor.

"I don't know what you're seeing," I cut in, "but you are dreaming. We can't possibly buy this." Malki looked at me smiling and said calmly, "I have violins playing in my heart, and that doesn't happen to me very often, but when it does, I know they are real. I'm not telling you to buy this, but I won't be looking at anything else." Emotion overtook me and I cried like a baby. "Malki please don't do this to me."

"I am not doing anything to you," she replied. "You can do whatever you choose, but for me this is it."

I knew that this was now the only option but I had no idea how we could buy it or how this could ever look like anything other than what met my eyes. It was not going to be easy.

We were introduced to the owners, two astute businessmen. I was advised by several people in the know not to get involved with this deal, because one had provided the funding and one was building the house, but it had come to a standstill and they were now fighting in court.

The price was $750,000, and that was only for the shell. We estimated that it would cost another $250,000 to finish it. We met with them with our lawyer present and they demanded a first payment of far more than we had. It appeared to be all over, when I said, "Gentlemen, let's face it. You are fighting each other in court. Neither of you will walk away with your investment because the legal costs will eat that up. I am offering you a way out. Become my partners in providing the opportunity to create a magnificent home for the Shalva children, work with me, and with a little patience you will have your money in full." No one was more shocked than our lawyer when after further haggling they worked out an agreement that required $249,000 as a down payment.

I turned to Malki and whispered, "This is incredible but how can I sign on a deal when that's all we have?" to which she replied, "That is not written on your forehead. This is heavenly so let's move forward." Indeed, it was the fact that the sellers were unaware that enabled the deal – and I was now in over my head.

We didn't have funds for architects or construction companies so Malki turned to Mohammed, an electrician we used who also did construction work for the city. He began to survey the property in detail and called us up excitedly, exclaiming, "You have won the lottery! The ground around the house isn't rock," he said. "It's compacted rubble. I can bring in a small tractor and excavate it and expand the building, while still on your half acre."

Malki was excited and gave the green light, but I cautioned that we don't have the money. She was unfazed. "Kalman, dear," she said, "this can only be done once, and the choice must be made now. I am so happy that you grew up in Vancouver with the comforts of a beautiful house, cars in the driveway, and membership in the golf club; my mother survived Auschwitz and if I am here, I am not going to allow this challenge to hold us back."

Additional funds were now desperately needed, and Esther Wachsman agreed to go with me to New York for a week. I introduced her to two friends, Harry Freund and Jay Goldsmith, who were partners in an investment firm and caring human beings. They were proud to meet Esther and spoke to her at length. She was sharing the dream of Beit Nachshon and its pressing needs when Jay suddenly turned to me and asked, "How much do you need to finish this?" "We need $500,000," I replied. "Harry," Jay exclaimed, "we can do this. I am telling you that we can do this." He then turned back to me and said, "And we will. You will come back in a couple of months for another meeting." Jay and Harry thanked Esther for the privilege of meeting her and we walked out, hopeful, but not knowing what to make of it.

Others also wanted to meet Esther. The names of Esther and Yehuda Wachsman were known as much for the grace and faith with which they met their tragedy as for the tragedy itself. I received a message that the esteemed Rabbi Avraham Yaakov Hakohen Pam requested to meet Esther. A humble, soft-spoken man in his nineties, Rabbi Pam was a deeply respected talmudic scholar and dean of the Torah Vodaas Yeshiva in Brooklyn, where he had taught for sixty years. Esther and I went to his home.

He was deeply moved to meet her. He couldn't forget her husband's words, which had been transmitted by Nachshon's rabbi when the Wachsmans had buried their nineteen-year-old son. "Your husband's message," he said, "touched hundreds of thousands of people who had prayed for Nachshon's safety. Yes, every prayer is heard, but in this instance the answer was no. I wanted to meet you and thank you personally." Subsequently, he painstakingly wrote his message for Esther and Yehuda, each letter meticulously formed by his aged hand.

Two months later I was back in New York in Jay and Harry's office, where they had gathered five others. Jay talked about the importance of supporting this project and shared the amount that he was donating. He then went around the room cajoling the others and getting pledges. He pulled no punches, and true to his word Jay and Harry raised the needed funds in thirty minutes. I was thunderstruck.

* * *

Malki was hard at work. She had no training in architecture, engineering, or interior design, but she knew the needs of the children, and so she knew precisely what she wanted and was able to work intimately and effectively with dedicated quality professionals, led by our tireless lead contractor Neal Scher.

Under the watchful eyes of Malki and our son Yochanan, then a student and obsessed with every detail of the building, the renovation progressed. Playrooms, exercise rooms, and therapy rooms; a library, kitchen, dining room, bedrooms, and an auditorium; a kindergarten, a training-for-independent-living space, and a space for arts and crafts all took shape. A small area was built under the sloping attic eaves to accommodate Shalva's administrative offices. Malki was on-site constantly, directing the workers with such requests as "I need another two feet for this room. Go deeper into the rock." The construction was tedious and took significant time.

It was early 1998. We had our own six children born in the span of less than seven years, the youngest of whom, Shlomo, was now sixteen years old. I was forty-seven and Malki forty-four. She sat me down over a coffee in our home, and I was anticipating some important update about the building – but this was a little different.

"I am not feeling well," she said.

"I'll get you an Advil," I replied. "It won't help." "Ok, I'll get you two." "It won't help." "What are you talking about?" I hesitatingly asked.

"I am expecting."

I was overwhelmed both with joy and with a sudden abundance of concerns because Malki had experienced numerous complications in pregnancy over the years. Sensing my thoughts, Malki reassured me calmly, "Don't worry; this one is different."

There had been no ultrasound technology available for the first six, but now there was, and we soon learned that we were blessed with a girl. It was strangely wonderful to share with our grown children that Mommy was carrying their sister. They began to suggest names and I urged them to leave that until after the healthy baby was born, G-d willing. So they began to refer to her as Mommy's little "princess" and that nickname stuck.

Due to her age there was concern during the pregnancy of a higher risk of Down syndrome. That is to say, the doctor and I were concerned, while Malki was at complete peace, ready and waiting to empower our daughter to be all she possibly can. We were informed early on that because Malki was over thirty-five, it was advisable to undergo an amniocentesis to check for Down syndrome. I asked about the risks and was told that they are very minor. My internet reading that night told me something different. I learned that a sample of amniotic fluid that surrounds the baby in the womb is removed by placing a needle through the belly, and that process can trigger a miscarriage in 1 out of 235 cases.

The next day Malki told the doctor that if G-d had put life in her womb at this late and unexpected stage, she was not going to take any such risk of losing it. He was a friend and explained the importance of the test, to which I replied, "It will not change a thing because even if the baby has Down syndrome, we will not abort and will know more at birth."

It was the summer of 1998 and the heat was oppressive. A by-then-very-pregnant Malki was quite the sight on-site, working intensely to complete the building down to the very last design elements, including walls painted in different colors and murals adorning the walls, a veritable Disneyland.

The grand opening was in October during the holiday of Sukkot, and many friends from Israel and abroad joined us. It was joyous and in our eyes, simply miraculous. I still carried significant debt, but the center was complete and the children were moving in. Our staff told Malki that they were petrified by the size of the building and she laughed and said, "In a year you will be crying that you don't have enough space," and so it was.

Malki now had other business to attend to – giving birth. A mere two weeks after Shalva's grand opening, our beautiful, healthy, ten-and-a-half-pound daughter Sara, Hebrew for "princess," was born. She brought the entire family so much joy, and no one was happier about her arrival than Yossi, who doted on her from the first moment. Even prior to her birth, Malki would place Yossi's hand on her stomach and he would laugh as he felt the baby kicking.

Malki went right back to work, planning and installing an elevator in the building for which we hadn't had the funds beforehand. Incredibly, she managed to get it done without interfering with the children's activities. But once she was digging, she decided to dig down two more floors to allow for the creation of a hydrotherapy pool, a multipurpose space, and a synagogue.

Shalva–Beit Nachshon came into its own, and new ideas and new ways to help youngsters with disabilities were pioneered, modified, and implemented.

The number of children served kept climbing, into the hundreds. Shalva was authorized to work with the army and host dedicated post–high school youngsters who chose to join the noncombat National Service program at Shalva (similar to the Peace Corps). Their numbers also grew, as did the number of younger volunteers. Once again we were reluctantly turning applicants away. The various programs used every square inch of the center throughout the day and we managed to do it all without lowering our standards.

Every level of the building had its own color scheme to help youngsters orient themselves. Each of the overnight respite bedrooms had its own unique theme and colors, from its murals and curtains to its bedding and light fixtures. In the clearest way possible, Malki's design declared: "Shalva is not an institution. This is our home and these are our children!"

The intimacy, hope, and love with which we'd embarked on this journey remained central to our philosophy, enabling families to raise their child at home and still maintain a high standard of quality of life. Shalva had grown in size but its core values remained intact.

Chapter 30

Me and My Mommy

I t had now been two years since we entered the new center and things were under control. The after-school program ran from 1:00 p.m., when the younger children arrived, until after dinner at 6:00 p.m. when they were bused home. Those youngsters who were sleeping over each night as part of the respite program had a great time with their peers and practiced important independent living skills; they stayed overnight and left the next morning at 7:30 a.m. when they were picked up by their school buses.

I arrived home from my computer work at Binational one day to find Malki crying. "Malki, what is it? Has something happened?" I feared the worst. She settled down and I slowly got her to open up. "I can't live with myself. At Shalva we are doing nothing in the mornings." "Well, that is pretty normal," I said. "Our programs run from 1:00 p.m. until 7:30 a.m. the following morning, which is an eighteen-and-a-half-hour span. Show me a school or a community center that provides eighteen hours of childcare each day. And in those morning hours we are busy with what you have always felt is critical – cleaning the building and making sure it is immaculate. So, in fact, it is in use around the clock."

"No," she responded, "that is not enough, and we will manage with cleaning. I need a program for mothers who have just given birth to a baby with problems, or mothers that have just been told by their doctors that their babies are not reaching their milestones. From that moment, that mother is not functioning. She is devastated, can't grasp what is happening, and doesn't know where to turn. She is depressed and above all lonely." Malki paused thoughtfully and continued, "The loneliness is devastating. I'll never forget it. I can still feel it. Yes, doctors will give excellent medical help – but emotional support is critical, and there is nowhere to go for that."

"OK, so what do you have in mind?" I probed gently. Malki began, "Humpty Dumpty sat on the wall; Humpty Dumpty had a great fall. All the king's soldiers and all the king's men, couldn't put Humpty together again." "So who can?" I queried. "Only other mothers," came her response. "I want a program where every day, Sunday through Thursday, a different group of these mothers will come together and receive all the different therapies for their babies, swim together with their babies in our pool, and most importantly, there will be half an hour mid-morning when the staff will back off and the mothers will have coffee and cake together."

"So it will be one day a week?" I asked.

"Yes, for each set of mothers, and there will be five such sets, one for each day."

"And what kind of therapies are you talking about?"

"Everything – speech therapy, physical therapy, occupational therapy, water therapy and more – but the program will not only provide therapy for the child. It will also actively teach the mother how to work with her child at home during the rest of the week."

"Sounds amazing," I commented. "If I may ask, we now have a budget of almost $1 million annually, and there are no fees. Your therapists will be professionals who have to be paid. Who is going to raise the money for this expensive new program?"

"You!" Malki replied without missing a beat. I took a deep breath. Malki now waxed philosophical and continued in Yiddish, "Kalman dear, understand once and for all, there is no shortage of money in the world; there is only a shortage of health. You will travel for another week and G-d will help you find it."

The cost, I calculated, would be $145,000 to get the program up and running and to see it through its first year. There would be no help from Israel's government for this new, unrecognized program. Not that I had government funding for anything else, but here at least I knew from the start that there would not be any such funding available, which meant that as usual I had to find the entire sum elsewhere.

Among those with whom I shared the vision was a dear friend from New York, Andy Lowinger. I had first met Andy ten years earlier at his home when he gave me a long lecture as to how important children with disabilities are and how much they add to all of our lives. I was amazed at his sensitivity and insight. He became a generous and thoughtful partner and always delved deeply into matters at hand. Over the years, I had the distinct privilege of meeting his elderly mother, Edith Lowinger, who together with her late husband Morris, Andy's father, had saved tens of thousands of Jews from starvation in the Budapest ghetto during the Holocaust. She was a giant of the human spirit, and I loved to listen to her schmooze about a vast array of subjects in her Hungarian accent.

I now presented the "Me and My Mommy" program to Andy in his Manhattan office, and we went through the plans and figures together. With Andy I was candid and shared my concerns that it may impact my ability to fund existing programs and so I wanted to start slowly, while Malki said it had to begin at full capacity with an adequate number of mothers participating. Andy

agreed with Malki, arguing cogently that "if you don't do it right –
if you dilute it and limit it – it will not be successful, and no one
else will ever be able to do this kind of program again because
you will have 'proved to them' that it is not doable. So either do
it right, or don't do it at all, and if you do it right, you will have
such a strong impact that the government will ultimately have to
come around and fund it. I am prepared to consider jump-starting
this," he said, "but you must get broad support, because once you
embark it will grow very quickly. And most critically, I am going
to give you some homework, and if you want my help, you will
have to do the homework and answer my questions to demonstrate that you are serious."

Back in Israel, I worked long and hard to prepare the materials and provide answers for Andy. He asked for further clarifications, which I provided, but it still wasn't enough. We met again
and again on successive trips, and each time he challenged me on
new details and wanted more information. I felt that the goalposts
were being moved and however hard I tried I could never quite
get there. Ten months down the line, going into what I expected
would be yet another such meeting, I spoke to Malki on the phone
from New York. "Kalman, if you respect yourself, do not go back
for another meeting." I said, "The meeting is today, Friday, at high
noon, and if indeed he moves the goalposts again, it will be my
last on this matter."

The discussion in Andy's spacious boardroom followed its
predictable course as he raised new issues for almost an hour. As
I stood up to go, I drew my breath and opened my mouth to say,
"I love you and we'll stay friends – but we won't talk about Me
and My Mommy anymore." But I never got the chance, for as I
rose, so did he. He then reached into his back pocket and produced an envelope and gave it to me. "Open it!" I did and was
shocked to see that it contained twelve monthly checks totaling
$145,000 to finance the program through its first year. "This is

seed-money to get things going," he said casually. "Find other funding for the future." My emotions welled up and I walked around the enormous table to hug and thank him. Yet another Shalva miracle. Given that it was already the Sabbath in Israel, I could not speak to Malki until Saturday night in New York. When we finally spoke she quipped, "I am learning to respect your lack of self-respect."

I worked hard in the coming year to find other significant funding, but had little success. With time running out, I went back to Andy. "Kalman," he said, "we had a deal. I told you, one year only. You've got to find another way to get it together."

He was no doubt a tough businessman…but he was not a tough son. On my way out, his elderly mother, my devoted fan, who was standing at the doorway and had overheard our exchange, said without hesitation in her sweet intonation, "Andy, he is a very good boy, and he's trying so hard. Give him one more time." On the spot Andy turned to me and said, "You just got another year for which you can thank my mother."

Me and My Mommy was a resounding success. It broke new ground and was awarded a prestigious national award for "the most exciting new program in the field of early childhood development." Down the road, the government hailed its unique and ground-breaking value and provided partial funding. It was the only such supportive, therapeutic framework for mothers and their children with disabilities at the beginning of life anywhere in Israel. Being part of a larger community empowered these mothers, and in a matter of weeks, mothers who had felt helpless and frozen with devastation and fear before joining the program were back on their feet. They often shared their feelings in notes to the staff, as did these two:

> I was completely shattered when our son was born. He was my first child, and it was so unexpected. I couldn't hold him.

I couldn't even look at him. Five minutes with him was too much for me. I am ashamed to admit I was ashamed. I remember the moment when everything changed. I was with him in the hydrotherapy pool for the first time and I suddenly had a rush of feeling toward the baby I was coddling in the water. I understood: you are my son and I love you. An enormous burden was suddenly lifted and I began to cherish him as the greatest gift I have ever received.

Another mother wrote:

He was born more than three months early. He weighed less than 2 lbs. He chose to live, but his care was 24/7. When he was a few months old, I took him to the doctor, with his food, his clothes, and a packet of diapers. The nurse said: "You don't have an appointment today." I replied, "I know. I'm not here for an appointment. I'm here because I can't do this anymore. I'm leaving the baby with you. You decide what to do with him." The doctor understood and referred me to Shalva for Me and My Mommy. Helpless, I called and went. It was love at first sight. I don't have words for what it meant to me. The program helped me to dream different dreams for this child, who is different but is my son. I learned to love him as much as I could love any healthy child. I treasure him and show him to the world with pride. When I look back, I cannot grasp the change in me.

Malki and I had walked that path and lived that shock of all the heavens suddenly falling on our heads. We knew that families need support and a framework where they can learn how to help their children. We knew how vital it is for parents to be embraced and to be shown that while their baby may be different from what they expected, he or she is their G-d-given child to be valued and loved.

Yossi had taught us that a child with disabilities impacts the whole family and the whole family impacts the child. So this too was built into Me and My Mommy, with support groups for fathers, brothers and sisters, and even grandparents. As one such sixteen-year-old sibling shared, "We were a family of five until my mother gave birth to my baby brother with disabilities, and then we suddenly became a family of one." Our mission was to restore it to a fully functional family of six.

Several academic studies on the program were conducted by the esteemed head of the school of education at Tel Aviv University, Professor Malka Margalit. A recognized authority and researcher in the field of developmental and learning disabilities, her findings were published in leading academic journals; the following is a short excerpt from one of her papers:

> The uniqueness of Shalva is that it focuses not solely on the difficulties of the child – his or her learning and developmental disabilities – but equally on how to empower parents and the entire family to cope better. Children with special needs may present major and continuous challenges to the well-being and quality of life of their families. Parental coping in caring for all their children is put to endless and demanding tests. Many families feel alone at critical hours. Perhaps the primary reason for this emphasis is that Shalva was created by the parents of a child with disabilities to help other parents.
>
> Shalva provides the most solid and advanced global curriculum for the changing needs of disabled children... from young infants to young adults. Every parent wants their challenged child to reach maximum potential. Every parent needs to know that all new therapeutic knowledge and every educational method is available to help *their* children lead fuller and better lives, regardless of the severity of their disability and the family's economic constraints.

Malka, as we referred to her, shared an insight with me: "As a professor, in spite of my academic degrees, I could never have created Me and My Mommy or any of the Shalva programs for that matter." Surprised, I asked, "Why?" "Primarily," she continued, "because it required a mother who had experienced the challenges of raising a child with disabilities and who had faced the gaps in services both here in Israel and in New York, and had the smarts to understand how to fill those gaps. But there is another critical component. Let us say I came up with the brilliant idea of Me and My Mommy. I would turn to the powers that be at the university and share it with them. Assuming that they were impressed, their next question would be, 'How are you going to fund it?' and I might say, 'I have funding from a foundation for the first two years.' Their next question would be, 'And where will the funding come in year three?' If I didn't yet know, I would be told clearly that I may not begin the program. Your dear wife didn't have that concern. She was able to establish her programs, including Me and My Mommy, because she had a fool like you, prepared to travel the world to get her the needed funds for her dreams. She recognized the problems, had her clear vision how to solve them, and had you to bridge between the two."

Malka smiled and I laughed, marveling at her wisdom.

Chapter 31

A Stressful Choice

With my fiftieth birthday in sight, I found myself visiting doctors and the emergency room too often. It was always for similar symptoms: a sensation of ants strolling through my shoulders and upper chest. I ran a constant low-grade fever and neither I nor the doctors knew what was wrong. As time went on, I grew increasingly anxious as to what it was all about. One day, when the symptoms were especially severe, I took myself yet again to the ER, where I underwent the usual examination, but then the consultation took a twist.

The doctor was someone I hadn't seen before, a tall, fair man with a strong Scandinavian accent. "I see you have been here for this before," he said. "Could it be that you're under stress?" I laughed. "You might say that!" "Tell me about what you do," he requested. "I have a full-time job in the computer field, and for over a decade I've been managing a growing nonprofit that my wife and I set up," I said. He asked detailed questions, about both my computer work and the nonprofit, and about the hours and responsibilities involved in each. Eyeing me carefully, he nodded and asked gravely, "Do you have children?" "Yes." "How many?" "Seven." "Would you like to see them stand under the *huppa* (marriage canopy)?" He continued, "Let me be clear. If you go on like this, I am very concerned you won't make it. The symptoms you are experiencing are, in my opinion, stress related. Stress is making you ill and ultimately may well kill you, as it has many others. You must make significant lifestyle changes immediately."

I was in shock. I knew that I couldn't continue this way, and if it was stress that was causing it, I must make a change. There was no question that the pressures and conflicts involved in working full time at Binational while also running Shalva, with its travel needs and ever-growing responsibilities, had led to this situation. The pressure had to be relieved somehow. It was one or the other.

I shared with Malki the doctor's dire warning. "Malki," I said, "I can't go on this way, and so I've decided to leave Binational. I guess there comes a time when I can't do everything and I must face reality." I could no longer risk my health and my family's future.

It took me a full year to extricate myself from Binational, during which I documented its entire computer system. Once I left, my medical symptoms disappeared quickly and never returned, in spite of the fact that I worked no less. I was now dedicated to one goal and not torn and conflicted by two different sets of responsibilities, and it became clear that the doctor had been right on target.

Chapter 32

Volvo

It was a festive Simhat Torah, the final festival day of the Sukkot holiday, and the synagogue was alive with lively singing and dancing. The kids were having a blast. As always I danced with Yossi and we took breaks to sit down. As we did so, an older man with a cane sitting in the row behind me couldn't help himself and asked in a caring manner, "What is the story with your son?" I shared that Yossi couldn't see or hear and his gait was awkward so we need to take breaks. Yossi sensed that I had turned around and he also did so, reaching out and touching the man's hands. There was a pause and a connection was made. There were further questions: "How do you understand him? How do you communicate with him? I am in awe."

Now it was Yossi's turn. "What is your name?" "Amnon." "What do you do?" "I am a pharmacist." "What kind of car do you drive?" "A Volvo."

That was all Yossi needed to hear and he went into an explanation as to why his favorite car is the Volvo. "But how does he know what a Volvo looks like?" "He identifies cars by their door handles," I said matter-of-factly. Amnon was in shock and there was silence. I was then in shock when he continued, "Listen, your son amazes me and I am going to try to arrange a visit for him to visit the Volvo factory in Sweden." I listened incredulously as he went on. "Last year, I attended a Rotary Club meeting in Sweden and befriended the local Rotary Club president who is also the president of Volvo. I can't promise anything, but he is a sensitive person and so I will send him an email requesting that he host Yossi."

Six months and many emails later, Yossi, Avi, and I were on our way to the Volvo factory and headquarters in Gothenburg, Sweden, as guests of the president. En route, we stopped in Amsterdam for two days.

When we returned from the trip Yossi wrote a detailed diary of the experience. Here are some excerpts from his "braille blog":

Early wake-up: My father and Avi and I got up at 2:00 a.m., very early. I hugged my mother and Yochanan and Princess. We took two suitcases and went in a Mercedes taxi to the airport. We boarded an airplane that belonged to the Dutch airlines for the 5:00 a.m. flight.

The flight attendant was named Monika and was very sweet. She brought the passengers bread, cucumber, mayonnaise, tuna, cake, omelet, watermelon, honeydew, black coffee, and cold water. I made a joke about [President Bill] Clinton's Monica. Our Monika said: "Not so fast!" I went forward to meet and talk to the pilots.

Rachamim, the driver, met our plane in an old '92 Ford. He brought me a wheelchair and drove us to a famous garden full of flowers [Keukenhof]. We went to a village and dressed up as Dutch people. I thanked the woman who helped me and I thanked Jon the manager. Then we went to a place where they make clogs and to a cheese factory. There are many German cars in Holland – Audi A4 and A6, and BMW.

We ate in the Jerusalem restaurant – French fries, shishlik, kebab, lamb, potatoes, ketchup, and hummus. I drank Amstel white beer, for my health! I met the restaurant manager Sammy. We stayed at the Sheraton Plaza Hotel. It rained heavily which upset me.... From the hotel, we called Ruth [a young Dutch woman who had volunteered at the School for the Blind in Jerusalem five years earlier, whom Yossi loved and whose phone number he had kept]. Ruth told my Dad that she really misses me, and was very happy to hear from me. She's coming to Israel in a month and will be in touch.

We went to see the place where Anne Frank's family hid from the Nazis – may their name be blotted out! I felt very sad there. Next we sat on a bench at the Royal Palace and fed pigeons, and then saw a 400-year-old synagogue. Rachamim took us to the airport for the flight to Sweden. I thanked him. I'd enjoyed being with him very much. In Sweden, a driver named Janna met us in a fancy taxi, a Volvo V70, 2000 model. He drove at over 150 kilometers an hour to the hotel.

I got up at 7:00 a.m. and dressed in nice clothes to go to the Volvo Company.

We arrived and were greeted royally by the president of Volvo and some ten directors. Yossi shook everyone's hand and said hello in Swedish. A conversation ensued. I translated Yossi's comments from Hebrew to English and translated their remarks via Hebrew sign language into Yossi's palm. Their initial amazement was quickly forgotten as we got into the conversation. Yossi indicated immediately that he had a question: "Now that Ford has bought Volvo, who is in control of design?" There was total silence and surprised looks all around. "What did Yossi say that is so puzzling?" I asked. After a few moments a young lady opened up. "Ford's purchase of Volvo is not yet well-publicized," she said, "and the key problem that arose during the negotiations was that Ford demanded that the design be in their hands, while Volvo responded that if you take the design, you might as well call the vehicle a Ford. But how in the world does he know this?"

The visit was meticulously planned and began with the Volvo designer showing Yossi precise models of each car and explaining the differences. We then were brought to see raw sheet metal, which they allowed Yossi to feel, and he understood that this was the material from which the cars were made. They then paused the production conveyor belts in order to allow Yossi to touch and feel every stage of the process.

Our Volvo hosts had gotten used to the rhythm of our conversations, and communication quickly became quite natural. Walking through the factory, Yossi suddenly stopped and told me he wanted to share something. We all paused and Yossi announced in a clear voice, "I want to thank the Swedish people for all that they did on behalf of the Jewish people during the days of the Shoah, the Holocaust." Our hosts were overwhelmed with emotion and quite frankly in awe of his sensitivity.

Yossi was able to stand and to walk, albeit awkwardly, and we now stood in front of the dashboard of their lead sedan, the Volvo S80. I stood behind Yossi and helped him use an electric screw driver to put in the bolts to secure the dashboard. He then pushed a button on the side and the software was thereby inserted into its various systems. Yossi looked over his shoulder and asked me, "Are they selling this car?" I didn't translate, so naturally they asked, "What did he say?" "He wants to know if you are selling this car," I replied. "Well of course we are. Why is he asking?" came their answer. Yossi had now turned around and I signed into his palm, "They want to know why you are asking." With a twitch of a smile, he quipped, "What are they going to tell their buyer about their quality control?" I translated and the response was a pandemonium of laughter and tears ruining eye makeup. Six months later there was further laughter when I shared this episode over a Sabbath meal in New York. "Kalman," my host shared somberly, "you have just clarified something for me. I recently bought a Volvo S80 and surprisingly, it has been a lemon from the day I got it. No doubt, it is Yossi's car."

Following the indoor tour, we were driven to the Volvo test track, which was some four miles of road leading through the hills and forest around the factory. We were met by a strapping individual named Matz who gave Yossi the time of his life, whipping him around the track in numerous Volvo models. He then performed Hollywood stunts, pressing the gas pedal to the floor for a few hundred meters and suddenly putting on the handbrake to make the car spin 180 degrees. Yossi was screaming with excitement. When they took him out of the car after his final ride, he wanted a photo with Matz, who, despite the communication difficulties with Yossi, had become deeply connected.

"You're all good but Matz is definitely the best," Yossi signed to me. He then hugged Matz, gave him a kiss on the cheek, and said "I love you" in Hebrew. With tears running down his cheeks, Matz suddenly whipped off his hat and put it firmly on Yossi's head and they hugged each other again. Everyone was now crying. From that moment for an entire week, Yossi didn't let the hat leave his head, including when he slept. He said his goodbyes and courteously thanked each of our hosts with the Swedish "*tack*" and told them, "I felt like a king today."

Upon arriving home in Israel via a greatly delayed flight from Paris, we were exhausted, but Yossi refused to go to sleep until he had sat nonstop in front of his braille machine for many hours typing a detailed account of his visit.

Chapter 33
From Crayons to Perfumes

Yossi had developed from an engaging, cute little boy into a charming, charismatic young man. He was handsome, happy, often smiling, and always smartly dressed, his restless body language broadcasting his energy and zest for life. He continued to wear stylish glasses, which somehow kept him focused, along with his more recent cochlear implant, an electronic device surgically placed behind the ear. Designed to bypass the normal hearing process, a sophisticated external microphone lays on the skin and transmits signals to electrodes placed in the middle ear, or cochlea, which stimulate the cochlear nerve. We had great hopes that Yossi would hear and understand spoken language, but after many months of intensive work with expert speech therapists, we came to the devastating conclusion that he was unable to grasp oral communication. Gross sounds such as the ring of door bells and phones were picked up and that was of great value, but Yossi's daily communication remained and still remains via the palms of his hands.

And what astounding hands he has. Through the light touch of a hand, he constantly picks up on things we miss with our eyes and often has uncanny insights into the personalities of the people he meets: introvert, extrovert, sensitive, excitable – not to mention, tall, short, fat, thin, and in the case of females, good looking. Teaching him to be polite and politically correct was a process.

Yossi loves people, never failing to attract them, whether the encounter is one-on-one or in a group. He's well aware of his magnetism and plays to the crowd, entering a room and enjoying the tumult he creates by simply being Yossi. His sense of smell has always been acute. When his young siblings opened a can of coke several yards away, he smelled the wafting scent and yelled, "I want a coke too." As teenagers, his buddies had fun blowing smoke from various brands of cigarettes that Yossi would easily identify: Marlboro, Kent, Lucky Strike. He is often tipped off as to who is approaching via their unique scent or by their favorite perfume or aftershave, and from any number of coats could always identify the right one via scent and bring it to the appropriate sibling or classmate. Yossi is blessed with the capacity to be in the moment. For him, life's pleasures aren't fleeting. Give him a good glass of wine and a cigar together with his buddies and his enjoyment is total and intense.

His close friends number in the hundreds and acquaintances in the thousands. He stays in steady contact via personal visits, his weekly blog, emails, and text messages that are read to him and to which he dictates his response. Yossi's phone conversations usually begin with his monologue, after which his escort signs in his palm what is said by the other party, and so the conversation continues.

Yossi's memory is astonishing and he remembers the people he spoke to in great detail. He will remind visitors of which car they drove ten years ago, inquire about their children, and yes, about the wife or husband from whom they are long divorced.

Upon experiencing this, one astute visitor observed with a smile, "The Bible (Numbers 15:39–40) tells us, 'Thou shalt not wander after your heart and after your eyes that lead you astray, so that you will remember.' Yossi," he noted, "doesn't see or hear so his memory is seemingly not distracted and he certainly remembers."

As he'd grown taller, his awkward gait had worsened and his balance had deteriorated. In the months following the cochlear implant, his struggle with balance became more acute. He was losing his confidence and walked more awkwardly. Over time, he could scarcely walk and the little independence for which he'd battled so hard was lost to him forever. When he surrendered to the wheelchair, our blind and deaf son said, "For the first time in my life, I feel handicapped." Yossi had never referred to himself as blind or deaf, but rather "low vision" and "hard of hearing." Now, he would not bring himself to say "wheelchair" nor sit in it until Yochanan coined it as his *Jeepon* (little Jeep). After all, he was cool and just one of the boys.

Unable to walk, Yossi got around via our car, or often, especially when he went out with friends, via taxis. As it became more difficult for him to get in and out of a taxi, the drivers did not always have the required patience and refused to take him. I had no recourse, but Malki did. She suggested we buy Yossi his own car and whoever happened to be with him would be able to drive him happily to his destination.

Subsequently, I learned that the government allows people with disabilities to buy an appropriate vehicle with less of the exorbitant taxes. I applied for Yossi based on his being blind and deaf and unable to drive himself, but was refused on several occasions without explanation. I was frustrated and complained bitterly to someone I met in the department. "Apply again based solely on the fact that he has totally lost his ability to walk," I was advised. I did so and it worked; Yossi was suddenly entitled to his own vehicle suited for disabilities, which changed the quality of his life. Now he could go out for a beer or visit someone who lives in another city. It gave him dignity and worked wonders.

Yossi's mind remains quick and often makes him impatient. He likes things to happen at once and also demands that they be done in the same precise order. A, B, C must be A, B, C and he will not allow it to be done as A, C, B. I shared this with a close friend, and several nights later he arrived, sat me down, and insisted that I watch *Rain Man*, a movie starring Dustin Hoffman which tells the story of a savant on the autistic spectrum. I was laughing and crying throughout the film as both sad and comical situations were played out in which there was no way that the Rain Man would allow a change in the order of any regular activity. It was so helpful to me and from then on, in the face of frustrating delays, we would chuckle, "The Rain Man."

Yossi feels and senses the world vibrantly and as Malki once said, "If he could actually see the world, he would probably be disappointed."

The challenges Yossi faces as a result of his disabilities sometimes leave him feeling like he is caught between a rock and a hard place, and that is not an easy place to live. Yossi is sociable, friendly, and outgoing, his brain hungry and fertile, and he's determined to get as much as he can out of life. Even though he can't see, he loves the thrill of a roller coaster and has never hesitated to attempt to ride a bicycle, to jump into a swimming pool, or to find his way around an unfamiliar setting. He takes many knocks but they have never stopped him, for he knows that the alternative is to sit in a corner and shelter himself, and that is something he categorically refuses to do. At the same time, his combined disabilities have become so challenging that he can no longer manage without around-the-clock assistance.

Yossi follows a consistent daily routine. Each morning, he looks in the mirror, meticulously washes his face with cold water, brushes his teeth, shaves, and gets ready for his coffee, which he enjoys with a couple of cookies. He then puts on his *tefillin*, says key prayers, and beseeches G-d on behalf of others. Then it's breakfast and an hour in which he is read the daily newspaper, which provides him with a platform to gain an enormous amount of general knowledge. He enjoys doing the weekend crossword puzzle, loves politics, and has an opinion on everything. When I once hosted an Italian government minister, Yossi went into a detailed discussion with her regarding various Italian officials, none of whom I had heard of. There was a pause and Yossi smiled and asked, "And how is my friend Berlusconi doing?" She buckled over with laughter because Mr. Berlusconi was the colorful billionaire prime minister of Italy.

Yossi's days are full. As he matured, he began working at the sheltered workshop for the blind but lost interest when the opportunity arose to work at the Israel-based electric car company Better Place. For a young man who loved cars and routinely was read every car magazine available, this was an extraordinarily exciting opportunity. When Yossi was introduced to the company's head of human resources, I translated. Holding my hand, Yossi leaned over and said something quietly. I smiled. The gentleman asked what he had said that was funny. I tried to avoid it but he didn't let me. "He said you smoke Marlboro." Astonished, he asked, "How in the world does he know that?" I signed into Yossi's palm, "How do you know that?" to which he replied, "When he shook my hand, I smelled it." There was laughter and amazement all around. Yossi was hired and his efficiency and single-minded focus were an inspiration to the staff.

Yossi had self-respect and knew his own worth. When Better Place closed down, Osnat Michaelli, Deputy Director of Route 6, Israel's national toll road highway, hired him at their corporate headquarters to assemble three-piece easy passes. After a year, he asked for a meeting with the CEO, Udi Savyon, because he wanted a raise. Udi invited Yossi for a beautiful lunch in his office after which they got down to business. Yossi explained that he had increased his production to six hundred pieces a day and that he deserved a raise. Udi agreed and suggested an increase. Without batting an eyelash, Yossi responded that it was not enough and he would like double that increase. Udi was amazed by his poise and self-confidence and told Yossi, "You are well worth it because not only are you efficient, you are an inspiration to all who work here." Later Udi called to share this with me and explained, "Yossi comes to do his job, period. He doesn't schmooze or busy himself with phone calls, emails, and internet, and he clocks out and then back in when he goes to the restroom. He stays focused and his production rate is impressive. He was right to demand an appropriate raise."

Udi's friendship extended beyond Yossi's work at Route 6, and he became a vital partner in Shalva, ultimately becoming president of our Israel Friends.

Yossi kept up his relationship with one of his teachers at the School for the Blind, Hagit, long after he left, and she remained an invaluable presence in his life. She said of Yossi, "He's very clever, he's wise, and he's full of joy and life. He's loyal and loving; he knows how to give love and needs to receive it. He's also very determined, very mischievous, and pushes hard at boundaries – without always grasping the full impact of his behavior. The long years of silence and darkness have left their mark. He is an enigma: brilliant, possessing a curious mix of audacity and fear, wisdom and childishness. In reading him the daily papers, we sometimes omit news that will upset or frighten him. He feels things so deeply, and a report of something like a terror attack can consume him for days, so I always encourage Yossi to focus on the positive and maintain his unbridled optimism."

Chapter 34

Forrest Gump

After leaving Binational, I traveled more frequently to keep the growing "good ship Shalva" afloat and sought to expand our donor base. At a wedding in New York, I was seated next to a good friend who questioned me as to why I work solo. Why don't I hire a development director, he asked, to create a Shalva office in Manhattan and move us to the next level? I explained that I simply can't afford the risk of that person not succeeding and I will then be unable to recover: "What if it doesn't work out and I end up paying that person more in salary than what he raises?" I questioned. "First, you don't hire the first person you meet," he replied. "You do your due diligence. And second, I'm going to give you a safety net." Puzzled, I asked what he meant. "If it does go awry and he raises less than he costs you, then let him go and I'll cover the difference." Overcome with emotion, I gave him a hug. With his generous offer, he ushered in a new era for Shalva. It took me a year to find Leo Klein, who has been the outstanding executive director of our American Friends of Shalva ever since.

My children called us "the odd couple" because of our differences, but in fact, like me, Leo grew up nonreligious and became observant in college. We were both children of the sixties with shared interests in sports and music. While driving to appointments, Leo loved to flip on the radio to a classic rock station. "OK, Kalman, you must know this. Which group is it?" I would immediately identify one of the sixties bands. If I didn't recognize it, I would say that that song must be from after my cutoff date of June 1970, after which I didn't hear such music for the next decade. Occasionally Leo would challenge me and claim it was in fact a famous sixties classic, but I remained obstinate because for me it was a no-brainer. So he would call his music guru, yet another sixties guy who became religious but stayed with his music. "Sorry, Leo, but as usual, Kalman is right. That song came out in January 1971."

Leo rented space and hired an office manager. I breathed deep. I found myself spending more time in New York because he was now connecting me with good folks who, he claimed, wanted to hear the story from the horse's mouth. Up until then, on my trips to New York, I had stayed in Brooklyn with friends, but it no longer made sense for me to stay there and commute an hour by train, morning and evening. So I found a small, low-end hotel about a hundred yards from our office to stay at during the week and went elsewhere to stay with various friends on the Sabbath.

On one trip, Leo arranged a Shalva fund-raising event that took place on a beautiful summer night at the vacation home of Andrea and Harry Krakowski in the Hamptons. They asked me where I stay when I am in New York, and I named the hotel.

"Why on earth do you stay there? I can't believe this!" Andrea exclaimed. "Because the location and the price are just right," I replied. "Next time you come, you'll stay in our hotel," she said firmly, and then brushed aside my objection of, "I couldn't possibly accept your kind offer because I am here too often and for too long." "When are you here next?" "In September, for ten days." "Fine. You'll try our place."

"Where is it, if I may ask?" "Eighty-First and Columbus," she said, and with that, she began talking to another guest.

I stepped away and nervously called a friend to share that I am at an event with wonderful hosts who are inviting me to stay at their hotel for free, but it's halfway to New Jersey at Eighty-First Street and Columbus Avenue. He laughed and set me straight. "They call that the Upper West Side and it is a block from Central Park and she has just solved a problem. You no longer have to leave your hotel for the Sabbath because now you will have friends in the area who would be happy to host you for the Sabbath meals, and you will be within walking distance of your hotel." September saw the beginning of my having a home away from home during my many extended stays in New York, and this stability greatly contributed to my health.

Leo introduced me to wonderful people and new communities. Toward the end of a Shalva fund-raiser in a beautiful Long Island home, a guest approached me. "Rabbi, I'm told you're a single-digit golfer and quite frankly, I don't believe a word of it!" "Whoever told you that is seriously out of date," I replied. "As an eighteen-year-old kid in Vancouver, my handicap was single-digit, but I left Vancouver in May 1970 and apart from a game with my Dad many years ago, I haven't touched a club since. The only handicaps I know these days are those of the children I try to care for."

He grinned. "Listen, Rabbi. Next time you're here, we're going to play eighteen holes. I want to see if you were ever a single-digit player." I told him that he would undoubtedly know very quickly. Back in Israel, I laughed the whole thing off – but he didn't. He pestered Leo time and again, "When is the rabbi coming to play eighteen holes with me?" Leo felt it was important that I play with him and urged me to find a way to get my game back in shape.

I made some calls and discovered that Israel has one and a half golf courses: a full eighteen-hole course in Caesarea, an eighty-minute drive from home, and a nine-hole course at Ga'ash, north of Herzliya, about sixty minutes away. Ga'ash also had a driving range, which was all I needed. I was there on Friday morning, clad as always in a white shirt and black slacks, drawing some stares. It didn't take me long to realize that what was in my head was no longer in my hands or body. It was frustrating and I needed help. At the pro shop I found Basil, a man in his sixties who wore a large, broad-brimmed sun hat and had a strong South African accent, who told me he had run a pro shop in South Africa before coming to Israel. Great, I thought, the guy isn't even a pro. He's a pro-shop manager. But with no other choice, I booked a lesson for the following Friday morning.

Basil turned out to be an excellent teacher and we became good friends. My game was erratic at first, but he helped me develop a feel for it and regain a rhythm. Over the next five Friday mornings, I became more consistent and more confident.

On one occasion, I arrived home with my clothing covered with sand. Sarah, then a young child, greeted me with a shocked "Daddy, what happened?" I didn't quite know how to explain to her that I'd spent my morning hitting hundreds of wedge shots out of a sand trap.

Back in Long Island, I met my new buddy at the Coldstream Golf Club with Leo on hand. I found it exhilarating and surprisingly I shot in the eighties. "You know Kalman," Leo pondered, "I thought I knew you by now, but here I see the real you, the little boy who feels so natural and happy on the golf course." "When you begin to play at six years of age," I replied, "that little boy stays with you."

My daughter Nechama also noted the phenomenon of the little boy within me. She had just seen the movie *Forrest Gump* and urged me to see it. "Nechama," I said, "you know that I don't have time to see movies, so why don't you just tell me about it."

"I can't," she replied. "You must see it." "Why must I see it?" I probed. "Because you *are* Forrest Gump."

Sometime later, I was on a flight to Belgium when out of the corner of my eye, I noticed the words "Forrest Gump" scrolling down my neighbor's little monitor. I breathed deep, opened mine, and began watching. The main character, Forrest Gump, brilliantly played by Tom Hanks, is mocked by peers for his physical disability and his simple-minded intelligence and faces numerous challenges growing up, yet experiences an extraordinary and full life.

I laughed and cried so hard that the poor fellow sitting next to me didn't know what my problem was. In the character of Forrest Gump I saw my beloved Yossi who has so much to give and has surpassed all expectations, yet in spite of all of his and our efforts, his limitations are just enough to keep him from living a typical life.

When I returned, I sat Nechama down and shared, "OK, I understand that Yossi is somewhat Forrest Gump because their lives have many similar, unique elements. But I don't understand why you think that I am Forrest Gump."

"Oh Daddy," she said. "You missed an important line at the beginning of the movie. When bullies were pursuing Forrest to attack him, Jenny screamed, 'Run, Forrest, run!' From that moment he never stopped running, and that running becomes key to his life experiences. Mommy had her dream and told you, 'Run, Kalman, run!' and you've never stopped and it has colored your life and all of ours." I couldn't argue.

When I later shared this with Leo in New York, he commented, "Your daughter is right. You *are* Forrest Gump, and not only because of the running, but because of the floating feather that opens and closes the movie. Like that feather, you drift where the currents take you. You're all over the place like a child, Kalman. You take whatever comes your way and try somehow to make something out of it, and that is how your life experiences have played out in the extraordinary way that they have."

Chapter 35

Pushing Forward, Expanding the Network

Over the years, Malki was involved successfully with management as well as with architecture and interior design. I was puzzled as to where it all came from. "Malki, I married you when you were eighteen, just out of high school, with no training in these fields. In less than seven years you had six kids with Yossi as number two, so how do you do it?" "Kalman," she responded, I don't have special talent; I simply feel like a conduit for the Shalva children to help them realize the wonderful world that they deserve to live in."

My initial knee-jerk response to Malki's vision of what would become Shalva had been, "I'm just not the guy who can make this happen!" With the twenty-twenty vision of hindsight, however, I realized that much of what I'd learned and lived through had helped equip me for the task.

Raising Yossi was, of course, the seminal experience that had imparted the understanding and motivation that continue to fuel me. But my life – from its nonreligious beginnings, through my participation in individual and team sports, student activism, and weekend jobs, and on through my years of intensive Talmud study and computer-skills training and work – had seemingly all been part of an unconventional preparation.

My experiences as president of the eighth-grade student council and later as vice president of the largest high school in the province in my senior year were a crash course in organization and leadership skills. The shoe store job was humbling and taught me about salesmanship and hard work. Sports, my passion since childhood, contributed valuable life lessons, teaching me how to win but also that sometimes losing is inevitable, despite one's best efforts. Playing sports also taught me discipline and the importance of patience when striving toward goals, and that when working with others, it is about the team, not the individual. The years of rigorous Talmud study and structured logical reasoning gave a grounding that helped me greatly, as did the addition of Hebrew and Yiddish language to my native English and hesitant French. My computer skills made it possible for me to create a viable database for Shalva, built at home over the course of many late nights, in which we tracked everything relating to our participants and donors. That initial database was the basis for later, more sophisticated systems that were developed in collaboration with professionals.

My mom often said, "Variety is the spice of life"; indeed, I deeply enjoy meeting and working with good people from all over the world who hold different beliefs and values but come together to help the Shalva children.

The separation of responsibilities between Malki and me came to us naturally. She worked closely, behind the scenes, with Shalva's children and families, overseeing its programs and its staff. I became the front man, the public face of Shalva, and was responsible for securing continued funding. Malki's nonpublic role was so near complete that a donor who had visited Shalva several times but had not yet met Malki commented, "Kalman, as you know, you may not be the brightest light, but if you ever had a stroke of genius, it was inventing your story about having a wife!"

From the outset there were naturally steep learning curves for me. In Shalva's early days, I felt comfortable sharing the Shalva story, but in spite of appearances, I found it challenging to ask acquaintances and strangers for money. It was even uncomfortable to phone for an appointment, which was always my first step. I was often rebuffed, but on the whole my perseverance payed off and I met many extraordinary people, some of whom even thanked me for providing them with the opportunity to help.

Advice came cheap. Early on, I was told by a communally involved gentleman that I was wasting my time and efforts. "Kalman, you have a problem. Here you are, running around trying to meet people individually to get them to donate to what is basically an unknown cause, while the Israeli hospital that I am involved with has a large development staff here in New York that creates big events that can reach many people at once, and has sufficient name recognition to allow it to raise significant funds."

Without missing a beat, I replied, "I have a problem? They have a problem. They are largely in their offices while I am hitting the pavement meeting good people and carefully crafting my team, one by one. It is only a matter of time." Many years later, as a Shalva board member and significant donor, he reminded me of our conversation.

I learned a great deal about different philanthropic philosophies. There are those, I discovered, that focus on programs that give direct and immediate benefits. Others prefer capital projects – buildings that stand the test of time. Early on, I received an unsought lesson from a man who ran a large corporation and was known as a significant philanthropist. He was a genuine and nice person who greeted me cordially, extended me every courtesy, and listened patiently to what I had to say.

"I am taken with you and want to help, so I'm going to write you a check for $5,000," he said, "but I won't be contributing this amount again, and I'm going to tell you why. My family has run a successful business for many years and we apply the same philosophy to our philanthropy as we do to our business. We look for the best return for the smallest investment – least in for most out, and sadly, your children are the reverse – most in for the least out."

I was taken aback but regained my composure and responded, "I appreciate that there are many philosophies in charity. May I ask where you do contribute? Where do you get the most out for the least in?" "Money for scholarships to medical schools" was his immediate answer. "We invest in creating doctors who then return to the community over the next forty years."

"It's true that the Shalva children probably won't become your doctors," I clarified, "but with Shalva's support, their parents and siblings certainly can. Our program enables each family member to reach their fullest potential." My new acquaintance smiled and thanked me for the insight, but it didn't make a dent in his thinking.

Without mentioning his name, I shared this conversation with an elderly friend, a passionate and successful businessman. He blurted out a series of expletives, which was very unlike him. "Why are you so upset?" I asked. "It's his money. He can do what he likes with it." He wasn't mollified, so I continued, "My impression is that he's a sincere and good human being and extremely generous. He simply has a different view from ours of children with disabilities." He wasn't buying it and responded, "The utilitarian view of life where one is measured by one's value to society is a slippery slope. It begins with children with disabilities and moves on to elderly parents with Alzheimer's whose care is expensive and who are no longer able to make contributions to society. These were the views of those I fought against in World War II."

* * *

From time to time, I also met people who provided guidance in unexpected ways. One was Hillel Weinberger, a senior assistant to a major American philanthropist. He and his wife Elaine were friends of Esther Wachsman, and it was Esther who introduced us.

We met on the last afternoon of one of my early fund-raising trips to New York. It was a stormy day, with thunder growling, lightning flashing, and rain pelting, and I was thoroughly soaked by the time I got to Hillel's office at Loews Corporation. Our meeting began on time at 3:00 p.m., which gave me exactly an hour until I'd need to leave and race to Brooklyn via subway to get my luggage and then rush to the airport for my flight home. My first sight of Hillel was his back. He sat facing three large computer screens, each displaying data that I assume concerned stock market trading. And that was how he remained through most of our meeting – pleasant, chatty, but with his back toward me.

After the getting-to-know-you pleasantries and before I could tell him about Shalva, he began talking at length about an organization in which he was clearly very active. "We are helping women who are pressured to abort their babies for financial reasons," he told me. "Often it is just the financial pressure that causes women to terminate their pregnancies, and if we provide them with some money and psychological help they are able to see it through." "So, you are buying babies?" I said. "Not at all," he replied. "We are leveling the playing field at a difficult moment, and once the baby is born, these mothers are ecstatic." He expanded and expounded as the clock ticked on. By the time I was outside, running through the downpour to the subway, I'd gotten in only the briefest mention of Shalva. All the way back to Brooklyn and all the way out to the airport, and even on the plane, I kept thinking: What's with this guy? I came to see him about Shalva, and all he could talk about was his project.

Malki met me at Ben Gurion Airport. With hardly a hello, she exclaimed, "Kalman! You must save Sonya's baby!" Sonya was a recent immigrant to Israel from Russia who came on Tuesdays to help around the house. Beyond that, I had no idea what Malki was talking about. She clued me in on the way home. "Sonya told me she is not coming next Tuesday because she is having an abortion. I asked her what the problem is and she said, 'There is no problem, but we have two children already, my husband's mother lives with us, and there's no room or money for another baby. My husband will shoot me with his Kalashnikov if I don't get rid of it. I know that to you this sounds strange, but for me, this is just the way we did birth control in Russia.'" Malki continued, "I begged Sonya to postpone the procedure for one week because you are coming home and you'll speak to her. She's almost three months along and next Tuesday is the last date she can do this, so you must deal with things at once!"

I solemnly said to Malki, "Don't worry. This is one baby that will not be aborted," and told her about the strange meeting I had just had with Hillel Weinberger. The reason for that meeting and its message was now clear.

Upon arriving home, I called Sonya. "Kalman, it's not me who doesn't want this baby," she said. "It's Boris, and he will become upset and won't listen to you." We knew Boris. A Russian immigrant like Sonya, he delivered groceries for a local vender. Wary about his storied Kalashnikov, I decided to tackle him on his delivery route. Settled into the passenger seat of his van, I cautiously broached the subject. He abruptly pulled the van to the curb, put it in park, and turned to me.

"Now listen very carefully," he growled in his thick Russian-accented Hebrew. "I know you talked to Sonya about keeping the baby, but that won't happen. I live with my mother and can't do it." Gently, I turned to him and said, "Boris, I understand that you are pressured and you can't afford the baby at this time, but that isn't a reason to end a life, your child's life. I am giving you $5,000 to help out." At that, his eyes filled with tears. "In Russia, I was a successful engineer," he said. "Now we're in Israel, and because of the language barrier, I'm a deliveryman. What are you trying to do to me? It's not about money. It's about not being able to cope with another child. I don't want your money."

Clearly, I'd read things wrong, but I wasn't ready to give up. I couldn't believe that my frustrating meeting with Hillel had been random. Boris and I continued talking, and our conversation became calmer. We talked about where he lived, and he mentioned that he was proud that he owned a small apartment rather than renting. "Do you have a mortgage?" I asked him. "A mortgage?" he exclaimed. "I have three!"

"How big are your mortgages and how much do you pay monthly?" I queried. It was now a friendly conversation. Hesitantly and with a quiet sigh, Boris shared the amounts. "I'm taking over your mortgages," I said. "We'll go to a lawyer, right now, to draw up a contract." Boris broke down and wept. "A lawyer, with you? You must be joking. Do you really think I don't want this baby? But there is no choice." "Boris," I said taking his hand in mine, "there is now. Come with me to your bank and I will assume responsibility for your mortgages." It was genuinely difficult for him, but after an extended silence, we went.

Six months later, Sonya gave birth to a beautiful little boy. His *brit* (circumcision) was surely the most joyous I've ever attended, and the happiest among the many guests was Boris. When I next met Hillel in person, I shared with him what he had taught me and what had transpired and told him, "This baby is yours."

New Shalva friends were coming on board at every stage. Hillel introduced me to his boss, Jim Tisch, president and chief executive officer of the Loews Corporation, and he and his wife, Merryl, became dear friends. Jim suggested I come to a United Jewish Appeal dinner he was chairing, where Charles and Edgar Bronfman were to be honored and where then First Lady Hillary Clinton was to speak. "Why don't you come and see what a real New York charitable dinner looks like?" he said.

It was impressive. I turned up in my usual dark suit, white shirt, and tie to find everyone else dressed in formal evening wear, the men in tuxes. The guests milled about, cocktails in hand. Jim came out of a side door and spotted me. "So what do you think?" he asked. "Well, there's good news and bad," I answered. "Give me the bad news first." "There are hundreds of seemingly significant people here, and I don't know any of them." "And the good?" "There's a lot of potential!" And indeed, there was. Over the years I made new friends who introduced me to their friends. Eventually, I got up the guts to ask Jim and Merryl to host a reception for Shalva at their home, and they not only readily agreed, but made it into a prestigious annual event.

On one of my other early trips to New York, it was my final night of a two-week visit and it was pouring. Tommy Rosenthal, my acquaintance who had set up the immensely helpful parlor evening on one of my first fund-raising trips to New York several years back, told me that he would set up some meetings in his neighborhood and that I should be at his house at 8:00 p.m. I arrived and Tommy kindly asked me if I would like some coffee and cake. "Tommy," I said, "it's getting late. Who is our first appointment with?" "Oh I haven't yet made any appointments, but let me call a friend, Mordechai Hager." I was crestfallen, but fifteen minutes later we walked over to Mordechai's house.

Mordechai listened intently to what I had to say about the then four-year-old Shalva, and while watching my short video on the large screen in his den, he called loudly to his wife, "Lois, come here!" "I can't; I am busy," she yelled from upstairs. "Lois, come now. I want you to see this." Lois watched while standing at the den doorway, then joined us at the dining room table while Mordechai wrote a generous check for Shalva. I thanked him profusely, and he added, "I'm going to give you more than this check," he said. "I'm going to give you my wife as well."

I was shocked but noticed Lois smiling, clearly used to his humor. "Put him on the map, honey," he said to her. "What do you want me to do?" she asked. "Another dinner?" "Lois, this guy's for real," he said firmly. "I want you to help him." "OK," she said. "Give me time to think how."

A week later, back in Jerusalem, my fax sprang to life at 1:00 a.m., waking both Malki and me. We watched it churn out forty-two pages. In fifteen to twenty words per page in heavy black marker, Lois laid out her detailed action-plan to put Shalva on the map. In disbelief, Malki asked, "Who is this woman? She should be managing General Motors or the Israeli army." The plan was to hold a New York dinner in four months' time. Lois had been in touch with a close friend, who via his corporate connections was able to get the prestigious Jewish Museum on Fifth Avenue to waive their exorbitant rental fee and host the evening at no cost.

The venue could not have been better. A hugely popular Chagall exhibition was then on display, with the daily lines of people eager to see it stretching around the block. Lois offered a tour of the exhibit as part of our program. The evening began with a buffet eaten at small intimate tables with no fixed seating, which allowed people to mill around and mingle. Its Shalva content ran fifteen minutes, including a video, after which the exhibition could be viewed. This evening set the format for all of Shalva's future annual New York dinners – a buffet with short programs in an interesting setting – a format which later became standard for many other organizations' fund-raising events. Shalva was indeed now on the New York map.

At that dinner, I was introduced to Leon Wagner. "Leon Wagner?" I mused. "Your name rings a bell." "From where?" he asked. "Well, if I have to dig deep, I would say it is somewhere from my childhood interest in baseball or football." "You're right on," Leon conceded. "There was a professional baseball player of the same name, and he played for the Cleveland Indians." "Correct," I continued, "and he began his career with the San Francisco Giants. He was a big, black, burly left-hander with a 270 lifetime batting average. I had his baseball card." Leon was shocked. "That's incredible, and I am yours. I am giving you $5,000 now and am going to get involved in this organization of yours." And indeed, he did.

It was at Leon's home that I first met Norm Alpert, who was, like me, a sports enthusiast and who warmed to me as we spoke about his beloved Boston Red Socks, Boston Celtics, and New England Patriots. With initial common ground established, he and his wife Jane listened intently to what I had to say about Shalva and became the best of friends. Ultimately, Norm assumed the role of president of the American Friends of Shalva.

Chapter 36

Stepping Up to the Professional Plate

An aspirin may alleviate a headache, but it will not suffice for a more serious malady, which requires in-depth diagnosis and treatment. To that end, Shalva developed a comprehensive programmatic response to the multifaceted challenges faced by the child and family, enabling them to enjoy greater quality of life.

In Shalva's early days, one professional pointed out that we were "spoiling the parents" by stretching the child's day until 6:00 p.m. five times a week and returning them fed and ready for bed. "I'm so glad that you have no idea what you are talking about," I replied, "for clearly you are not a parent of a child with disabilities. In relation to their challenges, nothing we can do will be too much. When these children arrive home at 6:30 p.m. their parents and siblings still have ample work on their hands, and our goal is make sure they can cope and have the highest possible quality of life."

The combination of extended days along with one overnight respite each week made all the difference, enabling each family not only to survive, but also to thrive.

Together with its fun carnivals and celebrations, enthusiasm and love, Shalva continued to focus on professional standards in all areas of care. Front and center were the therapies that help the children increase and improve their daily living skills. This allowed them to advance as far as they can possibly go and helped them reach their maximum level of independence so that they can lead normative lives with their families and integrate into the community.

Academic leadership and guidance came on board with the participation of leading professionals, including Professor Malka Margalit, the Israel Prize laureate in education whose research on Shalva's Me and My Mommy program was published in leading academic journals, as well as Professor Arie Rimmerman, an Israeli academic in disability policy research who is often referred to as "Mr. Disability." Arie has often been an advisor on the topic of disability policy to senior government officials and committees; he is a foremost international expert on social inclusion and has published several books on the subject.

Shalva also developed a professional relationship with the Hebrew University–Hadassah Medical Center in Jerusalem and held annual joint academic conferences on World Down Syndrome Day, March 21. This date, 3/21, was designated since persons with Downs have three of the twenty-first chromosome rather than the normative two. The conferences regularly drew hundreds of medical and paramedical practitioners, social workers and psychologists, local and national legislators, educators, students, parents, and many others with roles in treating those with Down syndrome. The MC was often Efrat or Raphael, well-spoken young adults with a great sense of humor who have Down syndrome.

They spent years attending Shalva and went on to be employed in its programs, Efrat in the preschool and Raphael in the café.

Occasionally our relationship with Hadassah brought colorful characters to our door. Gerry Casey was a captain with the UN Peacekeeping Division's Irish contingent and visited Israel on a pilot trip ahead of his one-year posting here. Looking for a suitable framework for the youngest of his four children, sixteen-month-old Rachel, who was born with Down syndrome and a serious heart defect, he arrived at Hadassah Hospital only to be told, "You must go to Shalva. They will help you."

Gerry made the call and a couple of weeks later, baby Rachel and mother Theresa began in the Me and My Mommy program. On their first day, Gerry created quite a stir as he drove through the quiet residential street behind the wheel of his massive UN Hummer jeep clad in camouflage fatigues, high-laced leather boots, and green UN beret.

The Caseys immediately became part of the Shalva family. Theresa bonded quickly with the mothers, and Rachel began therapy – hydro, massage, physio, multisensory, and speech. Not only did she make sustained and visible progress, but Theresa and Gerry progressed too, and by the end of the year felt that they were better equipped to help Rachel.

They were part of Shalva's world during their year in Israel, and before they left, they took Shalva into theirs. Gerry invited tens of UN Truce Supervision Organization (UNTSO) representatives and diplomats – who managed to arrive from Lebanon, Syria, Egypt, and the Gaza Strip, requiring special travel documents to enter Israel – to a farewell buffet lunch. The Foreign Ministry told us that it wasn't happening, but it did, and they came. At the lunch, Gerry and Theresa cried as they expressed their heartfelt gratitude for the productive year they had, which had laid the foundations for their and their child's future.

Chapter 37

Batting a Thousand

Over the years, I have come to terms with the injury to my son and the resulting challenges that our entire family has had to face as a result, and that has enabled me to cope calmly with unexpected confrontations.

On one of my fund-raising trips, I was scheduled to spend Shabbat with friends in a beautiful New York suburb, but upon arrival to their home on Friday afternoon my hosts shared that they had an emergency and were leaving immediately, and they had arranged for me to stay with the family of a young rabbi in the community. Among the many guests at the Friday-night meal was a middle-aged couple and their son, a strapping young man in his early twenties who clearly had developmental issues. I was seated opposite the three of them, and I saw the father striving throughout the evening to keep his son calm. The father and I talked easily. I tried to make conversation with the young man but realized quickly that it wasn't happening. They made no mention of their son, and their seeming discomfort with him made me uncomfortable, but I respected their obvious wish not to talk about him.

The next day, they were once again among the guests at lunch. After the meal, we moved into the living room for tea and cake. The young rabbi turned to the father and said, "Mike, I don't think I mentioned that Kalman also has a child with developmental issues. He was injured by a faulty batch of vaccine."

The mood changed in an instant. Mike went rigid, his head raised and his neck tensed, and I sensed I was facing a cobra. He glared at me and offensively barked, "You're full of it. No child has ever been injured by a vaccine."

There was dead silence and the rabbi's face paled, registering shock. I didn't flinch and wasn't perturbed. "Interesting you should say that, Mike," I replied. "I fought a nine-year legal battle against the Israeli government for compensation for my son, and in Israel there are no juries who can be swayed by emotional arguments, so it all came down to the professional decision of the judge. He was very skeptical at first, but thoroughly convinced by the end, and he forced the government into a compromise."

Mike came venomously back at me with "So your judiciary is full of it too!" Turning to his wife, he said, "Marj, we're outta here." And with Marj obediently on one side and his bemused son on the other, an enraged Mike abruptly opened the side entrance screen door and marched out into the misty summer day.

The rabbi was mortified. "I'm so very sorry. I had no idea..." he spluttered. "I've never seen him like this." I reassured him, "Don't worry about it. I understand that Mike is a pediatrician." The rabbi gaped at me. "How did you know that?" "I've seen this kind of reaction before," I told him, "though not to such an extreme."

At that moment, the screen door burst open again, and Mike reappeared. "Rabbi," he said to me, "my apologies. It's nothing personal you know." "Of course," I replied, "I understand." With that, he exited, apparently having fulfilled his wife's demand.

"Kalman," the rabbi said, "forgive me for asking, but could he be right?"

"No," I replied. "It's ludicrous to claim that no child has ever been injured by a vaccine. Vaccines are given in the millions, and like any other medical procedure large or small, there is a risk factor. When we drive a car, we are aware that it carries risk. We are aware that we can injure ourselves, our passengers, pedestrians, or other drivers, and that awareness influences our decision as to whether we drive or stay home. Similarly when we walk across a busy intersection, we know there is a risk, but given that this is an everyday activity we don't give it much thought. Similarly, with vaccinations, they are part of early life and most people don't give them much thought. They are not aware that babies will react to a vaccine in different ways and to different degrees. Pertussis, or whooping cough, has been a major cause of infant death worldwide, and immunization against it has drastically reduced its incidence and saved countless lives. That is an enormous gift and blessing. But as every neurologist and pediatrician knows, there will be a very small number of infants who have a severe neurological reaction."

"So why do we risk giving it to our children?" he asked.

"Because that's a price that public health authorities have judged worth paying," I continued. "The benefits of vaccines vastly outweigh their risks. The problem is that in a case like ours, over and above the tragedy of what happened to Yossi, some members of the medical establishment turned us from victims into aggressors. Our son was incurably injured by a government-mandated medical procedure, but when we asked questions of knowledgeable doctors, there were suddenly no responses, only accusations."

"After Yossi's tragedy, are you opposed to the pertussis vaccination?" he now asked.

"The batch of vaccine that injured Yossi was faulty," I replied, "and resulted in a far higher than usual incidence of irreversible neurological reactions, and we cannot make judgments based on an exception."

The rabbi was still troubled. "So why do you think that Mike, whom I know to be a generally reasonable person, would have reacted as he did?"

"A vaccine differs from other medication in that it's designed to protect the entire community," I explained. "If I don't take an aspirin for my headache, that doesn't impact anyone except me. But if I refuse a vaccine, I am said to be endangering the herd. I think the problem here is one of balancing two extreme opinions: the view that vaccines should be avoided at all costs, and the view of our friend Mike that vaccines are entirely benign."

I continued, "Let me share a funny anecdote from a financial advisor for significant clients. A few years back, client after client approached him asking, and in several instances outright complaining, about why he wasn't investing their money via an unusually successful financier named Bernie Madoff. 'Why aren't you using Bernie?' they demanded. 'Everyone else is, and he's making a killing for them!'

"My friend explained why. He said he had met with Madoff, and in the course of conversation Madoff mentioned that he had never lost on a stock. My friend tried to clarify, asking Madoff, 'You mean you've never had a losing year?' 'No,' said Madoff, 'I mean I've never lost on a stock.' 'Kalman,' my friend said to me, 'this would be statistically similar to an all-star baseball player claiming to have a lifetime batting average of a thousand when we all know that that is impossible and a .333 average will get him into the Hall of Fame.'

"Rabbi," I said, "on this particular issue, your friend Mike and others like him simply have the Madoff mind-set. Madoff's claims turned out to be a hoax and so are theirs. No one can bat a thousand."

"OK, Kalman, I am sorry to have tormented you but I am sure you can understand how important this subject is to me as a father of young children," my host said.

"Of course I appreciate that," I replied, and with a pained smile, concluded, "Isn't it nice that the two of us can have a civil discussion on the subject?"

Chapter 38

Bombs and Bombshells

Shalva–Beit Nachshon had become an enterprise of hundreds of children and families, staff and volunteers, with a substantial annual operating budget. After more than a decade, our lives were finally settling down. I had turned fifty and we were enjoying our late-in-life daughter Sarah who ruled the roost, we were embracing children-in-law, and we were discovering the great joy of grandparenthood. Yossi and the life he lived were sources of pride. I'd left the Binational Science Foundation and could focus my energies exclusively on Shalva. My two sons Yochanan and Avi were now fully on board and leading Shalva, Yochanan from the world of law and Avi from the world of business. The realization of Malki's pact and of our shared dream was so deeply meaningful for us.

Events, however, were already in motion to disrupt this brief calm. A young man named Menachem Moskowitz was about to burst into our lives. The very fact that he was alive to do so was a miracle.

Just before 2:00 p.m. on a hot August afternoon in 2001, eight months before we met him, he was walking in a crosswalk at the busy Jaffa Road and King George Street intersection in downtown Jerusalem in front of the popular Sbarro Pizza eatery. That was the moment a suicide bomber walked in and detonated twenty-two pounds of explosives laced with nails, nuts, and bolts. In seconds, Sbarro Pizza was a charred and smoking shambles, and the street around it was covered with the bodies of the injured, dying, and dead. Fifteen people lost their lives that summer afternoon – one of them pregnant, and seven of them children; 130 more were grievously wounded.

Menachem was among those 130. The watch he'd bought himself for his twenty-fourth birthday days earlier ticked on undamaged, but its metal bracelet had been blasted through his flesh into his bone. That arm and his head had taken the main impact, and he lay unmoving, unconscious, covered in blood, and slated for a body bag.

Menachem had been a volunteer medic. A fellow volunteer medic paused, bent down, and recognized the torn body as Menachem's. Instinctively, he intensively tried to resuscitate him but with no success. Over and over again he breathed into Menachem and suddenly there was a faint response. An ambulance was on the spot and Menachem was hurriedly redirected from the mortuary to the emergency room of Hadassah Hospital. Against all odds, Menachem survived. Shrapnel and bolts scattered throughout his body, but he still had the greatest gift of all – life.

When Menachem walked past Sbarro that afternoon, he had never heard of Shalva. The connection came several months later, while dating Yael, his future wife, who was a secretary at Shalva.

We first met Menachem with Yael at Shalva's Independence Day party. He was not anxious to come, for he thought he had seen it all in the nonprofit world and wouldn't be witnessing anything new. He had volunteered with an ambulance team, with a disaster relief organization, and with a nonprofit that created happy events for kids with severe illness. He had indeed seen a lot.

Shalva blew Menachem away. "I've never seen anything like this!" he exclaimed. "And I've been involved in volunteer work for years! How is it that I've never heard of you?" I gave him what he later described as a "typically Kalman" answer. "You haven't heard of us because our resources go into taking care of the kids, not into promoting ourselves," I told him. And he came right back with a "typically Menachem" response. "Fair enough," he said, "but I'm going to see to it that many more people know about Shalva!"

From that first meeting, Menachem took Shalva to heart. When he came to see Yael, he routinely dropped in on me unannounced. "You're desperately overcrowded here," he once noted. He was right. Beit Nachshon, so spacious when we'd moved in several years earlier, was already full to capacity with a long waiting list to get into our programs. "We know," I told him, "but there is nothing we can do at this time."

"Why don't you build another, bigger building?" he queried. "Because I am not prepared to build, thank you," I said, "and besides, the city is not exactly giving away land." I'd lived in Israel for thirty years by then, but had grown up in orderly Canada, and in some ways my head was still there. Menachem simply laughed at me. "Kalman," he said, "this is the Middle East! Being told there's no land doesn't mean there's no land. It's just the opening gambit in the battle to get it! There are children who don't have Shalva because there's no room for them here. If I bring you land, will you build?"

I looked at Menachem wondering if he was really serious. I knew that a twenty-something-year-old didn't have that kind of pull, even if he had the passion. The memory of my experience with city hall years earlier, when they had offered a subterranean bomb shelter for Shalva's home, still irked me. I was getting impatient and told Menachem, "OK, here's the deal. If you bring me such an enormous parcel in the heart of the city that I will have to view it as heaven-sent, then we'll have to build." As he jubilantly headed for the door, I added, "Not so fast. I am sincerely not interested in this. And before you begin to waste your time trying, you should speak to Malki."

Menachem found her and had a similar conversation, and received a similar response: Unless Menachem came up with a piece of land that was so *meshuga*, so crazy, that Malki recognized it as a G-d-given challenge, she would not consider getting involved.

Menachem was off and running. His first discovery was that the city's Land Allocations Committee hadn't met for several years because of a court restraint on the municipality. Undeterred, he made the acquaintance of a city executive who was familiar with these matters and inquired about available land for public buildings. Today, Jerusalem's zoning maps are computerized and a couple of clicks bring them up in glorious color on a PC, iPad, or smartphone. But then, they were still stored as large paper maps in an archive located in a neglected sub-basement of the Jerusalem City Hall. Menachem obtained entry to this restricted area in his own inimitable way, and spent years of after-work hours pulling giant colored maps off the shelves, unrolling them, weighting them down, and carefully scrutinizing them for an available land parcel that fit all the criteria. His Herculean search was eventually rewarded.

"I've found it," he announced with undisguised satisfaction. "It's seven acres, it's in the middle of the city, zoned for everything Shalva does – and the view is amazing! Jerusalem is at your feet!"

That was in late 2004 and our opening shot was fired almost at once. The court gave permission to the City's Land Allocations Committee to resume allocations after its lengthy hiatus and our application was one of the first to come before it. The approval process was no longer allowed to be only political but was divided into two processes. An allocation request had to first come before a five-person committee of senior professionals and only after their recommendation could it come before the political city council. The committee of professionals examined both the request and Shalva operations in great detail and approved it unanimously. They then made the required public announcement of their intention to allocate the requested site to Shalva, allowing forty-five days for objections. A counterclaim was filed almost immediately – to Menachem's intense chagrin. "I'd spent years of my life in dusty airless archives searching for that land," he says, "and out of left field comes someone who seriously wants us to believe that he's known about it all along, and was about to put in his own application!" Aggravating as it was, the professional committee ruling came unanimously in our favor.

On September 29, 2005, I noted in my diary:

It's almost midnight and I'm completely exhausted, but if not now when? I must jot down a few things that are truly amazing. Menachem Moskowitz delivered on his messianic promise to secure a big piece of land in the heart of Jerusalem for Shalva, and against all odds, the professional committee of the city rendered a 5 to 0 verdict in our favor for a plot near Shaare Zedek Hospital, without conditions. This is an open miracle, given that we have no political clout, and it obligates us to build. We now await the approval of the politicians in the city council.

On November 24, 2005, the thirty-one-member Jerusalem City Council came together and, in an unprecedented manner, unanimously voted to award Shalva the largest remaining land parcel in Jerusalem designated for nonprofit use. It was a resounding vote of confidence; nothing could say more clearly that the city recognized

Shalva's role in helping children with mental and physical disabilities and its extraordinary efforts to leave no child behind.

We knew that we wanted a first-rate architect, capable of building Shalva as a world-class center, and we began to interview several firms. Each came with its vision for the project, and this made me uncomfortable. I sensed that there was a lot of rightfully deserved ego in play and that these firms would not work well with Malki, who had very clear ideas of what was needed.

"My phone rang one day," recalled Randy Epstein of the award-winning architectural firm of Kolker Kolker Epstein. "A man introduced himself and said he was calling from Shalva and was looking for an architect. I said, 'Shalva? Who are you guys?'"

Before meeting us, Randy did his homework. "I asked several people about Shalva, including the Hebrew University's dean of social work," he said. "There was a consensus: 'They're the best in terms of giving a framework for the development of children with disabilities,' I was told. Then I remembered that I had, after all, heard of them. My son Eran, commander of the elite Golani unit in which Nachshon Wachsman had served, had represented the army at the ceremony marking the tenth anniversary of Nachshon's death that was held at Shalva–Beit Nachshon two years earlier. I recalled Eran's excitement in describing the beauty and warmth of that building."

Randy, three years my senior, is New York–born, and educated at the illustrious all-scholarship school of architecture Cooper Union. He had been living in Israel for thirty years when we met. His impressive portfolio included Israel's new Foreign Ministry building, which had won the Royal Institute of Architects of Canada Prize for Design Excellence five years earlier and was lauded as a "sophisticated essay in the play between solid and void, mass and volume, and light and shadow."

"What do you know about children with disabilities?" we asked him. "Nothing," he replied, "but I'm a good student. If I am selected as the architect, I will spend two months at Shalva, observing and studying every detail of the programs and operations. My professor taught us that a good design is like a hand. The hand is not overly aesthetic, but is far more functional than meets the eye. Each finger operates both independently and together with the others, making the hand extraordinarily efficient. I will design a beautiful edifice but my key focus will be to make sure that it is fully functional."

I was relieved to hear his attitude and said, "I don't know if you are sincere or just presenting a good sales pitch, but I am impressed." There was immediate chemistry with Malki as she sensed Randy's positive tone and humility, and we all felt comfortable. She made her intentions perfectly clear, telling him, "We're building a home, not an institution, and if you think you are building an institution, please don't take this job. As large as the building may be, it must be intimate." Randy smiled and replied, "That is precisely what I intend to design."

We felt that we had the right land and the right architect, and it was time to move forward. But without money, how?

Chapter 39
Paying the Bill

Back in 1992, Malki and I had given ourselves three months to either cover Shalva's $40,000 debt or close the organization down. Now I found myself in need of many millions of dollars to build Shalva a new home.

The day Menachem had called with news that the Jerusalem City Council approved the gift of land to Shalva, I was excited but felt overwhelmed and helpless, not knowing where to turn. How was I going to move this forward without a penny? Instinctively, I emailed six close friends who had been there for Shalva in the past, and I shared my feelings. One response that I received was not anticipated.

It was early evening in Israel and I was helping my friend Danny Siegel, a giant in the field of Jewish education and mitzvot (good deeds), sort clothing he had brought with him from Washington to distribute to needy families. My cell phone rang. A very formal voice said, "Mr. Kalman Samuels?" "Yes," I confirmed. "Mr. Roland Arnall would like to speak to you."

Born in France in 1939 and hidden during the Holocaust, Roland was six years old when the war ended. From new, humble beginnings in Los Angeles after the war, he ultimately became a most successful businessman and later a diplomat, serving as the US ambassador to the Netherlands. Among his many communal activities was his position as cofounder of the Simon Wiesenthal Center in Los Angeles, which was how he met a fellow board member, Gordon Diamond. And it was via Gordon that I had met Roland and his wife Dawn two years earlier when they were in Jerusalem together.

Gordon had called me then, saying, "Hello, Kalman! I'm here in Jerusalem with Leslie, pressed for time as usual, and I'd like you to show Shalva, my project in Israel, to two good friends of mine. Please be there with Malki in thirty minutes." The two good friends were Roland and Dawn. Clearly moved by the center and by meeting Yossi, upon their return to the States they sent a generous donation. I called their corporate office to get Dawn's email and sent her a heartfelt thank you. Dawn responded, and our email exchanges continued and grew into a friendship. Roland and Dawn came to know Shalva well. They knew its needs were real and recognized that it needed to grow.

So that evening, when the call came, I stepped out on the porch and waited several long minutes until Roland came on the line.

"Kalman!" he said. "Dawn and I are so proud you got the land. We know Shalva is the real deal, and we want to help. How much is this building going to cost?" "I don't know yet," I told him, "because we have only just submitted an architect's preliminary set of plans to the municipality." "Yes, I understand that, but give me some idea of how much it will cost." Again, I hesitated. "The proposal is still raw; I am not yet sure." Clearly irritated, Roland repeated tersely, "How much, Kalman?"

After years of playing catcher, it suddenly hit me, "three strikes and you're out!" and I was about to strike out. Hesitantly and uncomfortably, I finally stammered, "I am told it will cost $18 million." "Good," Roland continued without missing a beat, "Dawn and I will give $1.8 million and we will get a *minyan* (a group of ten) together. Do you know anyone capable of being in the *minyan*?" "Yes, I know a few, but I am not confident that they will give me that kind of money. I have never dealt in such figures." "OK," he continued. "We will get a few, you will get a few, and we will get the job done," and with that Roland bid me good night and hung up.

I had to sit down; I was in total shock. Did this really just happen? One million eight hundred thousand dollars? I rushed home and shared the news with Malki. We were awed.

Several days later, Dawn emailed me to say that they were scheduled to have dinner with a business associate in New York and she was hopeful that he would come on board and match them. I was incredulous. Following their meeting, Dawn emailed, "He is on board and we now have $3.6 million for the building; what's with Gordon and Leslie? Can you ask them to match us?" "Sure," I replied, "but I doubt they will respond to me in that manner." "So leave it to us," Dawn wrote. "We're friends of the Diamonds and will find the opportunity." Six weeks later, she emailed me that she and Roland had just visited with Leslie and Gordon and they too had agreed to join the *minyan*. Incredibly, we now had $5.4 million.

Once this solid financial foundation was laid, other Shalva friends began to come forward, with both funding and with ideas for the building. One such friend, John, was the chairman of a major corporation, a brilliant man who was avowedly secular. He always spoke his mind and our conversations tended to be challenging, but also stimulating.

On one of my New York fund-raising trips during this period, I came to his office with plans to share the news about the new center, hoping to get some vital support, but he was upset by another rabbi he had just seen appearing on a leading talk show. "The interview was ridiculous!" John griped. "Belief in G-d is so irrational," and looking at me, he repeated, "it is just irrational." I asked whether he was referring to belief in a specific religious doctrine, or the belief that the world has a creator. "Both!" he responded. "They are both irrational."

Keenly aware that this was a sensitive issue for John, I thought, should I or shouldn't I, but that didn't stop me. Placing my wristwatch on the table, I asked, "Do you believe this watch that keeps perfect time and has various functions that interact together had no design, that someone simply played around with the materials and this emerged?" I asked. "Anyone who believes that should go down the road," he answered, nodding in the direction of the Bellevue psychiatric hospital not far from his upscale Manhattan office.

I put my iPad on the table. "So a watch couldn't have just happened," I said. "What about an iPad, with its hardware and multileveled software? Did this just happen?" "They have a lotta rooms over there," John smiled back.

"So let me understand, when it comes to a watch or an iPad, it is rational to think that there was a designer. Why, then, do you think, when we discuss the infinitely more complex universe, suggesting that there is a designer is irrational?" To my great surprise, he paused and admitted, "I don't know."

"Well, perhaps this can explain it," I said. "The design of the watch and iPad have no personal relevance to us, but the idea that the universe has a designer suggests that it may also have purpose. And if it has purpose, perhaps we should try to understand what that purpose is." John was clearly becoming uncomfortable and I was not interested in pushing his buttons, so I cut it short and said that I hope I didn't upset him. "Oh, no," he assured me, "I found the conversation most interesting."

Conversations like these only strengthened our friendship and we truly enjoyed our visits. As I got ready to leave, he noticed on our brochure the logo of the ISO – the International

Organization for Standardization of Geneva – given for compliance with the highest standards of quality management.

"What is that?" he inquired. "That is the ISO," I began to explain. "I know that that is the ISO but you can't have it. I have it."

"You," I clarified, "have it for what your company does and we have it for what we do." I explained: "When we got land, I knew that our growing organization had to stand on solid foundations, so we brought in experts from the ISO to help us review and optimize all our activities and therapies to be the most effective and professional. Initially, our staff was not enthusiastic about this and it was a challenge to introduce new ways of doing things. But it was important for us all to work in the same way, and we gradually got used to it, and now it's become an indispensable part of our DNA."

"OK," John said decisively, "now that I know you have the ISO, I want to help you, and for that I must get further information. He proceeded to specify a dozen different financial documents he wanted to see. I didn't know what several of them were, but upon my return to Israel I worked with our CFO for a week, gathered the comprehensive information he wanted, and emailed it to him. Two months later I was back in New York and reached out to him to see if he wanted to meet, to which he replied, "Please come over."

"I've examined all of your documents," he told me. "John, you must be kidding; how did you have time to read all that?" I queried. "As you know, I'm a venture capitalist, and a significant part of what I do is to assess companies. I would be proud to have Shalva in my portfolio, and since that is not feasible, I am going to invest in your new center," and with that he made a significant commitment.

I was very moved, for while I had done my best to prepare the financial reports, I certainly didn't expect to get that kind of positive review. Our ISO status had been the clincher, but the differences in John's and my worldviews remained.

At the end of what I had felt was a positive meeting he surprised me, asking, "Why do I give you money? Why do I even like you? We live in different worlds." He paused, and then postulated, "I guess it's because you're doing G-d's work – if He exists." "I'm only able to do what I do because of your partnership," I responded. "So it looks as if we're both doing G-d's work – if He exists."

John smiled, so I took the liberty to share a related story told about the nineteenth-century hasidic leader known as the Kotzker Rebbe. "When the Rebbe was a five-year-old boy, he was approached by an older man who said, 'If you show me where G-d is, I'll give you a ruble.' The child's answer was instantaneous: 'And if you show me where He isn't, I'll give you two.'"

"Kalman," John said. "I know you identify with the boy, but I'm still with the old man."

Malki also had to occasionally cope with potential donors who asked tough questions. In our initial meeting with the director of a substantial charitable foundation that was showing interest in our new center, Randy spread the architectural plans across a table in the Shalva dining room and explained them in great detail. They were totally absorbed in the presentation until the director, who was around our age, suddenly turned to Malki and said, "Young lady, I can't agree with your design because you are wasting a lot of money on the four protruding verandas on each of the top three floors that create what you refer to as pavilions. It would be far less expensive without them."

My heart sank and I sensed it was over. Randy was silent and we had seemingly just lost what I knew was a great opportunity. Calmly, Malki rose and said, "May I trouble you to come with me for a moment?"

She led him to the far side of the dining room, where large windows offered a panoramic view of the valley and beyond.

"Can you see that large building in the distance?" "Yes." "Do you know what it is?" "No." "It's Hadassah Hospital. Have you ever been there?" "Yes." "Have you ever been a patient there?" "No." "Well, I've been hospitalized there twice. The first time, my bed was next to a window, and it was as pleasant as a hospital experience can be. But the second time, I was in an inner corridor with no natural light or air. It was miserable – and I will not build a dungeon for our children."

There was a tense pause, and then the potential donor said, "OK. You have convinced me. Thank you for clarifying."

I breathed a deep sigh of relief. The meeting continued and ultimately resulted in a significant grant.

Chapter 40

The Exorbitant Cost of Free Land

While the size and location of the land were ideal, its critical shortcoming lost little time in making itself known. Soil experts, sinking their exploratory shafts, made the unwelcome discovery that this enormous hill with its tree-lined surface and park was in fact once a ravine that had been filled with hundreds of tons of compacted rubble from the construction of the adjacent neighborhood many decades ago. It was unfit for foundations of any kind, they said.

We brought in engineers, and charged them with making the site safe to build on. Their expert opinion was that the fill must be completely cleared. But it wasn't as simple as that. Hollowing out the valley could destabilize the ground along its upper rim where several large buildings stood. The experts came back with a challenging engineering solution that demanded shoring up the valley's sides from the top down and building a retaining wall.

We got our excavation permit and began the Herculean task of slowly excavating the mountain and building the ninety-foot-high retaining wall. It worked – but it delayed the start of construction, added $7 million to its cost, and left one entire side of the future Shalva building without windows.

Malki cried herself to sleep at nights. "How did we get into this?" she lamented. "For the millions it's costing to make this 'free' site safe to build on, we could've bought any piece of land in the city!" "I'm sure we could have," I told her, "but on this land we can build something far larger and far better. At the end of the day, it'll be worth it, you'll see. In any case, we've no choice now but to move ahead." Her tears continued unabated.

As the detailed planning began, we saw that the preliminary proposal's estimated $18 million price tag for a sixty-thousand-square-foot design was history. The new plan for a vastly larger building would cost far more. And then the value of the dollar suddenly plunged – so while the budget in shekels remained unchanged, it shot up in dollars by more than $3 million. At the same time, there was a global increase in the price of building materials, due to the huge supply demand for construction for the Olympics in Beijing, and that translated into an additional $3 million-plus increase to the original budget. We were now looking at an outlay of at least $35 million.

While all this was going on, we had another setback. Out of the blue, the city called Randy. "There is a problem. The hotel above you has filed a request that the city build a new road going directly from the lower road up the steep slope to their hotel, and their plan is for the road to run through the middle of your site." We checked. There indeed had been such a request, but it was ridiculous because it would require a costly road that would have to be elevated as on stilts, and it was clear that no one would build it. It was the proprietors of the enormous old hotel above, who also owned the adjacent wedding hall and retirement home, who wanted the approach road through our site to replace the existing circuitous access road that snaked around it.

The hotel soon revealed itself as our implacable foe. We hired an excellent real estate lawyer named Uri Yamin to represent us, and the hotel owners hired three of the most prestigious legal teams in the country to block this gift of land to the Shalva children. It was David against Goliath. They sued the Jerusalem Municipality, the Ministry of the Interior, and Shalva, demanding that the gift of land not be allowed, claiming that the new center would create terrible traffic jams and present a security risk. We were forced to bring experts to court who asserted that in fact if there was a traffic problem, it was the hotel and the other nearby buildings that were the cause.

Some seven months later, the judgment came in our favor. We thought we were done, but soon there were other claims that took extended periods of time to bring to court and resolve. One after the other, their claims were thrown out of court and they were accused of simply not wanting the Shalva children in their vicinity – NIMBY, Not In My Back Yard – but somehow they always managed to enter yet another claim via the side door.

In August 2007, we celebrated the groundbreaking of the new center with great fanfare together with donors who flew in from many cities around the world. There were numerous public figures in attendance, and popular Democratic congressman and Holocaust survivor Tom Lantos joined us as the keynote speaker. There was a joyous, carnival-like atmosphere that day on the site, with over a thousand guests. Elderly residents of the retirement home – including some who could hardly walk or were in wheelchairs – were brought by the home's owner to picket with colorful signs, screaming that our center was going to destroy their quality of life. But thankfully, their protest did little to put a damper on the festivities.

Meanwhile, an extraordinary building was taking shape on Randy's drawing board with the help of our gifted landscape architect, Barbara Aaronson. Its entrance on the street level, opposite the hotel, would be a large welcoming lobby, flanked by the auditorium and other public rooms. Above street level, three stories would house the bedrooms, lounges, dining room, kitchen, independence-training, and life-skills areas. And below it, three more stories, terraced down the mountain, would accommodate the therapy rooms, sports complex, pool, and outdoor space, backing onto what would be six acres of public parkland, extending from Shalva to the ring road.

"It had a flow and a language of its own and I was proud of what we'd created," Randy shared. Malki, too, was delighted and loved working with an architect who understood what she needed and embraced her input. Reading blueprints as if she had years of training, Malki worked hand in hand with Randy, bringing to the table her eye for detail, her knack for design, and her unfailing instinct about what was right for Shalva's children. Every time she changed something in the design, she apologized for driving him crazy, and Randy would always respond with a smile, saying, "Malki, this is the process and don't worry because we are getting there." Still, there were some tense and challenging moments, as when Malki suddenly told Randy that she wanted to move the entire building some eighteen feet away from the retaining wall in order to have light and air on that side. Randy explained how much internal space would be lost across the length of the building, but Malki didn't care. She was not prepared to allow any part of the building to be a "dungeon." Randy, with his special smile, agreed and made it happen.

A similar discussion took place when Randy told Malki that her insistence on creating wide corridors would once again eliminate vital space across the length of the building. Malki reminded him that her biggest challenge was to make sure the center did not feel institutional, and for her, these were not corridors but living spaces that would provide a liberating feeling.

We hadn't yet raised all the necessary funds, but we were making progress. The plan was complete and we were thrilled with it. We submitted it to the city with an application for a building license – and that was when everything came crashing down.

Chapter 41

Back into the Legal Labyrinth

The hotel launched further lawsuits against the building, raising objection after objection, and creating delay after delay. Whatever challenges we might have anticipated facing in the planning and building process, we had certainly not anticipated that we would be spending our days in court and our nights agonizing over those days. We tried to meet the hotel owners and suggest a compromise to make it smaller, but it was made crystal clear that in spite of their talk, the only compromise they would actually agree to was no building at all. So we were back in the legal jungle – preparing for hearings, appeals, and more hearings, while construction approached a standstill.

It's hard to describe the pain and frustration of these years that we spent fighting to build. It put not only our new center at risk, but also the future of Shalva itself. We were asking our donors to fund a large state-of-the-art building, but year followed year in which we had no more to show them than the massive retaining wall and the completed foundations in an enormous dusty crater. Our credibility had never been in doubt, but now there was a legitimate concern as to whether we would be able to overcome the opposition. The thought that I had invested millions of dollars of charitable funds raised from the dearest of friends who had placed their confidence in me, when in the end, I might not be able to carry through with the plan, was crushing me. And the hotel's strategy was to drag out the process, so whether they won or lost in court, they would delay us long enough that I would lose my donors and they would win by default.

We couldn't understand why this was happening. All we wanted to do was to help more kids and families – and the need was only getting more urgent with every passing day.

We were dragged though fifteen different courts at various levels and there was no end in sight. Our detractors were influential, wealthy real estate owners whose family was connected politically for two generations, and they freely applied pressure on the municipality. But the city's chief architect, Yael Karma, was undeterred when she presented her report before the Regional Appeals Board, and stated, "This is a project of which we can be very proud, from both the social and architectural aspects. In my humble opinion, the aforesaid building complies with all the elements and characteristics of good and correct architecture for the character of the neighborhood, as well as for all the residents. It expresses an architectural language that distinguishes it from other buildings that surround it. The development of extensive public areas is an integral part of the project and it displays architectural excellence and planning sensitivity." In spite of their pressure, the hotel's opposition was not accepted.

Early in 2009, the case came before Judge Moshe Sobel, who sat as a one-man authority on the high court for zoning issues.

It was their last resort and our last hurdle. There was nowhere else to go.

Shalva, the municipality, and the hotel were in the courtroom. We sat nervously, ready for our lawyers to present their cases, and waited for the judge. He entered briskly, sat down, and began.

"Good morning to all. I have taken the time to study this case in great detail. It has gone on for far too long and I am going to put an end to it now. What I am about to share with you can either be accepted as a compromise now, in the next fifteen minutes, or you can spend some nine months fighting in my court, but my position will not change. There is a clear three-point resolution, and this is it.

"First, this building will go up with its full size as planned and approved by the municipality and courts." The hotel owners didn't hold back and began to scream that this is impossible and they can't agree.

The judge paid no attention and continued. "Second, to address the hotel's long-standing complaints about noise and traffic, which have in fact been rebutted in other courts, the planned entrance to the new center will be relocated from the road above, near the hotel, to the other side of the structure far below, toward its base."

Before we could jump to respond, the judge quickly stated, "And third, the city will allow Shalva to build a two-hundred-yard access road from the nearby street to this entrance through the public parkland."

We all went ballistic. The judge had carefully calibrated his decision, which would give Shalva its home while sparing the hotel and its guests the sight of youngsters with disabilities, but it pleased none of us. The hotel didn't want the building at all, and if it had to be, they wanted something far smaller. The city was incensed at "the dangerous precedent" of being compelled to build a road through public parkland. And we were being told to completely redesign a building we'd worked on for years, and which we felt was flawless to its smallest detail.

Randy leaped to his feet. "Your Honor, our building plans are approved. You are sending us back to the drawing board. These kids have the same rights as anyone else!" he stormed. "You're letting people into the hotel, the wedding hall, the retirement home, and the apartments through their front doors. It's only our children you're sending in through the building's *tuchas* (rear end)."

The judge snapped, "Mr. Epstein, that language will not be used in my court. Please leave immediately."

The municipality's lawyer followed. "Your Honor, every architect and builder wants access through public land of one kind or another and we refuse steadfastly. You are setting a precedent we cannot live with."

The judge repeated, "Gentlemen, you have fifteen minutes to decide if you will accept this compromise."

Everyone was stunned and huddled with their lawyers. We conferred with Uri. "I am sorry to tell you that there's little to discuss," he said curtly. "When the judge takes a position like this, there's nothing more to do. And in fact, you have just received what we have been fighting for, the full size of the building. I know that you cannot appreciate what has just transpired, so I will explain. This case has been dragged out far too long. I appreciate that this comes as a shock to you, and I do understand that it will take you considerable time to redesign the building and get the permits, but in the end your entrance will be far away from this hotel and I know that you will thank the judge."

We exited and discussed all the options heatedly, with different opinions expressed. They ran the gamut, from "we will not surrender" to "we have no choice but to accept." Within half an hour, all parties realized that the judge was resolute and that his decision would ultimately remain unchanged; and so, against our wills, we accepted the compromise.

For months following, Malki and Randy were virtually paralyzed. They were unable to think about the building design differently, and Malki in particular couldn't understand why the perfect place for Shalva's children had been disallowed.

"Entering on the first story instead of the fourth changed everything," said Randy. "It wasn't a matter of simply moving the entrance lobby down to the bottom and piling everything else on top of it. There has to be a relationship between Shalva's different areas and functions – say, the bedrooms and dining room, the entrance and the therapy rooms. Then there was the difficulty of the large spaces: they're usually put higher up in a building so they can be supported by the walls of the smaller rooms beneath. That would mean putting the auditorium on top – and it doesn't belong there. It's for visitors and should be close to the entrance." Moving the entrance invalidated the whole concept of the design. Everything would have to change.

None of us had the heart or the energy to start over. It was Dawn Arnall who looked at things with fresh eyes and turned around what had seemed like a disaster. "It's a wonderful decision!" she said. "Don't you see? Instead of being dropped off at the public roadside – a road which also serves a bunch of public buildings and private apartments – our kids will come into Shalva through its own road in a green park. And instead of Shalva being a building with parkland behind it, the park is now an integral part of the entrance, and Shalva's National Center will stand in its own campus!"

The six acres of green space allocated for parkland would become a park for those with and without disabilities, accessible to the public, and bringing many visitors. This was truly inclusion in action. The judge's decision to move the entrance and to direct the municipality to build a two-hundred-yard access road to Shalva suddenly created a new reality.

After almost half a year, Randy and Malki were finally able to edge themselves back into planning the new design. The municipality named the new road Shalva Way, and now that Shalva was to become a campus, Dawn decided to dedicate the entrance plaza and parks in memory of her beloved Roland, who had passed away unexpectedly the previous year.

The center, perched on a hill overlooking the valley and the busy road below, was conspicuously visible from a distance. But there was more good news. A decision was taken to build the new Route 16 highway, a tunneled entrance into Jerusalem, with its main portal in and out of the city located at the base of our park, thus making Shalva the welcoming face of Jerusalem for some sixty thousand cars each day. As then-Jerusalem Mayor Nir Barkat observed, "It is fascinating to note that the new entrance to Jerusalem will not be graced with a government office, an IDF facility, or a museum, but rather with the Shalva National Center that proclaims the timeless message of the prophets: that of caring for the weak among us."

When we'd first hired Randy, I'd told him, "In the course of building this center, you'll see things for which you'll have no explanation. You'll have no choice but to ascribe them to a heavenly hand." This was one of the occasions when he reminded me of what I'd said. "I don't believe in miracles or guiding hands," he said, "but there's no doubt that inexplicable, special things have transpired in the process of building Shalva."

I reflected on the idea of good and bad angels. The word "angel" in Hebrew, *malach*, has a second meaning of "messenger" or "agent," and for many years we had no choice but to view our new neighbors as bad angels who had made our lives miserable with endless court cases in their efforts to block the gift of land and the building of the center. But now it became apparent that without their remorseless opposition to Shalva, no legal authority would have allowed public access to the building through the park, which was critical to making the campus design feasible. So were they in fact good angels, good messengers, albeit very heavily disguised? I was not about to send them flowers of gratitude, but the answer seemed uncomfortably obvious.

Chapter 42

Moving On

We had now overcome the key legal hurdle to getting our building permit and completing the building, but alas our dear neighbors were not yet ready to allow us to move on. Incredibly, with powerful connections, they were still allowed to bring an additional lawsuit designed to further delay our ability to get the coveted building permit. This continued to impact the confidence of several major donors.

Yochanan and Avi began to feel out the possibility of compromising with the hotel owners, and Malki was all in favor, for as she often said painfully, "I wanted to help children and families but not to spend my life in court." To me and Menachem, this was capitulation, and we would have none of it. I was adamant that I would not agree to give them land for peace, to reduce the size of the building – but rather only peace for peace. I would leave them alone and they would leave us alone. In spite of my feelings, my sons were also adamant and felt that a compromise was the only way to bring closure and be able to proceed. And so they began meeting with the owners in a challenging effort to create basic trust and a plan to move forward.

The continued impasse and its potential consequences took me off my feet, and one day, my breathing was short, my pulse racing, and I was sent to the emergency room. I did not have to wait for medical attention because I became a VIP patient immediately, rushed through unfamiliar tests. The electrical impulses in the heart were off, and nothing, including electric shock and medication, helped to rectify the situation. I suddenly felt twenty years older, found it challenging to function, and was unable to travel. Feeling quite lost, a friend suggested that I consult with a medical adviser named Rabbi Elimelech Firer. I chuckled and thought, why didn't I think of that? Several days later I met my old classmate at 6:30 a.m. in his office in Bnei Brak.

There were many others waiting with me. After warm hellos, we discussed my medical issue, and he advised a procedure called ablation to fix the problem. He referred me to the head of a cardiology department in a Jerusalem hospital. Upon returning home, I made the call and told the doctor that Rabbi Firer had suggested I call him. That was all I had to say, and he saw me the next day. He confirmed that I was an excellent candidate for ablation, something that other prominent doctors at another hospital had not mentioned. The following week it was done at the hospital's outpatient clinic, and I awoke and immediately felt that, miraculously, I was back to normal. I promised myself that I would tone down my anxiety but had limited success because the agonizing legal delays continued.

We were not alone in this struggle for the center. The Director-General of the Jerusalem Municipality, Yossi Heymann, and members of his staff picked up the gauntlet and worked tirelessly to facilitate the process of getting the building permit. Yossi saw the situation as black and white and was determined to see it through. Our American Friends of Shalva was actively and intimately involved, and two dear friends and board members, president Ari Storch and Mitch Presser, flew in to help assess the situation and provide their business and legal acumen.

In early 2012, it came down to a final court appearance in which our antagonists realized that they were finally going to lose their case and may well have legal problems of their own. The afternoon before, Uri Yamin received an urgent call from their lawyer that he should come immediately to Tel Aviv and they would settle with a compromise. There was no trust, but Uri too now reminded us, "Every time we thought we were home free, they managed to get the court to delay further, so a compromise that bars further court activity is what we must get. Kalman you must come to terms with the fact that after all their years of fighting, the reality is that they will not go away without receiving something significant in return."

I felt unable to accompany Uri, but Yochanan and Avi did. It was a grueling, long night, at the end of which we agreed not to build the top floor as planned, as well as to make 40 percent of the new top floor into an enormous veranda so as to minimize blockage of their view. I was frustrated and furious, but deep inside I realized that we had no choice. Malki was comfortable knowing that the battle could be over and we would finally be able to finish the building, which was still a whopping twelve floors with 220,000 square feet. The court session the next morning now became a matter of closing final details to legally certify and seal the compromise. As expected, that too proved to be taxing and challenging, but it got done and paved the way toward making the center a reality.

Chapter 43

Jerusalem! Our Feet Stand within Your Gates

It took a full year to redesign the building, and what emerged was extraordinary. Funding was a critical issue so rather than give the project turnkey to a contractor who is responsible for all subcontractors and costs significantly more, we hired a leading construction management company but retained full control of everyone working on the project. This also enabled changes in midstream. Yochanan and Menachem, now both lawyers, worked tirelessly, hand in hand, to get it done. Yochanan was our agent who oversaw the day-to-day construction, and Menachem, who had his own practice, made sure that we got maximum help and minimum hindrance from the folks at the municipality. Malki was on-site, making difficult decisions and assuring that the plans were executed with the level of quality she demanded. The entire structure was concrete and the building process was tedious. She was on top of every detail of the construction and simultaneously began the process of interior design. Working with professionals, she took part in many long and intense meetings over a period of several years. As endless as it seemed, this too began to take shape.

Complex design and engineering solutions were required in order to place large open spaces on the lower floors with minimal supportive pillars and beams. The sports center, one floor underground, sits over two levels of parking and consists of a full-size gymnasium, a fitness center, and two pools, one therapeutic and the other semi-Olympic in size, with large windows that provide natural light. This is cleverly made possible because the sloped ceiling of the pools is the underside of the floor of the 340-seat auditorium directly above it; since the outside wall is two stories high, it allows room for the windows, even though the pools are underground.

The entrance lobby evolved into a three-story atrium, filled with space and light. The various levels flow together thanks to elements such as interior balconies that look down into the lobby, giving the atrium the feeling of a buffer-zone where youngsters can both decompress and transition into a different setting as they come into and leave Shalva.

Late one night as I was falling asleep, Malki called me from the car while on her way home from Tel Aviv. "Kalman, are you up?" "Of course," I replied. "I know what I am going to do in the atrium," she continued excitedly. "That's great. What are you planning?" I said groggily. "I am going to create an enormous mobile of butterflies hanging from the ceiling." "That's nice," I mumbled. Sensing my silence, she asked, "Don't you want to know why I've chosen butterflies?" "Of course." "Because a butterfly begins life in a cocoon and has to struggle its way out until it ultimately becomes a colorful flying creature. If you try to help it out of the cocoon, it will never make it. Our children have challenges early on and we can't do the work for them. Our job is to provide the appropriate environment and stimulate them to do the work they need to do on their own in order to develop and ultimately fly to the best of their ability."

I was now wide awake. "Wow," I exclaimed. "That is incredible!" Malki added, "And do you want to know who is going to create this for me? David Gerstein. We will invite him to the building, and I have a wonderful feeling that he will want to make it."

The following week, we hosted David Gerstein, a man in his late sixties and one of Israel's leading artists, who is best known for his colorful, steel, cut-out sculptures. We were impressed by his soft-spoken, delicate manner and immediately felt comfortable with him. Malki shared her vision and David loved it from the get-go. He was deeply moved by the Shalva story and the design of the building and told us that he wanted to partner with us. This was totally unexpected and without a doubt, in no small way, made it feasible.

Over the coming year, David designed and created a twenty-foot-high, ten-foot-wide majestic mobile consisting of hand-painted metallic butterflies that revolve slowly with the flow of air. Above it, Malki placed colorful insets in the ceiling representing cocoons from which the butterflies emerged. Though David employs a team of talented artists, he insisted on painting each butterfly himself.

One flight up, conveniently close to the main entrance, would be the 340-seat auditorium where Shalva children would entertain and be entertained, and where professional seminars and national and international conferences would take place. Adjacent to the auditorium we planned to have Café Shalva, a full-service café that would be open to the public and provide gainful employment for young people with disabilities.

Security in the center was critical and we worked with top consultants. The two underground parking levels and the next three floors, which included the sports facilities, the main lobby, the auditorium, and the café would be public spaces and accessible to visitors, but the upper seven floors, which related solely to the Shalva children, would be sealed tight and require a security pass to enter.

Retaining a sense of intimacy in an enormous building was one of Malki's major concerns. To that end, she and Randy designed each of the upper floors as a series of five pavilions separated by a veranda that provides light and air. Each has its own color scheme and story theme, and each has its own focus. "The concept of pavilions solved a multitude of issues," explained Randy. "Perhaps most important of all, their scale gives intimacy and hominess to what is a very large building. But they contribute much more than that. They define different kinds of space, so that the right relationships can be established between everything that goes on in Shalva – from entering, eating, and sleeping to therapy, activity, and public events. They answer the problem of light and they help connect the structure to the ground: the building is terraced along the steep slope of the mountain, so we have outdoor balconies on every level, not only to enjoy the sunshine, fresh air, and the view, but also to create extra settings for therapy and care, and as an additional safety feature, providing emergency exits."

Malki summed up the design process in one concise sentence: "We didn't follow an instruction booklet because there wasn't one. We wrote the book ourselves, as we went along."

"Malki was my active partner," said Randy. "She had her design completed in its entirety in her mind and never forgot anything. She was always utterly consistent, and she would never compromise when she knew she was right. Even when we were all exhausted, she'd find the strength to go on."

One such instance concerned the color of stone that Malki wanted to use for the facade of the building. A law dating from the British Mandate in the first half of the last century requires that all Jerusalem buildings be faced with Jerusalem stone, a regulation which enhances the city's beauty but greatly adds to its construction costs. The limestone known as Jerusalem stone comes in different tinges – white, yellow, ochre, and pink, although there's very little pink still available. For Malki, there was never a question that the building must be faced in pink-tinged stone. "It will bring warmth and distinguish it," she told a perturbed Randy, who tried vainly to make her understand that the supply of pink-tinged stone was virtually exhausted, and even if they found some, it was unlikely to be of good enough quality or in sufficient quantity.

Randy, however, like others before him, learned that Malki can't be dissuaded on things that matter to her. He kept on searching, and to his utter surprise, eventually found a supplier with good-quality pink stone in sufficient quantity. "And you know what?" he said. "Malki was right. With the pink stone, the building doesn't disappear into its background. With that and with all the glass we used glowing in the sunlight, the structure looks almost magical."

Chapter 44

Bologna

When it came to choosing ceramic tiles for the flooring, Malki was no less adamant that she wanted a warm, rustic hue. After much time spent searching, it became clear that what she wanted was not available anywhere in Israel. Pressure was brought to bear on Malki by the management company, who were saying that her delay in selecting tiles was going to cause significant and expensive delays in the construction. She had just agreed to use a different color tile when her phone rang.

"Malki, hi. This is David. Don't make any decision on your tiles until we have met!" "Excuse me? Who are you?" "You don't know me yet but trust me, I will get you what you want. I am now in Tel Aviv and will be in Jerusalem tomorrow morning." "I have already made my decision, so you have no reason to come," Malki replied firmly. "That is OK, but I must meet you. Please allow me to come in the morning." David left little room for discussion and yes, there was something about him that piqued her interest, so she agreed to meet him.

David arrived at 10:00 a.m. In his forties, he was Israeli and newly religious, with a full beard and a black yarmulke on his head. He was a real character, full of energy and truly engaging, whether he was speaking Hebrew or English. He generated excitement and you couldn't help but be charmed.

He shared that he had been in the tile business for over twenty years; he had worked for the biggest companies and now had his own firm. "Malki, I know that you can't find what you want here, but come with me for two days to Bologna in northern Italy, the capital of the ceramic industry, and I will introduce you to friends who own factories larger than football fields who will have what you are looking for."

When Malki told the owner of the large Israeli tile company that she was delaying her order until she visited Bologna the next week, she was met with derision. "We have every color of tile manufactured in Italy, and if it existed we would have it. Malki, you are wasting your valuable time." Pressure was also brought to bear by our construction team that they needed to move forward with the tiles. But David insisted that she should wait, and he would deliver.

It was September, and several days later Malki and Yochanan flew with David to Rome and on to Bologna in a small plane through stormy weather. They were met by Lorenzo, a lanky Italian man in his forties who spoke broken English. David clearly knew him well. Lorenzo was welcoming and drove them quite a distance to their hotel in preparation for the coming day. It had been a long trip and Malki was exhausted.

Lorenzo picked them up early in the morning and drove them to an enormous factory. He was well received and Malki realized that David had meant what he said. The factory was seemingly endless and one could spend days walking through it viewing a myriad of different tiles. They spent hours looking at tiles and realized that there was not a color or shade that they didn't have in stock – except for the rustic hue that Malki was looking for. In fact, they had nothing close.

"Don't worry," David assuaged her. "We are off to another even larger factory, and we will find what you want." This scenario continued in a number of such factories on that day and well into the next. Malki was too tired to be angry. David and Lorenzo were wonderful people trying their very best, but the tile salesman in Jerusalem had proven right. If he didn't have the tile or know about it, then it didn't exist in Italy.

Yochanan and David tried to keep Malki's spirits up, but there was little they could do, because even David had lost hope. They were ready to return to the hotel and prepare to fly back at noon the following day. Lorenzo felt terrible. "Let's go to visit a friend of mine," he said, and so it was into the car and on to one of the largest tile design centers in the area. Lorenzo entered into a long, animated conversation with the owner in which he shared that Malki had come from Jerusalem in search of a certain style of ceramic tile for her new center for children with disabilities, and was crestfallen to return empty-handed.

The man looked carefully at Malki, turned to Lorenzo, and said, "The lady is very dedicated. We design for corporations and not for individuals, but in this case, come with me," and with that, he walked to a large office with oversized computer screens. He spoke to a woman who was seemingly the head honcho, and then he extended his hand toward a chair, indicating to Malki to sit down next to her. Lorenzo explained to Malki that she had touched the owner's heart and that he was going to have his lead designer create the exact tile she wanted. The Italian woman spoke no English but that didn't stop them from working together effectively. Over the course of several hours, she and Malki combined colors and styles on-screen until they got the design of the tile just right.

It was, in fact, not one tile, but nine tiles of the same color, each with a slightly different design, so that when laid out over large spaces the floor would appear not uniform but rather delicately varied.

The designer explained that the high-resolution images would undergo a complex printing process; it would take many hours to produce the precise print of the nine enlarged sample tiles in a three-by-three table. The resulting print would be some nine feet wide and six feet high. Malki was to review two identical copies, sign on one, and send it back to confirm the order.

Back at the hotel, the threesome were emotionally spent but overjoyed. Rather than returning home empty-handed to the mocking response of "I told you so, Malki," the "lady" would arrive knowing that the tile she wanted was on its way toward production.

Shortly before departing for their return flight, Lorenzo arrived at the hotel with a long cylinder from which he pulled out the master print of the tiles. Malki looked at it momentarily and it was stunning, but it was very late and Lorenzo quickly inserted the print in a cylinder and drove them to the airport.

Malki made her trek back to Jerusalem via Rome amid serious delays due to further inclement weather, but with a very happy heart.

Once home, she excitedly took out the oversized print and spread it out across the living room. It was spectacular. As she examined it more closely, Malki's face turned from joy to great concern. "I can't believe this," she exclaimed. "Look at it. This is not what I created with her. It has an added tinge of pink in it. The designer changed it after I left."

I too could not believe this scenario. Here Malki delayed the purchase of the tiles and went to Italy, and miraculously a famous designer created specifically the tile she wanted, and now it would be back to the drawing board. Not having been in Italy, I was not in a position to argue, but I tried my best to point out that it was only she who saw this minute difference and no one else would even notice it. Time was flying and it was now several days before

Rosh Hashana, the two-day Jewish New Year holiday in which the country comes to a standstill.

Malki couldn't accept this situation. She had not traveled all the way to Bologna in order to put a tile in her building that was not what she wanted. And so she decided to return to Bologna immediately after the holiday and work with the designer until she got it right. A week later, between Rosh Hashana and Yom Kippur, the Day of Atonement, Malki, Yochanan, and David headed back to northern Italy once again. It was enormously taxing and stressful.

After many more hours with the designer, Malki was hopeful. Arriving home exhausted just before Yom Kippur and its twenty-four-hour fast, she now had to wait until she received the printed proofs once again to know if this time they were on target. Ten tedious days passed until the cylinder arrived. We once again spread it out in the dining room and immediately Malki saw that this was it. The hues were right; the variations in the tiles were right. She finally had her ceramic tile.

We sent the signed copy back and the design went into accelerated production to produce enough tiles for the 220,000-square-foot building. Malki was now asked by her Italian friends what she wished to name this design. We thought they were kidding but they were in fact serious. The Italian designer suggested "Malki," but she preferred "Shalva." The process moved forward and miraculously, the precision, high-quality "Shalva tiles" arrived at a significantly lower cost without causing any delay in the construction schedule.

Chapter 45

Unforeseen Security

Despite the forethought and meticulous planning that went into the large building designed for our needs, changes and additions came up even as we moved toward completion.

The disagreeable discovery that the allocated site was in fact a mountain of compacted rubble, and the vast engineering and construction project that was then required to shore it up, meant that the lower 54,000 square feet of our building were well protected by the massive retaining wall.

This discovery and the subsequent engineering, design, and construction challenges it brought had all seemed an unwarranted burden, until Gideon Shalom, the Deputy Director of the Ministry of Social Affairs, visited the building under construction. "It's astounding that you have so much secure protected space here," he said. "The government needs to create a National Emergency Center for persons with disabilities, and this site would be perfect."

Once again, one comment and one new perspective was enough to feed our imagination. He was taken aback by how fervently

I thanked him for pointing this out. "You've put in focus something my wife and I have agonized over for years," I told him. "At last I understand why we had to carve Shalva's home out of the mountain."

With Israel's borders frequently under attack, its population is well acquainted with warning sirens and well drilled in seeking shelter in protected rooms and public bomb shelters. During the war with Lebanon in the summer of 2006, the residents of northern Israel spent thirty-four days running for safety from barrages of missiles. Throughout that period we brought groups of children with disabilities and their families from northern Israel to our Shalva–Beit Nachshon center, providing them with freedom from the fear and danger they faced at home.

During the summer of 2014, missiles once again rained down, but this time from Gaza in the south, and when the warning sirens wailed people living in adjacent areas in Israel had less than a minute to run to shelters or safe rooms. For those with disabilities and mobility problems, that was insufficient, so they simply moved in – spending days and nights eating and sleeping in the claustrophobic shelters and rarely venturing out into the sunlight.

Once again, we brought children with disabilities and their family members to our Shalva–Beit Nachshon center in Jerusalem, but it was frustrating since we were very limited in terms of the number of people we could serve.

Now, motivated by Gideon's comment, we entered into lengthy discussions with the Ministry of Social Affairs and the IDF Home Front to plan an efficient facility, and the new National Emergency Center for Persons with Disabilities became a reality at Shalva. Vital equipment for every circumstance was stored on-site by the IDF Home Front, and in the case of emergency, whether natural disaster or war, Shalva is able to admit up to 1,200 youngsters with disabilities within twenty-four hours, where they will continue to benefit from appropriate programs and therapies on-site. Clearly, the hope is that it will not be needed on a massive scale, but prepared we must be.

Chapter 46

Of Dentistry and Oral Hygiene

Well aware of the problems we dealt with when we had to bring Yossi to a dentist for even the most mundane procedure, I was bent on providing children with disabilities the dental care they required in an atmosphere tailored to their needs in which both they and their parents would feel comfortable. This thought had been brewing in my mind for years, and, convinced of its need, I had been looking for the right person with whom to share it. Avi and I were attending the wedding of Leon and Leesa Wagner in Miami when I was pulled aside from the bustling reception by Leon's dear friend Great Neck, and introduced to a burly man with a short greying beard, with the words, "the two of you have a lot to talk about and you should do just that." We found our way to a quieter corner and began to schmooze. I sensed I was talking to someone with a powerful personality and we bonded quickly. We soon realized that our common ground was dentistry. The man's name was Steve Kess; he was a senior executive at Henry Schein, an enormous dental supply company headquartered in Long Island, and much of his role focused on running their charitable endeavors. Naturally I shared my vision, and Steve showed interest and suggested that we meet for coffee in the coming days in a quieter environment where we could have a more focused discussion.

Back in New York, Steve and I spoke at length about the dental project. He concluded by saying, "Kalman, I am on board and that means that Henry Schein is on board. Go home and write a full proposal that I can share with my colleagues and let's move this forward." I returned to Jerusalem elated in the knowledge that unexpectedly, one more dream was now being realized.

To my surprise, my excitement was not shared by others. Yochanan was concerned about the complexities involved in such an undertaking and invited me to a meeting with an expert who designed and built operating rooms and dental facilities at hospitals. He was very pleasant but wasted no time in lecturing me about the sensitive issue of anesthesia and sedation in dental care in general, and more specifically for those with cognitive disabilities. "This is far more complex than you realize," he said, "and such care must be introduced only after taking each person's complete medical history into account in order to assess the proper degree of sedation. The complications can be many, ranging from under-sedation that can cause great pain to over-sedation that can cause many side effects, even death. Trust me; with all your goodwill, you should not take upon yourself this responsibility and the resulting liability in your new center. Leave these matters for dedicated dental facilities in hospital settings."

There was silence as others in the room waited for my response. There was none. The wind had been knocked out of me and I was speechless. I slowly gathered myself and said, "OK, I understand and thank you for sharing." Subdued and crushed, I walked out. No one could appreciate the intense level of disappointment I felt upon realizing that my dream, which I had been planning for years in my own mind, had just been shattered. But I had no choice but to accept that reality because I knew that they were right.

Somberly, I wrote Steve an email and shared in detail what had just transpired, thanking him for his goodwill but telling him that it would not be happening. To my surprise, he replied that he had only gained greater respect for me, because in his experience, when people have passionate dreams they often cannot back off even when the facts change, but I had just done so. He looked forward to having another coffee with me in New York in the future.

Several weeks later, I received a phone call from my cousin Eyal Botzer, the director of pediatric dentistry at Tel Aviv University and an expert on complex procedures for children with severe disabilities. "Kalman, I know it is 5:30 and late in the day, and I do apologize, but I am just leaving an international dental conference at Hadassah Hospital in Jerusalem and would love to visit Shalva, however briefly, with my mentor from NYU, Dr. Barry Grayson." Half an hour later they arrived, as the Shalva children were getting ready to return home in their many minivans, and I showed them the colorful seven floors of our Shalva–Beit Nachshon center. Barry was very moved by all that he saw and heard.

We sat and spoke for some time and I shared my recent disappointment. Thoughtfully, Barry paused and said, "I understand how frustrated you must feel, but I do believe that you made the right decision. There is, however, something that I would like to suggest to you, and that is an oral hygiene program. When a child has a disability, he or she is often unable to brush their own teeth properly, and due to the daily pressures of getting the child and his siblings out to school in the morning and caring for them in the evening, brushing this child's teeth is often not a high priority for parents. The resulting poor oral hygiene puts the children at increased risk for gum disease and tooth decay, and if the bacteria migrate, they can be a catalyst for other severe medical issues too. Add to that the range of health problems associated with developmental disabilities and you're looking at a horrific dental situation. This can mean that by the time that child is six or seven, it is often no longer a question of visiting a dentist, but rather a complex situation that requires dental surgery in a hospital setting. The sad thing is that their pain and suffering can in large measure be prevented or minimized if these children benefit from proper oral hygiene from a young age and are referred to a dentist in a timely manner for issues that come up."

Barry continued as if reading my mind. "I understand that a dental hygiene program is not what you had in mind, but I would suggest that you now recognize its significance and consider it."

Bingo. I was overwhelmed with excitement. It made perfect sense and would bring great benefits to the children and their families; it was doable, and presented no side effects or liability risks. I couldn't thank Barry enough for enlightening me.

Eyal and Barry left and I immediately wrote Steve an email sharing this development and the new idea. He responded that this is indeed very exciting and that he is on board.

A few months later Steve was in Israel for a dental convention and visited the new Shalva center under construction, together with the dean of the Temple University dental school, Professor Amid Ismail, and Dr. Allen Finkelstein, the CEO of a large health insurance company. Between the three of them lay an enormous amount of talent and knowledge.

To my amazement, they spent a couple of hours in the frigid weather climbing up and down all of the twelve concrete floors and were amazed by the sheer size and myriad planned facilities. That night I joined them at an international dental conference in Tel Aviv, and Amid shared his excitement about Shalva. He wanted to come back to Jerusalem the following day and see the current center and the children we serve, and so he did, absorbing every detail of the colorfully designed and decorated floors and all of Shalva's programs.

Meeting Yossi was the high point of his visit. Amid was amazed by Yossi's inquisitiveness. Unable to contain himself in Yossi's presence, Amid emotionally shared that this was a life-changing experience for him. "When I was growing up in Mosel, Iraq, these services didn't exist and children with disabilities were viewed as a sad fact of life but not more. Here at Shalva I see the impact that love and education can have on them. I am immediately ordering for Yossi an online subscription to *The Economist* because his brilliant mind will be stimulated by the wide range of articles that will be read to him, and please tell him that I expect to receive an update as to which subjects were of interest." Yossi enjoyed the weekly experience and shared his interests with Amid. An article about the new phenomenon of Wi-Fi on flights hit close to home for him. He was distressed to learn that though Wi-Fi was being installed on more and more flights, my regular flight between Tel Aviv and New York lagged behind and didn't allow us to be in email contact. I have to admit that, personally, I enjoyed the eleven hours of solitude and the rare focused, undisturbed time.

The night after his visit, Amid expressed his deep feelings in poetry:

The House at the Gate of Heaven

I visited a house like no other
The angels roam happily
They take care of children in need
Who do not differentiate between human deeds
Yet they have a feeling of joy
Enjoying simple acts that others forgot

The fish in a tank can excite their senses
A swim ignites their joy
Music awakens their souls with laughter
Their view of life is refreshing
They do not look at the color of your face
Nor religion nor faith
Nothing material matters to them
They only look at your heart
And that is all that matters in life
The lesson is simple in the House at the Gate of Heaven
Our free souls should guide us to see the heaven inside and
Guide our eyes to see the beauty in the angels around
The House at the Gate can only be seen by the lucky ones
whose souls are free

Amid and I bonded on many levels and an extraordinary friendship developed. When he invited me to give the keynote address at the graduation of the dental faculty in Philadelphia, I balked. "I am not an academic," I told him. "I am a rabbi." But Amid had a persuasive manner, and I found myself on a magnificent theater stage in front of thousands of attendees, donned in what appeared to me as a take on biblical Joseph's multicolored dream coat, but to others was just the traditional graduation gown and cap.

We designed and built the oral health center at Shalva, and Steve had two dental chairs and other dental equipment donated by Henry Schein. Named by Amid as OHEV, Hebrew for "love," the name stood for Oral Health for Everyone, but the vision didn't stop with ensuring that every child attending Shalva had impeccably clean teeth. We created an educational agenda to teach children, families, and staff about the importance of oral hygiene, and the focus on oral health permeated all of our programs and went beyond. The subject of oral health for youngsters with disabilities raised great interest, and conferences on the subject were developed. Under Steve's vision and direction, an international oral hygiene coalition and program called Program Accessible Oral Health (PAOH) was formed to promote this agenda, and its impact has been astounding. A distinguished advisory board was created on which I was privileged to be a founding member, and vibrant new partnerships were developed.

Chapter 47

Of Sheep and Prophecy

The new center was taking form and we began to think about art that would contribute to its beauty and inviting feeling. One of the ideas that came up was to place a significant sculpture at the entrance. When I discussed this with Malki, she asked, "Like what?" "Like the Ten Commandments," I replied confidently. "Like the Ten Commandments?" Malki began, and I could hear the skeptical tone in her voice. "Why that is brilliant. No one has ever done the Ten Commandments before." She paused and then continued, "If you want to do ten, you'll have to look elsewhere." "Like what?" "Like the ten divine utterances of creation." Her words surprised me, but I immediately realized her stroke of genius and its depth.

My mind was spinning. Of course I knew that the ten divine utterances appeared in the biblical story of creation, but I needed a review to remember it more precisely. Later that night, I pored over ancient classical Jewish texts looking for the sources of the tradition that the world's creation did not cease after six days;

rather, it is renewed daily through G-d's divine utterances and the dynamic partnerships among people.

I knew that this was mentioned at the opening of the fifth chapter of the two-thousand-year-old compendium known as *Ethics of the Fathers*: "In ten divine utterances the world was created." But there were no specifics. I looked further and found that the same statement appeared in the Midrash, the rabbinic compilation that contains thought-provoking interpretations of the biblical narrative and was compiled in the same period as was *Ethics of the Fathers*. The Midrash went into more detail, providing the words from the biblical account of creation that made up each utterance:

Genesis 1:1 – In the beginning G-d created the heavens and the earth.

Genesis 1:3 – G-d said, "Let there be light," and there was light.

Genesis 1:6 – G-d said, "Let there be a firmament in the midst of the waters, and let it separate between water and water."

Genesis 1:9 – G-d said, "Let the waters beneath the heaven be gathered into one area, and let the dry land appear."

Genesis 1:11 – G-d said, "Let the earth sprout vegetation: herbage yielding seed, fruit trees yielding fruit each after its kind, containing its own seed on the earth."

Genesis 1:14 – G-d said, "Let there be luminaries in the firmament of the heaven to separate between the day and the night; and they shall serve as luminaries in the firmament of the heaven to shine upon the earth."

Genesis 1:20 – G-d said, "Let the waters swarm with swarms of living creatures, and fowl that fly about over the earth across the expanse of the heavens."

Genesis 1:24 – G-d said, "Let the earth bring forth the living creatures, each according to its kind: animal, and creeping thing, and
beast of the land, each according to its kind."

Genesis 1:26 – And G-d said, "Let us make man in our image, after
our likeness."

Genesis 2:18 – And the L-rd G-d said, "It is not good that man be
alone; I will make him a helper corresponding to him."

I was elated and in the days ahead Malki and I delved into it. She
envisioned ten pillars, almost nine feet high with one element of
the Shalva logo placed at the top of each one, representing a parent stretching arms heavenward, and a smaller pillar in the middle
representing a child. Together they convey that every person is a
beautiful and important part of creating a world community.

I called an old friend, the well-known Jerusalem artist Sam
Phillipe, and began to discuss which famous artist might we ask
to create it. We thought of approaching one artist for each pillar.
Many names were discussed but there was no simple answer and
much time passed. One day Sam met Malki and me and shared
that he often does his own sculpture work at a large foundry in
Netanya, and the proprietor, Yossi Ben Dror, had just agreed to
introduce us to Israel's most famous sculptor and artist, Menashe
Kadishman, who also used his foundry.

Yossi made an appointment, and he and Sam met Malki and
me, together with our artistic teenager Sara, outside Menashe's Tel
Aviv apartment. It was a hot, humid afternoon. We entered and
found ourselves standing in the presence of an imposing eighty-
year-old man sitting up in bed wearing a T-shirt. He greeted us
warmly.

Yossi asked me to first give some background about Shalva
and then share our request. Menashe was deeply moved by what

Shalva does and emphasized that he has always had a very special love for children with disabilities and a strong will to help them. I described the sculpture and said that we want him to interpret each of the ten divine utterances through his own artistic expression. Menashe listened pensively and a lively discussion ensued, not only about art but about life and values. He was clearly a very thoughtful and spiritual being, deeply connected to Jewish tradition. He asked a number of questions and concluded with a broad smile, "I would love to be your partner in creating this exciting art piece, and I want to draw a sheep on the smaller pillar in the middle."

There was a collective gasp as we realized what had just transpired. Menashe Kadishman had just accepted the challenge and would grace it with his signature sheep.

Menashe then turned to Sara and inquired about her interests in art. It was remarkable to hear him conversing respectfully with her, as if she were his peer, asking her where she studied and what kind of art she liked. He called his assistant and asked her to bring one of his small sheep paintings on canvas. He then wrote a personal inscription on the back, "To Sarala, the Princess, Best wishes for love and health and a wonderful life with smiles, Amen. Love, Menashe Kadishman." This sensitive interaction had significant meaning for Sara and for us; it was a mark of Menashe's humility.

Sam began to facilitate the process; he met with Menashe as needed and would update us on the progress. On one occasion, we were sitting in my office with Malki and Sam on one side of my desk and me on the other next to my computer. The discussion focused on precisely how to present the ten verses. Malki shared with Sam that since Menashe's motif is always about sheep, she wants in some way to include two words from the biblical Prophets, *tzon kodashim*, meaning "holy sheep," which in Israeli literature and culture has become a figurative way to reference the Jewish community, or more specifically, its children.

"Kalman," she said, "find these two words and tell me where exactly in the books of Prophets they are found." "OK," I replied, "I will, but let's first finish our broader discussion while we have Sam here with us." "No, please look up the source of the phrase *tzon kodashim* – I must know where it is from." With little choice I googled the two Hebrew words and immediately found them in Ezekiel 36:38. "OK, I found it." "Read me the verse," Malki continued. I did: "As the holy sheep, as the holy sheep of Jerusalem in her appointed seasons, so shall the destroyed cities be filled with flocks of men; and they shall know that I am the L-rd."

We were taken aback by the ancient prophecy, from the time of the destruction of Jerusalem, in which the image of sheep bore the promise of Israel's return to its destroyed cities; and here we were, some 2,600 years later, sitting in rebuilt Jerusalem, filled with flocks of people, and discussing these same sheep mentioned in the prophecy. It was a powerful moment.

As we spoke, I gazed at my computer screen and suddenly, the two Hebrew words seemed to jump out at me. I bent over and looked more closely. Malki asked, "What are you doing?" "Just a moment, I want to be certain," I replied. "Oh my G-d, I don't believe what I see. I can't believe this." "What is going on?" Malki probed impatiently.

I was shaken and gathered my thoughts. "Malki, you wanted me to look up the two words *tzon kodashim*, 'holy sheep,' and you didn't let go until I did. Well an extraordinary riddle has just been solved." I turned my computer screen for Malki and Sam to see it and pointed with a finger. "Look at these two Hebrew words. What do you see?" They looked and saw only the words themselves, *tzon kodashim*.

I highlighted six consecutive Hebrew letters of the verse in red and said, "Now look again.... Look at the final letter of *tzon* (sheep) and the five letters of *kodashim* (holy). These six letters are the precise letters of Menashe's last name, Kadishman. And it is perfectly clear to me that this is why Menashe's signature art is sheep. He is a deeply spiritual person, and his sheep symbolize this prophecy that the Jewish nation will ultimately return to Jerusalem and see it rebuilt and teeming with life."

"Kalman," Sam scoffed, "that is fascinating, but believe me, Menashe is not aware of it and that isn't why he paints sheep. Let's move on." "Not so fast," I said. "When are you going to visit Menashe next?" "In a few days, together with Yossi." "Before you leave today, Sam," I said, "I am printing out this verse with the highlighted letters in red and you are going to show it to Menashe and ask him if, indeed, this is why he paints sheep." "Kalman, I really don't know if I should do that..." I cut him off. "Sam," I said, "either you will show Menashe or I will come with you and ask him myself." "OK," Sam replied. "I think it would be more appropriate that I ask him, because this might be a sensitive subject."

Several days later, Sam showed my page to Menashe. Menashe stared at the letters for some time, looked up, and stated pensively, "Kalman has revealed my secret." Sam was taken aback and tried to continue the conversation, but Menashe said tersely, "I don't want to talk about this again."

On his way back to Jerusalem, Sam called and confirmed what I had suggested. I was overwhelmed, because with the new depth and dimension of Menashe's art that I was now aware of, I felt even more privileged that his creation would grace the entrance to Shalva.

Menashe's health, which wasn't good when we first met, continued to deteriorate. He told me that if there is one place he would love to visit, it is Shalva and the holy children whom he loved, but he was unable to make the one-hour trip to Jerusalem. His masterpiece was finished, but to our great sorrow, Menashe passed away at age eighty-two before the new center was complete. He deeply touched our lives and we knew that his *Ten Divine Utterances* piece at the entrance to the new center would inspire and educate new generations.

Chapter 48

Toward Opening

The building was taking shape, but transforming an enormous, cold, concrete structure into a warm home for our children was now the challenge facing Malki, and the finishing details were seemingly endless. Each floor was a fully accessible 20,000-square-foot world unto itself in function and in appearance. Even the most rudimentary working list of floors and facilities to be completed was daunting for me, let alone the level of finishing detail each required.

Somehow Malki was not overwhelmed. She worked intensely with a talented interior designer and architect, Ben Biran, who, like Randy, was patient and attentive to Malki's requests. Later she worked closely with Yael Lichi, another gifted interior designer, who was passionate about the project and helped Malki facilitate the finishing details. Watching these two powerful personalities work together and attack a given hurdle was often comical, but they were a wonderful team.

On many occasions, Malki was told by a variety of professionals that she was using too much color, and Malki would quietly proceed to tell the workmen to just use the colors she specified. When it came to the facade of the building, Malki wanted the trim highlighting the windows to be colored in a peach hue, and everyone freaked out. "Malki, don't go there; you want a classy building," someone said. So much pressure was brought to bear from all corners, including from Randy, that Malki felt she had little choice but to give in. I stood with her outside the entrance as the painters readied themselves to go up on the scaffold and begin to paint, when she quietly said to the manager, "Yaakov, tell me, is it too late to change and make the highlighting trim peach?" "Not if you tell me right now," he replied. There was a pause and Malki continued, "OK, so please do it as I want." When completed, after the initial shock, all sincerely agreed that it was delicate and embellished the appearance.

In addition to the works of Menashe Kadishman and David Gerstein, Malki filled the entire edifice with color and art, giving it a vibrant life of its own. She worked for over a year with Anna Kogan, a superbly talented Russian artist who brought the walls to life with hand-painted glorious murals, each of which Malki and Yael chose and whose painting they oversaw. The enormous dining room showcases the soft, colorful art of Mel Corin, while the synagogue hosts four large panels of biblical scenes created by Mexican artist Flor Esses, made from thousands of pieces of broken glass which make up a magical mosaic. Weighing over a ton, its shipment all the way from Mexico and its installation proved challenging but well worth the effort. The stunning *mezuzot* on every door are also Flor's handiwork.

One of the key figures in getting the building finished was a talented contractor whose expertise was precisely in moving from structure to finished product. Edward Borochov is a Russian immigrant and totally on top of his game. From day one, Malki referred to him as Putin, and that always brought a smile to his face. When he commented to me that this center has one of the highest level of finish that he has ever seen, I doubted him. "You have worked on large commercial projects and many of the biggest and fanciest homes of Russian oligarchs, so surely you must have seen a far greater level of finish when dealing with that kind of wealth." "Come with me, Kalman, and I will show you that in the highest-end projects that I have worked on, the public spaces are indeed very beautiful, but often the technical areas in the back that the public doesn't see are left unfinished. Your wife told me when I was hired that every centimeter of this building must be finished with the same quality workmanship, and that is what we are doing."

It was during this process that the various technical systems designed to provide functional life to the center were installed. At every stage, decisions had to be made regarding the quality of the long-term infrastructure that we would purchase and install. Our mantra was "you can only do it once," so in spite of a lack of funds we went with the best, without being excessive. It was a challenge to design the building in such a way that the flow between secure areas, which are closed to the public, and publicly accessible areas be as smooth as possible, so that the flow of Shalva children and visitors would be seamless.

Time was moving quickly and we were up against a serious deadline. We were determined that our preschool, consisting of classes for children with disabilities as well as three parallel classes of normative peers, would open as scheduled on September 1, 2016. In order to get the preschool classes licensed by the Jerusalem Municipality we had to commit a year in advance that those classrooms would be ready for the beginning of the school year on that day. We committed even though we knew that it was going to be tight, because we couldn't contemplate completing the center several months later, leaving those who chose Shalva without preschool. Registration opened in February and in spite of the fact that all were aware that the center was not yet finished, families showed great confidence, and registration filled up quickly.

* * *

Getting the building finished was costing far more than anticipated and we were simply out of funds. I was having an extremely difficult time and felt helpless. Often, I shared my anxiety with Malki, and her calm response was always the same biblical verse in Hebrew, "G-d will provide Himself the lamb for a burnt-offering, my son." Her reference was clear: In Genesis 22, G-d commands Abraham to take his son Isaac to Mount Moriah to sacrifice him. Isaac, unaware that he himself is to be the offering, delicately asks, "The fire and wood are here, but where is the lamb for the burnt offering?" And Abraham responds, "G-d will provide Himself the lamb for a burnt-offering, my son."

"Why is there the seemingly unnecessary word 'Himself'?" Malki asked me. "It could have simply said, 'G-d will provide the lamb.' The reason is that it wasn't only Abraham who faced a test of faith; G-d Himself faced a seemingly insurmountable problem. He had promised Abraham that future generations would descend from him, and Isaac was miraculously born while Abraham and Sarah were very old. Now that He told Abraham to sacrifice this future, what was to be with His promise? G-d Himself now needed a lamb."

Malki continued, "You too are in a seemingly impossible situation and you can't see any way out for G-d's special children. He provided a lamb then and He will show you your lamb too, when it's time."

I tried to comfort myself with my wife's optimistic words as I headed, yet again, for the USA and a hectic schedule of Shalva meetings, which included Los Angeles. At Gordon's request, I was to spend a Sunday with him at his winter home in Palm Desert, California, playing eighteen holes of golf at the Bighorn Golf Club next door, and follow that with a relaxing, long, afternoon schmooze on his scenic deck and pool.

It was a gentle California day, and walking down the fairway I suddenly noticed movement at the back of the green. Moving closer, I gestured excitedly to Gordon. Grazing contentedly behind the green was a magnificent bighorn ram, its enormous curved horns brushing the ground as it tugged at the grass. Far less excited to see us than we were to see it, the ram strolled majestically up into the rocky hill behind and out of sight.

"I've played here for twelve years, and I've never seen a bighorn before, despite the club's name!" Gordon marveled. "Where on earth did it come from?" Silent, I was stunned as I recalled Malki's words and the subsequent verse: "And Abraham lifted up his eyes, and he saw, and behold! There was a ram behind him, caught in the thicket by his horns. And Abraham went and took the ram, and offered him up for a burnt-offering in place of his son" (Genesis 22:13).

After teeing off on the next hole, Gordon turned and said matter-of-factly, "I have something important to share with you, but I will do that back at the house."

My curiosity was killing me but I respected his wish. Back at his home, relaxing next to his pool, Gordon poured drinks and began to open up. "I gather Dawn hasn't shared her news with you." "No," I replied. "I will be meeting Dawn tomorrow in Los Angeles." "Well," said Gordon, "she's planning to give another big gift to Shalva for the new center," and he shared the figure. I gasped not only because of the news but because of the ram.

"And," he continued, "I have a major problem because she's asking me to match her contribution and I just can't do it. You know that I am no longer running my charitable foundation alone;

my dear children are partners, and the local Vancouver community's needs are great."

I understood well, but in the coming hours of conversation there remained one image etched in my mind. It was now
getting dark and I had a two-hour drive back to LA ahead of me.
As Gordon walked me to the door he paused, took a breath, and
said, "You know – about that gift, when I get back to Vancouver
in a couple of days, I'll see what I can do."

The following day, as Gordon had said, Dawn told me she
would be giving another significant gift, and before the week's end,
Gordon called me to share that he and his family foundation would
be matching Dawn's gift. I felt dazed, moved by the generosity of
two exceptional friends and partners, and dumbfounded by the
bighorn that heralded these developments.

* * *

As spring and summer moved on we felt like we had a gun to our
head. On August 1, one month before opening, the task appeared
to be beyond impossible. Yochanan was pushing forward with all
his might and was steadfast and confident that we would finish in
time. Malki gave him a helpless look and asked, "Yochanan, why
are you so selfish? Clearly, you are smoking something and hallu-
cinating. I also need it. You're putting up your best appearance, but
you know as well as I do that sadly it is impossible to be ready in
one month." Yochanan took a deep breath and replied, "Mommy,
in spite of how it looks now, with G-d's help it is doable, and I
promise you that it will be ready on time."

Miraculously the upper three floors, used by the preschools,
were ready three days before the opening date. The auditorium,
the gym, and the semi-Olympic pool still needed work, but they
were not critical to the opening. Over the previous few weeks
Menachem had been pushing to get the myriad operating permits

in place, and for days on end the fire department had been there en masse checking every inch of the building to ensure that all systems conformed precisely to their specifications. It was nerve-wracking and down-to-the-wire, but they came through.

How stunned we were to suddenly learn that the early childhood program licenses from the Ministry of Social Affairs and Social Services from the previous center were not valid for the identical programs in the new center. Getting those licenses had been a long and complicated process and getting new ones would take several weeks. I made an urgent call to Gideon Shalom, the deputy director of the Ministry of Social Affairs programs and operations, whom I had come to know well. Gideon confirmed that we needed to apply for new licenses via the standard process. Shocked, I said, "Gideon, this is unacceptable. We have worked so hard to get the classrooms ready and now we're going to leave scores of families without a preschool over a technicality?" He blasted me. "A technicality? This is our license, and your staff should have known that it was required. We are now three days before the start of the school year and the person responsible for this process, along with several of her key committee members, are all on vacations out of the country. There is nothing to be done; it will get done when it gets done." I was speechless, between a rock and a hard place. The silence was deafening. Surprisingly, Gideon changed his tone. "Kalman, I do want you to be able to start the school year at your new center on the right foot. Leave it to me and I will get back to you."

Given the complexity of the application process, I now realized that it was indeed an impossible task, but Gideon undertook to make it happen and he went to work moving mountains within his ministry. On the morning of September 1, several hours prior to the opening of the school year, the required permits were finally received and were a source of great celebration.

And what a celebration the opening of the preschool was! Jerusalem Mayor Nir Barkat was present together with other distinguished guests to welcome the beaming preschool children and their families, and it was an exciting feeling to see our first educational activity in the new center. The after-school program as well as the overnight respite and the Me and My Mommy program remained in the old center until their new facilities were completed. They made their move, one program at a time, two months later in November. After eighteen years of nonstop activity, it was an emotional, heart-wrenching moment to see the old building devoid of activity, a body without its soul, but it was reassuring to know that same soul was alive and well in the new center.

It was as if the walls spoke calming messages. Full of colored murals and art, each floor was inviting in its own unique way, bringing joy and dignity to all. It was as if the edifice were extraterritorial; when one entered, the world outside was forgotten and left behind. Upon exiting, one gently returned to the outer reality.

Over the coming months we continued to work nonstop to complete the finishing touches on the entire building, and in April 2017 we celebrated its grand opening in the presence of many close friends who flew great distances to join us. It was a moving two-day event, and one of its highlights was the outstanding performance of the Shalva Band.

Chapter 49

The Shalva Band –
Ambassadors of Change

From its earliest days, music therapy played a vital role in Shalva programs on both the individual and group levels, and in-house productions were developed.

It was 2006 and I was sitting in my office at Shalva when there was a knock on my open door, and in walked a scrawny young man who asked if he could sit down. Before I had a chance to answer, he was sitting. "Shalom," he said with a smile that seemed a little painful, "my name is Shai Ben Shushan." "Shalom," I returned, "my name is Kalman Samuels. To what do I owe this unexpected pleasure?"

"I understand that you have a music therapy program here at Shalva. I am a music therapist and would love to work here."

"That's nice," I said, "but we already have one."

"I understand that, but I will take your children much further," he said with confidence.

"And how precisely will you do that?"

"I will create a real performing band."

My curiosity was now piqued by his mild-mannered audacity. "OK, so tell me more about yourself Shai."

He began.

"I was born and raised in Haifa and was considered a gifted musician and played several instruments, but focused on percussion. My musical training was in Israel as well as in Europe, and I was one of the youngest musicians ever accepted into the Young Israel Philharmonic Orchestra. At age eighteen, I was scheduled to join the army in the IDF music corps where I would get three years of additional training. But as the time for enlistment neared, my friends were all focused on getting accepted into various elite combat units and I decided that I would too. I trained intensively, and to my and their great surprise, I was accepted into the elite Duvdevan unit."

Here I had to stop Shai. I was well aware that Duvdevan are brazen, highly trained special forces units doing undercover operations and often disguised as part of the local populace. He didn't fit the bill.

"Forgive me for asking, but you don't look like what I would expect from a Duvdevan fighter."

With another painful smile, Shai said, "Allow me to clarify," and with that he pulled out a photo of himself with friends, all shirtless. "That's me a few years ago in my unit. I was thirty-five pounds heavier and a little taller." What he didn't mention was that both he and they were clearly very muscular young men. Without pause, he continued, "I was part of a commando unit sent into the West Bank town of Jenin to apprehend four terrorists preparing a suicide bombing in central Israel. All went well and we captured three and had another one in our sights, when a woman and children stepped in between us. Upon sharing this information with our superiors via our headset, we were instructed to wait. A few seconds later the terrorist launched grenades that exploded on me. Bedlam broke out, and over the next three hours I was hit again and again; my jaw and body were riddled with shrapnel. I continued to shoot into the house where the terrorist now hid. Reinforcements finally arrived and captured the terrorist. As I was placed in the ambulance, I learned that my beloved Duvdevan commander had been killed by a booby-trapped wall that collapsed on him, and I fell unconscious. The next thing I remember is being taken into surgery. Surviving was far from a certainty. I underwent three additional surgeries to fix my shattered jaw and to remove shrapnel from all over my body. Like a baby, I had to learn again to eat and to talk. My life was destroyed." Shai paused and I was silently spellbound.

He continued, "I learned what it was like to be helpless and dependent on others. I had a lot of time to think about how I could move forward, and I began to think about going back to music and sharing it with others who face similar challenges. It seemed improbable. But here I am sitting with you today and asking for the opportunity to realize my dream."

I was shaken. "Shai," I said, "you are a hero of Israel. How long will it take you to build a band?" "One year," he replied. "OK, so let's go for one year and see how you and the band are doing then." I got up and, moving to the other side of the table, gave him an emotional hug.

Shai began to teach the kids and to identify those whom he felt had the musical potential and cognitive ability to train for the Shalva Band. It was a process. Within a year, he had created his first ensemble and was invited to perform at a local music festival. It was very exciting but the festival plans fell through. The children were devastated, so we thought, why don't we create our own music festival?

With our therapists and seventy of our youngsters, we embarked on several months of intensive preparation. Word got out.

One of the rehearsals went up on a website. Stories appeared in the press. What had begun as an in-house talent show was becoming an event. It relocated to a major concert hall, and *FestiShalva* was opened by Jerusalem's mayor, who, despite a tight schedule, remained in his front-row seat for the entire performance. It was an evening for shattering stereotypes as our performers brought the house down. Those who could sing, raised their voices. Those who could dance, swayed and boogied. Those who could play, struck and shook percussion instruments. They were all joyous stars and the full house of their parents and siblings were so proud. The tone had been set, and from year to year the production grew and every child attending Shalva's after-school program had a role, with the Shalva Band taking center stage. The Masters of Ceremonies were of Israeli children's TV fame, Sharon Shahal and Asaf Ashtar, Dana Frider and Oded Paz.

Over many years and tedious hard work, the Shalva Band developed into a professional unit, touring the world, performing at concerts, and being hosted and recorded by Google as "The Shalva Band, Ambassadors of Change." The musicians derived great pride in making their living through their music.

The two talented soloists each came to Israel as youngsters with their families – Anael Khalifa from France and Dina Samteh from India. Both are blind. Both faced severe social challenges as they developed.

Guy Maman sings and plays the keyboard, and his lack of vision in one eye and 5 percent vision in the other doesn't even slow him down. He is super talented and holds a BA in Music Composition.

Yair Pomburg and Tal Kima have Down syndrome and attended Shalva from a young age, and it was in music therapy that their talent for percussion was discovered.

Yosef Ovadia has Williams syndrome and also came to Shalva early on. He has extraordinary musical talent and plays the drums.

Sara Samuels, my youngest, is creative and musically gifted, and composes and writes songs. While doing her post high school national service at Shalva, she became the guitarist and was responsible for the well-being of the band members. Sara forged deep and unique relationships with each of them, and her love and deep friendship proved to be a critical element in keeping them unified and in good spirits.

Spending time with the band is to experience love and seemingly endless laughter, and they melt all who meet them. Harry Krakowski, our dear friend in New York, was captivated by their rich personalities and provided them with the opportunity to go on their first international tour. Harry hosted them royally in his hotel and doted on their every whim, ensuring that their visit included Broadway shows and go-cart riding at a center that he arranged to be open following a concert after midnight. Anael and Dina drove the vehicles around the track with sounds of great excitement. Harry and Dina went at it in a fencing duel with each holding a long blind stick. Wherever they went, he went: Mexico, London, Moscow, and then back to Israel, and he was affectionately named "Uncle Harry."

Danilo Bracho is a professional videographer and joined the tour on their first stop in his home city, Toronto. With his long black hair, tattoos, and heavy Spanish accent, he and the band members made quite a sight. In city after city he not only shot video, he became their best friend and went to great lengths to provide for their every need. He too received a nickname from the band – *Ah Sheli* – Hebrew for "my brother." He was no longer Danilo but rather in every conversation and amidst heartfelt laughter, he was only *Ah Sheli*.

After a late closing concert in Mexico City we went out to a taco restaurant before flying out the next morning. There was a lot of emotion on display. Each of the band members spoke about their feelings at this sensitive time and Danilo filmed them. Finally it was his turn to speak.

313

He shared how much he had come to love each of the youngsters and said that he truly feels like a brother. "I want to remember these special moments with you for the rest of my life so this morning I did something to make that certain," he said with tears in his eyes. Danilo rolled up the sleeve of his T-shirt and there, emblazoned on his arm, were two Hebrew words spelled with a Torah-style script, *Ah Sheli*. Everyone burst out crying and there were hugs all around.

The Shalva Band's success was not overlooked by Israel's most famous musical talent contest on national television, *The Rising Star*, and they were invited to audition. A positive answer was quick to arrive, and the youngsters were soon filmed for the purpose of the program promos and readied to perform. Their excitement was palpable; each of the eight band members who took part was about to become a household name. The competition would be fierce because it was open to all, including seasoned professionals who hoped to win and thereby become the Israeli representative to the world's largest song contest, Eurovision, with its forty-two participating countries and a television audience of almost 200,000,000.

The night before the first performance, the band relaxed with a meal in Café Shalva, and I told them that they had reached the pinnacle of success and are impacting society by demonstrating their extraordinary abilities. "Whatever happens further," I said, "is wonderful but of little consequence. Now you must relax and enjoy these enchanted moments."

On Saturday night, November 24, 2018, the Shalva Band appeared on the program's season-opening show singing their version of "Here Comes the Sun" by the Beatles, and literally brought the house down. After thirteen years of preparation, I was overwhelmed with emotion as I watched them perform so magnificently.

The judges and the audience scored them with an unusually high 91, which sent them handily to the next round. Yair strolled off the stage and approached the judges, hugging each of them. They in turn became emotional and the feedback was amazing. The video clip of their performance went viral with millions watching it. The Shalva Band had come of age and was now impacting disabilities and inclusion globally. They exemplified Shalva's mission of empowering persons with disabilities to become ambassadors of their own change, and they did so with great dignity.

From the outset we knew that since Eurovision was won the previous year by an Israeli singer named Netta Barzilai, this year's contest would be hosted in Israel. We also knew that the home country need not compete in the semifinals, but would automatically qualify for the finals held late Saturday night. Several band members are religious and Sabbath observers, and we understood that this would not be a problem, since the Sabbath would be over at nightfall with ample time to get ready. In any case, at the time this was not even a consideration because neither we nor the production company dreamed that the band would progress beyond a couple of rounds. We were both excited just to have them participate.

Surprise surprise. The Shalva Band wowed the audience with each new song, receiving the highest marks in the competition and becoming beloved household names. The judges spoke in superlatives and made it clear that this was no gimmick, and while the band brought to the fore a powerful message of inclusion, they were judged strictly on the merits of their musical abilities. They decisively won round after round and were now into the semi-finals of *The Rising Star* and recognized as one of the clear favorites to win and advance to the Eurovision contest.

And then the news from Eurovision arrived.

Yes, the finals were on Saturday night, but the dress rehearsals were to be on Friday night and they were not optional; they were mandatory. Tedy Productions headed by Tmira Yardeni, and Keshet, the host Israeli network, conferred with Eurovision representatives in an effort to find a way for the band to participate. The network requested that the Shalva Band be allowed to perform a couple of hours earlier, before sundown on Friday afternoon. Many got involved, and the Israeli Minister of Culture wrote an impassioned letter to Eurovision: "The question at stake is not hypothetical but is rather a matter of principle, underlying the very foundations of equal opportunity and true acceptance of the concept of diversity that the Eurovision Song Contest proudly symbolizes."

News of the problem hit the press and struck a deep nerve, with countless newspaper articles about it in many languages and an inordinate number of items on prime time television news and leisure programs, often several times daily. They turned to each of us at Shalva for a response, including band members and their parents, and received one unified response: "The production company and the TV network are intensely conferring with Eurovision in an effort to find a solution, and any information will come from them." This fueled further articles and speculation.

During this process, Shalva performed in the semifinals and defeated two strong contenders, thereby winning the first of the four coveted slots in the finals. Now there was real shock. What would happen if Eurovision refused to budge? We were informed that we would not be allowed to compete in the finals, for if we won and then withdrew, that would mean that the runner-up would represent the country in the Eurovision contest, and that was not an option. On the other hand, we could also not quit now and thereby leave only three finalists.

Eurovision's final answer arrived. The Shalva Band would receive no concessions of any kind.

It was time. The band, consisting of both religious and non-religious members, met and came to a unified decision: They had entered the competition as a family and would respectfully leave as a family; they would forfeit their clear opportunity to fame and fortune, and honor the Sabbath.

The news spread like wildfire and once again countless articles appeared, all respectful and positive, filled with great pride and unity. As Anael expressed it to a media outlet, "There was fame and bright lights and it was easy to lose focus and get confused; but we didn't. We stuck to our principles."

An additional Rising Star contestant who had previously lost and left the competition was now brought back and added to the finals, ensuring that there would be four finalists. The Shalva Band appeared on television for an emotional goodbye interview with the MCs Rotem Sela and Assi Azar. In the middle of it, there was an unexpected news update from Eurovision that while they couldn't bend their rules, they were extending an invitation to the Shalva Band to perform as guest artists in their semifinals, two days prior to the Saturday night finals in May.

The band would yet have their day in the sun in front of their massive viewing audience. All were in shock, and an atmosphere of sorrow rapidly turned into one of joy. Assi, avowedly secular, pointed his finger upward and looking in the direction of Heaven exclaimed, "You are the ultimate Director, You played one on us, only You could have arranged this matter so perfectly."

The five program judges also wanted a chance to say goodbye to the band members, to whom they had become deeply attached, so the band was invited to sing a final song on television several nights later, and were once again given an emotional send off.

As the performance drew to its final moments, Dina asked all to rise, and she quietly read moving lines of thanks from a page in braille, to the accompaniment of a soft melody that Sara strummed on her guitar while Anael hummed. Mesmerized by the unexpected power of the moment, tears streamed down the faces of the judges and audience.

The band was subsequently chosen by Bank Hapoalim to lead an effective social campaign via their first single, "The Door

Will Be Open," that, together with an emotional clip, conveys the process of acceptance of the "other."

They prepared intensively for scores of major concerts that awaited them, including a concert in New York, the opening ceremonies of Israel's Memorial Day and Independence Day, and their Eurovision appearance, with its slogan "Dare to Dream."

The day arrived, and on May 16, 2019, the Shalva Band stood on the Eurovision stage and magically performed "A Million Dreams" from the film *The Greatest Showman*, and truly dazzled Europe and the world. Dina began by reading from braille a powerful, short message, accompanied by Sara's soft guitar.

> John Lennon once said,
> A dream you dream alone is only a dream.
> But a dream you dream together is reality.
> We dreamt and here we are on the biggest stage we can imagine.
> Don't stop dreaming no matter what people say.

Anael and Dina's singing was described as heavenly and emotional, and the viewers were moved by Tal signing the refrain in sign language.

As I listened to the lyrics from Anael and Dina, I sensed that they sung from the depths of the hearts of their fellow band members – and from mine: Only with a million dreams can we embark on a journey of change. No matter they mock us or consider us lunatics – we can live in a world we design that only dreamers can realize.

The audience jumped to their feet and gave a deafening standing ovation, and within minutes the Shalva Band dominated the Eurovision conversation online. The internet exploded, and their performance was soon seen and praised by millions of online viewers and media outlets around the world as a source of great inspiration. Many declared the Shalva Band the real winners of Eurovision.

The Shalva Band has always had a goal – to create social change via their music – and their astounding impact is achieving precisely that, inspiring the world to take note and rethink disabilities and inclusion.

Chapter 50

Inclusion and Reverse Inclusion

Inclusion is a buzzword in programs for persons with disabilities. For Malki and me, Yossi was all about inclusion long before we even knew it was a concept. While well-intended voices spoke of the negative impact he could have on our family, Yossi in fact had the opposite effect. He united our family and was a blessing in our lives. We raised our children to know that Yossi was special, loved, and wanted, and they absorbed that message.

Great pride in having Yossi as a family member was instilled in each of Yossi's siblings, and that was critical to our family's health, as it is to that of any such family. A sibling that understands that Mommy and Daddy are proud of their child with a disability has been given the tools to grow up to be a healthy adult, spouse, and parent. On the other hand, if there is a sense of embarrassment, or even a hesitant attitude, the emotional damage will not only be to these siblings, but will be generational, extending to their children as well.

Yossi was often hosted by our dear friends Ita and Ephraim Sheinberger at their home, where they pampered him with goodies and he played with their young children. It was naturally an amazing help for us. When I picked him up, I was always welcomed with hearty smiles and gratitude for the joy Yossi brought them. Ita claims that Yossi's visits contributed enormously to her children's healthy upbringing.

Malki was in a fancy gift shop when four-year-old Yossi knocked over and broke an expensive vase. One customer gasped while others turned in horror. Without hesitation, Malki smiled and asked, "Who is paying for that vase, me or you?" There was silence and the message was heard.

Our young children sat around the Shabbat table when their conversation turned to Yossi and what kind of girl would he marry. One suggested a girl who is blind and another suggested a girl who is deaf. Suddenly Shlomo, who was six years old, erupted into heartfelt sobbing and said, "Why can't Yossi marry a regular girl?" Shlomo's view of his older brother stemmed from our view of Yossi, just a regular guy with a couple of disabilities.

Years later, Yossi returned the favor. Orit Tanenbaum did her national service at Shalva, and Yossi loved to go out for coffee with her and other girls. Given that his walking had become awkward, help was needed, and so Shlomo occasionally joined them. Yossi embarrassed both Orit and Shlomo by flashing a sign of placing a ring on a finger and insisting that they take his advice. In time, they did, and no one was happier at their wedding than Yossi.

Shortly after opening Shalva, our then eleven-year-old son Simcha came home breathless one afternoon. On his way back from school, he'd seen two thirteen-year-old boys snickering as they watched the Shalva children playing in the garden.

"What are you laughing at? There's nothing funny about these children," he exclaimed. With a burst of laughter, they replied, "They're very funny, and the only reason you're not laughing is because your brother is one of them." Simcha went after them with his fists, and in spite of the difference in size and age, they bolted.

Our experience of prejudice and lack of inclusion wasn't restricted to strangers and young boys, but at times extended even to professional caregivers. One Friday night, our family crowded into the small kitchen of our rented apartment in the Jerusalem neighborhood of Kiryat Moshe to ritually wash our hands before eating bread. Yossi, then in his late-teens, suddenly lunged back and bumped into the large urn of water kept boiling on the stove through Shabbat. It overturned, cascading its scalding gallons across the narrow kitchen floor. Yossi, Yochanan, and Malki, standing nearest, slipped and fell into the boiling water.

"Get the car," Malki yelled. We rushed to the hospital emergency room. Yochanan, who had suffered lesser burns, was released, and Malki determinedly ignored her more serious injuries. Yossi, whose skin had come off along with his socks, was immediately admitted, but the physician in charge of the burns ward clearly did not want him there. In spite of the obvious evidence to the contrary, his first statement was, "There's no need to hospitalize him," and did everything he could to get Yossi released and out of his way as quickly as possible. For the next two months, Yossi remained home-bound in excruciating pain, unable to walk on his badly burned feet. As for the doctor, following my detailed written complaint, he was removed from his position.

The Shalva center was designed to promote inclusivity throughout every facility in the building, and inclusion and reverse inclusion are reflected in all Shalva programs. Over 150,000 visitors a year come to Shalva for various reasons, whether to eat in Café Shalva, attend educational and professional conferences in the auditorium, play in the inclusive parks that are accessible to all, or participate in a wide range of other activities. They mingle with the Shalva children upon coming and going, and it is so very impactful as they all mesh into a single human fabric.

Shalva has developed into an international beacon of care, support, and research for those with disabilities, empowering the lives of countless individuals, families, and communities through an ever-expanding range of comprehensive programs. It has been referred to as a movement because of its continued impact not only on standards of disability care but also on generations of young people who have volunteered at Shalva and developed socially via their volunteerism, taking with them the lessons they've learned throughout life.

In fact, new generations often trace their beginnings to Shalva; we've had many "Shalva couples" who met when working or volunteering at Shalva and ultimately dated and married. Malki found this very meaningful and built a beautiful dedication entitled "Wall of Hearts" with the names of each couple listed on its own brick under the heading, "These young people came to give love, and love is what they found."

There is also a new generation of capable and passionate leadership moving Shalva and its vision forward to ever-expanding horizons. Yochanan and Avi have demonstrated their unique professional talents and leadership abilities that empower them to guide Shalva further. Yochanan has initiated successful management strategies and plans ensuring their alignment with Shalva's mission, while Avi has skillfully developed its global reach and partnerships, together enabling the present and securing the future.

As a center of excellence, Shalva is a strategic partner in effecting social change. Rather than seeing insurmountable walls, we see only hurdles to be crossed. Its impact continues to grow in Israel and internationally, with educational delegations from across the globe visiting regularly and relationships developing. The United Nations appointed Shalva as a consultant to the

UN Economic and Social Council (ECOSOC), and this marks an opportunity for Shalva to reach new frontiers in its international impact as a leading advocate of inclusion and equality for those with disabilities.

Shalva's core values of equality and supporting quality of life are reflected not only in its programs but in the superior standards of the physical center itself. Not everybody understands the importance of this, and sometimes people wonder why the center was designed with so much focus on aesthetics and so much attention to detail. What one person says, many others are often thinking, but hesitate to ask. So it was with Ron, an acquaintance from an affluent New York community. After touring the twelve floors of the building, he took a deep breath and turned to me. "Kalman," he said, "all this for whom?"

"Well, let's see," I replied. "As I recall, in your local community center, you have a semi-Olympic pool as we do." "Of course," he said. "And I believe you also have a beautiful auditorium as we do?" "Well sure." "And don't you even have a full-size gym like us?" "Yes, we do," he confirmed.

"Why do you have all those things?" I queried. "Kalman," he replied with a puzzled look, "it is called quality of life."

"Ron, who told you that because a young mother unexpectedly gave birth to a baby with a disability, that she not only has to cope with her new challenges, but she has thereby forfeited her and her child's rights to that same quality of life? This building is a statement to remind you and so many others that mother, child, and family are equally worthy and deserving of quality of life and living a quality life!"

My guest thanked me and readily admitted that he had simply never thought about it in that manner.

Chapter 51

Of Yossi and Dreams

Yossi has always been a dreamer and has been blessed with extraordinary friends who have set out to help him realize his dreams. His friendships are so sincere and mutually enriching. One friend is Shai Gross, who at age six was the youngest survivor of Entebbe, the audacious Israeli military mission in 1976 that rescued over one hundred Israelis being held hostage by Arab terrorists in Uganda with the cooperation of then-Ugandan President Idi Amin. Many decades later, another young Israeli soldier named Gilad Shalit was held hostage by Hamas terrorists, and Yossi couldn't accept this and would regularly attend rallies in support of making a deal to free him. Shai was involved in organizing many of those rallies. Ultimately, Gilad was freed and Yossi fulfilled his dream of meeting Gilad in person, together with Shai and another hero of Israel, Tzurin Hershko, a decorated IDF commander who was shot in the spine in Entebbe and became a paraplegic. A deep friendship between Shai and Yossi ensued, and Shai set out to help Yossi fulfill further dreams, arranging for him to meet leaders in

Israel's government, the IDF, and industry sectors, and to travel throughout Israel, where he experienced something new and yet more exciting with each trip. Each adventure ended with the same question: "And what is your next dream?"

Yossi dreamed of using his heightened sense of smell to professional advantage. We had first thought about something related to perfumes, until we were reminded that taste is all about smell, as anyone with a bad cold and a stuffed nose whose sense of taste is dulled will attest. Yossi could be trained to be a sommelier! He loved the idea.

We were put in touch with a young, dynamic Frenchman named Jessy Bodec, who had won the Israel sommelier competition several years earlier. Jessy drove an hour on his motorcycle from Tel Aviv to Jerusalem once a week with varied bottles of quality wine in tow. Over the next two years Yossi trained with Jessy and delved into the depths of the study of wine, and I was amazed at just how complex the subject is. He learned how to taste the many wines and to spit them out into a large bowl. He did enjoy swallowing a little of each, though, and at the end of each session, he was high. Given that Jessy didn't know sign language, there was need for an interpreter, and that position was willingly and ably filled by Yossi's brother Simcha, who became quite the wine expert himself. Upon graduation, Yossi received his diploma and then traveled to France with Jessy and his good friends Itamar Shevach and Elisha Weingot, where they visited famous wineries and vineyards. Some years later Yossi became the sommelier for quality wines of his own, and on the bottle appeared his name, an "I love you sign," and text about the wine in braille.

Yossi had traveled extensively on commercial airlines and now dreamed of flying overseas on a private jet. I laughed. He didn't. Yossi shares a deep friendship with Haim Taib, a successful Israeli businessman fifteen years his elder. The two love to spend quality time together at Haim's beautiful home in Kfar

Shmaryahu, schmoozing, sipping whiskey, smoking cigars, and driving in his high-end sports cars. It was at a large Shalva event that Haim approached me and said, "Your son has just shared his dream of flying on my private jet and I am going to make that happen." "Haim," I replied, "please don't worry about Yossi's requests. Sometimes he just doesn't have limits." He became very serious, gazed at me sternly, and said slowly and deliberately, "Kalman, do not ever get in between me and my dear friend. We will be flying in the next two weeks." I backed off, and sure enough, Haim and his wife Iris flew Yossi and his escort on their magnificent jet to London where they hosted him royally and showed him the town.

Like many young people, Yossi dreamed of meeting the president of the United States, but that did not seem to be within our reach. Yossi, however, always alert, recognized his opportunity. When I shared with him in 2006 that our dear friend and devoted Shalva supporter Roland Arnall was now the new American ambassador to Holland, he immediately suggested that Roland should be able to arrange a meeting with the president for him. I thought to myself, now why didn't I think of that? But I didn't feel comfortable asking Roland at the time and told Yossi that I just couldn't do it. Yossi persisted. Some time passed and I eventually felt more comfortable sharing Yossi's dream and did so via an email to Dawn in Amsterdam. Her reply was immediate. She said she had asked Roland, who told her to tell Yossi that he would do everything in his power to make the meeting happen.

In early November 2006, shortly after Yossi's thirtieth birthday, I received a large envelope in the mail whose return address read "the White House." With trepidation, I opened it carefully, and sure enough there it was, an invitation for Yossi Samuels to join President George W. Bush at his White House Hanukkah party in mid-December. Yossi was overwhelmed with joy, as were we. I couldn't help but reflect on the verse, "And Joseph was thirty years old when he stood before Pharaoh, king of Egypt" (Genesis 41:46).

Avi, Yossi, and I headed for Washington, bringing with us as a gift for the president a bronze cast of Yossi's hand signing the international symbol for "I love you," with a quote from Helen Keller: "The best and most beautiful things in the world cannot be seen or even touched – they must be felt with the heart."

Upon arrival at the White House, we had an emotional meeting with Dawn and Roland, who ushered us in to meet the president and First Lady. We were led into a room filled with bright lights, photographers, and security officers to meet the most powerful man on the planet. Sitting in his wheelchair in front of a portrait of George Washington, Yossi reached out at once for the president's hand. "I'm excited and honored to meet you," he said clearly in Hebrew, with me translating. "I admire your father, but I admire you more because of your war on terror." The president seemed floored, undoubtedly appreciating this sincere compliment. Yossi continued, "I urge you to please free the Israeli soldiers held by Hamas and by Hezbollah," and proceeded to name them one by one.

"Mr. President," Yossi continued, "before you leave this house it is your responsibility to take care of Iran." Spontaneously the president gave Yossi a playful slap on the shoulder, turned to the First Lady, and said, "Laura, this young man knows what he is talking about, and there is what to talk about." Photos were taken and we were gently escorted out of the other door where Roland and Dawn embraced Yossi. "I cannot begin to tell you how impressed I am," Dawn said. "Given that there are many other invited guests here this evening, each will be given the opportunity to quickly meet the president and pose for a photo, and will be ushered out in about thirty seconds, but Yossi kept him engaged a full six minutes. I am also impressed that the president was so sensitive and gave Yossi significant time."

As we began to push Yossi in his wheelchair toward the larger reception area, he became very agitated. "What is it?" I asked. "I forgot to talk to the president about North Korea!"

A long-time friend, Jay Lefkowitz, who was an advisor to the president, stepped forward and asked what is going on. I explained. He smiled and said, "Please share with Yossi that I am now serving as the president's Special Envoy for Human Rights in North Korea. Rather than take time now, ask him to write me an email with his suggestions and I promise to share with the president at our daily briefing those that I feel have merit." Yossi was mollified and we moved on with Roland and Dawn to enjoy the magnificent Hanukkah party.

The following day, long-discussed UN sanctions were finally passed and placed on Iran, and I began to receive emails stating, "Yay, Yossi did it," to which I replied, "What did you think, that he went in for a photo op?"

Upon arrival home in Israel, Yossi immediately sat down in front of his braille machine and knocked off a long list of important suggestions for Jay to share with the president.

Yossi continued to dream, and one dream in particular was very dear to him, but we were unable to find a way to make it happen. Yossi had studied world geography and learned about various countries and what they are known for, and riding elephants in Thailand captured his interest. Years passed. Yossi was now thirty-six and it didn't seem to be on the horizon.

How surprised I was to arrive home from yet another New York trip and hear from Malki at the airport that Yossi would be flying to Thailand a couple of nights later. While I had been on the flight back to Israel, Malki had received an email from Daniel Mandel, one of Yossi's close friends, stating that he was completing a post-army trip that has become a rite of passage for many young Israelis. "Malki, I'm now in Thailand," he wrote, "and I will be coming home in three weeks. There are elephants. Please send Yossi here immediately."

Recognizing the opportunity and not wanting to waste time, Daniel called Avi Cashman, another friend of Yossi who lives in Tel Aviv, and asked if he would consider making the trip with Yossi. Though his wife was expecting their first child, he didn't miss a beat and excitedly replied, "I'm in – let's make it happen."

It was clear that a ten-hour flight to Bangkok, including a flight transfer in the middle, with Yossi in his wheelchair unable to move himself, was a most challenging undertaking for one person to manage, but Yossi's friends have never focused on the challenges, only the end result. As we drove to the airport, Yossi was overcome with excitement while Malki and I were overcome by the dedication of his friends.

Naturally Yossi kept us up-to-date through his blog.

Would you believe it, I'm off to Thailand! My parents and my sister Sara came to see me off. My friend Avi is accompanying me. The flight was long and good with tasty food. I was so excited when we actually landed in Bangkok. Everyone was really nice and helpful. Soon after landing, we got to go on another plane to the island [Ko Samui] where my friend Daniel was waiting for us!! It was amazing to be with him again.

Two days after Yossi's departure, four American congressmen visited Shalva. Prior to showing these prestigious guests the center, we sat in the small guest room and introduced ourselves. I had explicitly told my secretary to be certain that neither she nor anyone else interrupt our meeting, so I was taken aback when there was an anxious knocking on the door. I opened it with a puzzled facial expression that conveyed a clear message: "Why in the world are you disturbing me at this time?" Picking that up, she blurted out in Hebrew, "I apologize, but for G-d's sake, look at your email." I excused myself and opened my phone but I wasn't prepared. Suddenly I saw a photo of Yossi with his two buddies sitting on top of an elephant, with his enormous smile spreading from ear to ear. Emotions consumed me and I burst out crying. It took a couple of minutes to regain my composure.

"Please excuse me and allow me to explain," I apologized, and briefly shared some background about Yossi and his visit to Thailand. Upon seeing the photo of Yossi atop the elephant, they too were deeply moved.

"My dear friends," I continued passionately, "Yossi has every reason to give up on life. He is blind, deaf, and cannot walk, but he never loses his zest for life, never ceases to dream new dreams and to make them happen. We must learn from him and continue to dream our dreams with the confidence that with G-d's help, we can realize them."

Upon their departure, still rife with emotion, I found myself reflecting on the fact that as a nonreligious kid in Vancouver, I had never dreamed of becoming a rabbi. When Yossi lost his sight and hearing, I never dreamed that he would learn to communicate. And never did I dream that Yossi's immense challenges and break-through to communication would lead to Shalva. Clearly, dreams never dreamed continue to unfold.

Acknowledgments

אוֹדְךָ עַל כִּי נוֹרָאוֹת נִפְלֵיתִי נִפְלָאִים מַעֲשֶׂיךָ וְנַפְשִׁי יֹדַעַת מְאֹד.

I will thank You, for I was formed in an awesome
and wondrous way; unfathomable are Your works,
though my soul perceives much. (Psalms 139:14)

I cannot adequately express my truly heartfelt gratitude
to each of my dear family members, friends, associates, and
partners in the private and public sphere, who have so deeply
impacted and enriched my life and enabled the realization of so
many dreams.

I thank Matthew Miller, publisher at Koren Publishers and
its imprint Toby Press, and his exceptional team of professionals
who enabled this book to become reality and spared no efforts
in the process. The wisdom and literary skills of Rabbi Reuven
Ziegler, chairman of the editorial board, are deeply appreciated, as
is his calm under pressure. Thank you also to the editorial team:
Sara Henna Dahan, Debbie Ismailoff, and Ita Olesker, as well as to
cover designer Tani Bayer and graphic designer Tomi Mager. My
very special thanks to marketing director Yehudit Singer-Freud.

My profound appreciation is extended to my Shalva family, who provide me with boundless inspiration daily.

No words can express my heartfelt gratitude to my dear sister and brother-in-law Sossy and Yakov Long, who were always there for us in raising Yossi and our children, providing our own personal Shalva, long before Shalva came to be. The untimely passing of Sossy, of blessed memory, so loved by all, is an abyss that cannot be filled, and she will be forever missed.

A huge shout out for my good friend Steve Linde, former editor in chief of the *Jerusalem Post* and current editor in chief of the *Jerusalem Report*, who voluntarily edited the manuscript and introduced me to my publisher.

Thank you to Wendy Elliman for her meaningful assistance.

I am deeply indebted to Gitty Shafer of Brooklyn for her dedication and critical assistance in Shalva's formative years.

I was blessed and thankful to have shared a unique friendship with Steven Diamond, a rare human being who touched the lives of all who were fortunate to meet him, and greatly impacted my and my family's lives. We often discussed the subjects of this book. Wise, razor sharp, funny, always calling it like it is, and so much more, his untimely demise left an irreplaceable void. Stevie D. we miss you.

And to the tens of thousands of children and their family members who over the years have entered the doors of Shalva, learned and developed, matured and blossomed, discovering in themselves strengths and abilities toward more fulfilling lives – you are always in my heart.

The author can be reached at
DreamsNeverDreamed@gmail.com

Glossary of Hebrew and Yiddish Words

Bar mitzva	A boy who has turned thirteen and is obligated to keep Jewish laws, and the ceremony that marks this occasion
Bedikat hametz	See *Hametz*. The ritual of searching for leavened food the night before Passover
Brit mila	Circumcision ceremony performed on Jewish males on the eighth day from birth
Bubby	Grandma
Chabad	See *Lubavitch*. Acronym of the Hebrew for "wisdom, understanding, and knowledge," the name by which the movement of Lubavitch Hasidim is known
Daven	Pray
Gett	Jewish divorce certificate, given to a wife by her husband
Gut Yom Tov	"Good holiday," a festival greeting

Hai	Life. The word's numerical value in Hebrew is 18, and it is traditional to give charitable contributions in multiples of 18.
Hallas	The braided loaves traditionally eaten on Shabbat
Hametz	Food containing leavened wheat, barley, oats, spelt, or rye
Hasid, *Hasidim* (pl.)	Literally, "pious." A member of a branch of Orthodox Judaism that maintains an insular lifestyle. Hasidism originally rose as a Jewish revival movement in the eighteenth century.
Huppa	Marriage canopy
Hutzpa	Audacity, nerve
Kabbala, *kabbalistic* (adj.)	Jewish mystical tradition
Kaddish	Public prayer of praise for the Almighty, recited daily in synagogue and in memory of those who have died
Kame'ah	Amulet
Kapo	Nazi concentration camp prisoner forced to supervise other prisoners
Kiddush	Special blessing recited on Shabbat and Festivals before a meal
Kosher	Ritually fit to eat or use according to Jewish law
Lahash	Kabbalistic formula

Latke	Fried potato pancake, traditionally eaten on Hanukkah
Lubavitch	Hasidic Jewish movement that is active in outreach to other Jews
Maariv	Evening prayers
Maven	Literally, "one who understands well"
Mazal tov/ siman tov	Literally, "good luck"/ "good sign." A way of expressing congratulations
Mensch	A moral, dignified, and responsible individual
Meshuga (adj.), *meshugene* (noun)	Nuts, crazy
Mezuza	Parchment strip inscribed with two passages from the Torah, encased, and hung on the right doorpost of the entrance to a house or room
Mikve	Ritual bath used for spiritual purification
Minha	Afternoon prayers
Minyan	Prayer quorum of ten men, aged thirteen and older
Mishna	Early compilation of Jewish oral tradition
Neshama	Soul
Patsch	Slap or spanking
Peyot	Side curls
Purim	Literally, "lots" as in lottery. Festival celebrating the rescue of the Jews from extermination at the hands of the Persian minister Haman

Reb	Respectful address to a learned man
Rebbe	Leader of a hasidic community, often believed to have mystical power
Rebbetzin	Wife of a rabbi
Rosh Hashana	Jewish new year
Schmooze	Cozy, friendly talk; gossip
Schnorrer	Beggar; charity collector (pejorative)
Shabbat	Saturday, the seventh day of the week, a day of rest and spiritual enrichment
Shaliah	Literally, "messenger." In Chabad, it refers to an individual or couple sent to spread Judaism and Hasidism in locations around the world.
Shalom Aleichem, Aleichem HaShalom	Literally, "peace be unto you, unto you be peace." A traditional Hebrew greeting and response to that greeting
Shamash	Synagogue assistant or caretaker
Shavuot	Literally, "weeks." Festival commemorating the giving of the Torah
Shema Yisrael	Central prayer in Jewish worship
Shidduch	An introduction arranged by a matchmaker
Shiva	Seven days of mourning following the burial of a first-degree relative
Shohet	Slaughterer of kosher meat in accordance with the laws of Jewish slaughter

Shtiebel	Literally, "little house" or "little room." An informal synagogue used for communal prayer
Shtreimel	Fur-rimmed hat worn by Hasidim
Shul	Synagogue
Shulhan	Table
Siddur	Prayer book
Simhat Torah	Literally, "rejoicing of the Law." Festival celebrating the end of the past year's cycle of Torah readings and the start of the next
Sukka	Temporary dwelling used during the festival of Sukkot
Sukkot	Festival of Tabernacles
Tallit	Prayer shawl
Talmud	Collection of Jewish oral tradition interpreting the Torah
Tefillin	A pair of black leather boxes containing parchment inscribed with biblical verses, worn on the head and upper arm during weekday morning prayer services
Tisch	Literally, "table." Gathering of Hasidim around their Rebbe
Tisha B'Av	Ninth day of the Hebrew month of Av, it is a fast day commemorating the destruction of the First and Second Temples and other Jewish tragedies
Tosafot	Medieval commentary on the Talmud

Tzaddik	Righteous man
Tzitzit	Fringes attached to the corners of garments as a reminder of the commandments
Yarmulke	Skullcap head-covering; *kippa* in Hebrew
Yeshiva	Academy for the intensive study of Torah and Talmud
Yisgadal veyiskadash	Literally, "May [His Name] be great, may it be blessed." The opening words of the Kaddish prayer said for the departed
Yom Kippur	Day of Atonement, the biblical holiday of fasting and repentance
Zaidy	Grandpa

Shalva National Center

Kalman,
age seventeen,
at his high school
graduation

Yossi before
the vaccination,
age seven months

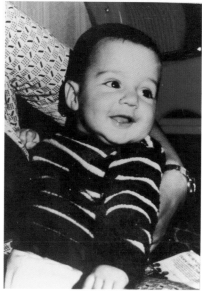

Kalman as a Torah scribe, writing with quill and ink

Left to right: Yochanan, Grandfather Norman Samuels, Yossi, Kalman, Simcha, and Avi

Yossi writing
using his
braille machine

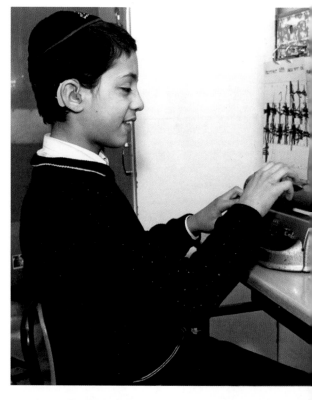

Yossi at home
in New York

Yossi dancing
at his birthday
party

Yossi falls asleep
while reading in
braille

Shoshana
reading Yossi
the news

Yossi sharing secrets with baby sister Sara, twenty-two years younger

Yossi on his favorite horse, Shosh

Yossi with
his friends
Daniel Mandel
and Avi Cashman
on an elephant
in Thailand

Yossi in Sweden,
zipping around
the Volvo test
track in one of
many models

Shalva –
Beit Nachshon
Center

Kalman and
Gordon Diamond
golfing at Bighorn

"You are the lead horse, and the Shalva children are right there with you."
(See chap. 22)

"And Abraham lifted up his eyes, and he saw, and behold! There was a ram."
(See chap. 48)

Yossi in a vineyard in Alsace-Lorraine, France

Sculpture by Menashe Kadishman at the entrance to the Shalva National Center

Schmoozing via
sign language
with his friend
Aviad Golian,
while taking in
the sights and sounds
in his way

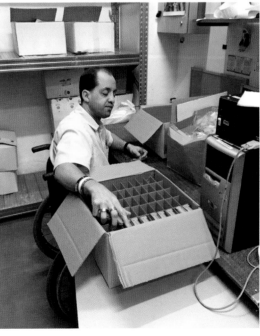

Yossi at work at
Israel's national
toll-road highway
headquarters

Roland and Dawn Arnall with Yossi at the White House

Yossi and Avi, conversing with former British prime minister Gordon Brown

Left to right:
First Lady Laura Bush,
Avi, Yossi, Kalman,
President George
Bush

Yossi and
Israeli President
Ruvi Rivlin
when he was
Speaker of the
Knesset

Left to right: Israeli Prime Minister Benjamin Netanyahu, Yossi, Avi, Yochanan, and Kalman

Kalman and his sons. Left to right: Shlomo, Yochanan, Kalman, Yossi, Simcha, and Avi

The Shalva Band on *The Rising Star for Eurovision*. Left to right: Shai Ben Shushan, Yair Pomburg, Dina Samteh, Anael Khalifa, Sara Samuels, Yosef Ovadia, Tal Kima, and Guy Maman

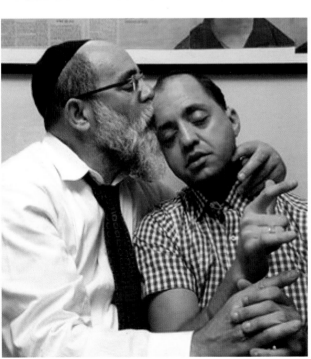

Kalman and Yossi signing "I love you" in sign language